Armoured Fighting Vehicles of the World
VOLUME 2

British AFVs 1919-40

Edited by Duncan Crow

Profile Publications Limited
Windsor, Berkshire, England

Uniform with this volume

Volume 1 Armoured Fighting Vehicles of World War I

Aircraft in Profile Series
(3rd Edition)

Volume 1 (Part numbers 1–24)
Volume 2 (Part numbers 25–48)
Volume 3 (Part numbers 49–72)
Volume 4 (Part numbers 73–96)
Volume 5 (Part numbers 97–120)
Volume 6 (Part numbers 121–144)
Volume 7 (Part numbers 145–168)
Volume 8 (Part numbers 169–192)

Classic Cars in Profile Series
(2nd Edition)

Volume 1 (Part numbers 1–24)
Volume 2 (Part numbers 25–48)
Volume 3 (Part numbers 49–72)
Volume 4 (Part numbers 73–96)

First Published in England 1970, by
PROFILE PUBLICATIONS LIMITED
Coburg House, Sheet Street, Windsor, Berkshire, England

Printed in England by
Mears Caldwell Hacker Limited, London, England

CONTENTS

Coloured illustrations by:

  Tom Brittain, Keith Broomfield, Gordon Davies, Terence Hadler, Martin Lee, James Leech.

ACKNOWLEDGEMENTS

The Editor, Authors and Publishers wish to acknowledge the help given, especially in the provision of illustrations, by Peter Chamberlain; Colonel Peter H. Hordern, D.S.O., O.B.E.; Colonel Robert J. Icks, U.S.A.R. (Retd.); the Imperial War Museum; and the Royal Armoured Corps Tank Museum, where examples of almost all the AFVs described in this volume are on view.

ERRATA

Page 19   Left caption, line one, for "A6E2" read "A6E1".
Page 20   Table, lines one and two, transpose W.D. numbers and Registration numbers of A6E1 and A6E2. A6E1 was T405/ML8699; A6E2 was T404/ML8698.
Page 35   The words "Vehicle modified to Indian Pattern and" should be deleted.
Page 83   The figures "2" and "3" under the illustrations should be transposed.
Page 106   Caption, second line, for "or" read "for".
Page 127   Right column, line 14, for "Jeffrey" read "Jeffery".
Page 167   A War Office announcement in August 1970 made it possible that the amalgamation between the 3rd Carabiniers and The Royal Scots Greys might not take place.

Mediums and Lights—the main British tanks of the inter-war years. In the foreground a Vickers Medium Mark II*, behind it a Vickers Light Tank Mark IV.
(Imperial War Museum)

Experiment in Armour

by Duncan Crow

TWO factors determined the types and numbers of armoured fighting vehicles produced in Britain during most of the 21 years between the First and Second World Wars. The first factor was the hypothesis about the army's rôle; the second was the small amount of money available for defence

The priorities of the army's rôle were seen to be: first, policing the Empire; second, minor expeditions and guerilla warfare; third, major expeditions; and fourth—an unlikely contingency, it was felt—a major war. Combined with financial stringency this order of priorities resulted, as far as AFVs were concerned, in vehicles that were small and comparatively inexpensive.

Because of the two prime factors—financial stringency and the continually renewed Cabinet statement that no major war was likely for ten years—there was no lever to overturn the rocks of reaction that were placed in the way of armoured progress. The road-block was all but impenetrable. And of crucial importance for the future was that this state of affairs caused not only the design and supply of tanks to dwindle to almost nothing but that it destroyed the

soil for future growth as well. For years Vickers-Armstrong were the only civilian firm which were interested in tanks, and after Johnson's Tank Design Department was closed in 1923 only the Royal Ordnance Factory at Woolwich did any tank work apart from Vickers. "Organization for tank design in the War Office was rudimentary in the extreme, and but for the solitary and pioneering efforts of the designers at Vickers-Armstrongs," wrote the historian of *British War Production*, "the country would have possessed no facilities for the design and development of armoured vehicles. As late as 1936 the total equipment of tanks in the hands of the Army was 375, of which 209 were designated as light and 166 as medium. Of the total number, 304 were officially classed as obsolete, and these included all the medium tanks with the exception of two, both experimental."[*]

The medium tanks were the first to be built by Vickers after an experiment with a light tank in 1921

* M. M. Postan, *British War Production*, p.7 (H.M.S.O. London 1952).

Policing the Empire—Light Tank Mark IIB Indian pattern on the North-West frontier of India. (R.A.C. Tank Museum)

which had been stimulated by Johnson's Light Infantry Tank. Johnson's tank was evolved from the Medium D, and the Vickers Light Tank bore a strong resemblance to the Medium B. Thus was the evolutionary link with the First World War tanks maintained. But from there on the link, in appearance at any rate, was broken, and only made a fleeting re-appearance in 1940 in a tank called TOG.

The Vickers Medium Mark I was taken into service in 1924, followed almost immediately by the Mark IA and by the Mark II in 1925. In all, some 200 Mediums I and II were built, many of them still being used in Training regiments for driving instruction in the early months of World War II.

In 1926 it was decided to build a tank to replace the Mark II and three A6s (also known as 16-tonners) were produced by Vickers in 1927 and 1928. On these were based the Medium Mark III, but because of the Mark III's high cost only three were built, of which one was destroyed by fire, leaving the only two non-obsolete mediums mentioned above.

Simultaneously with the development of the Medium Mark I had come a requirement from the War Office for a heavy tank to support infantry. This materialized in 1926 as the Independent (A1E1), but it was never made clear to anyone concerned whether the tank was meant as a prototype or a "one-off" or indeed what its purpose was. In any event, only the single tank was built and there was no more infantry tank work until 1934 when the design was started for an "I" tank to equip the army tank battalions, the first of which had been designated that year.

Another line of AFV development in the 1920s started with the one- and two-man tankettes built by Martel and Carden-Loyd. The Carden-Loyd light armoured vehicles Marks I to VI led to the first Vickers light tank after the Carden-Loyd firm had been taken over by Vickers in 1928. The Vickers Light Tank Mark I appeared in 1930, having evolved from the Carden-Loyd Mark VII prototype light tank, the

first to have a traversing turret. The Mark I was followed by the Mark II (1930) which was the pattern on which all subsequent light tanks were based up to Mark VI. Apart from the two Medium IIIs the only tanks the army had in 1936 which were not classified as obsolete were 22 Mark V light tanks (the total production of this Mark) and 47 Mark VIs which were just being introduced.

The Mark VI and its variants (VIA, VIB, and VIC) were the high-water mark of light tank development. Although there was a Mark VII (the Tetrarch) and a Mark VIII (the Harry Hopkins), the light tank was obsolescent as a type by the time these were produced from 1941 onwards.

Obsolescent or not, however, the light tanks had to play an important numerical part in Britain's armoured units in the fighting in France in May and June 1940 and in the battles in the Western Desert until the advent of the American Stuarts in 1941. Even some Mediums had to take part in operational service in Egypt at the beginning of the war, and after the disaster in France in May-June 1940 the Mediums, like everything else in Britain, had to stand ready to repel invasion.

The high cost of the Medium Mark III led to an attempt to produce a cheaper machine carrying the same main turret armament but without the subsidiary turrets which the Independent had brought into fashion. Known familiarly from their weight as the 14-tonners and officially as the A7s, three experimental tanks were designed and built by the Royal Ordnance Factory, two in 1929, the third in 1934. Development work went on until 1937 and although the tank never went into production the A7 contributed several points to contemporary and subsequent designs.

Vickers, too, started to design a successor to the Medium III based on the A7. Work on this other experimental Medium, the A8, continued from 1933 to 1937, when it too was abandoned.

"1st Brigade, Royal Tank Corps" on Salisbury Plain, September 1931. Liddell Hart called it "the most important step in tactical experiment since the training of the Light Brigade at Shorncliffe Camp, prior to the fight with Napoleon's armies in the Peninsular War." (*The Times*)

Less abortive, however, was the work that was going on at this same time on the A9. The A9 was designed by Sir John Carden of Vickers to a 1934 War Office specification for a close support tank, a "Woolworth medium tank" that would be cheap but effective. In fact there were two specifications—the A9 and the A10. Both had the same chassis but the A10 was to have additional armour. The reason for this duplication was that the current theory of armoured warfare demanded two classes of tank as well as the light tank for reconnaissance. These new classes were in fact an emphasized division of the two functions that the Medium tank might have carried out albeit ineffectively in war and did in practice carry out on manoeuvres: close support of infantry, and independent mobile operations. The first rôle remanded "I" tanks, the second "cruisers." The A9 was to be the first cruiser, the A10 the first "I" tank. In the event, while the A9 was officially designated Cruiser Mark I the A10 did not become the first "I" tank. Instead, after being dropped because it was not considered to be heavily enough armoured for infantry support, it became a "heavy cruiser" for a time and then took its place in history as Cruiser Mark II. Both the A9 and the A10 were regarded only as stop-gaps in the cruiser rôle, the future of the cruiser being seen as developing through the Christie chassis and the A13—the Cruiser Mark III—which was the first British tank to have this type of suspension. Cruiser development, including the A13, is dealt with in Volume Three of this series *(British and Commonwealth AFVs, 1940-45)*.

Before Carden had completed the A9 and the A10 he began the design of yet another tank, which was to be a "heavy I tank" with armour thick enough to withstand any existing anti-tank weapons but which, unlike the A10, would mount only a ·303-in. or a ·5-in. machine-gun. This tank, the A11, became the Infantry Tank Mark I. Even before it was finished it was apparent that its advantages of cheapness and mechanical reliability would not offset the disadvantages of a two-man crew and insufficient armament. Infantry Tank Mark II, of which only two were in service on the day Britain went to war on September 3, 1939, was designed to take its place. Both Marks were known as Matilda. In 1938 Vickers proposed a new infantry tank based on what they had learnt from the A9, the A10, and the A11 (the A12, Infantry Tank Mark II, was not a Vickers tank). The proposal was accepted and resulted in the Valentine, or Infantry Tank Mark III.

Two points stand out from this recital of different tank projects. The first is their multiplicity; the second is the compulsion towards heavier and heavier armour. These are the two characteristics of the immediate pre-war period. Throughout the inter-war years the accent in Britain was on tank development, not tank production. Not until 1938 did production begin to override development and the realization strike home that quantity was imperative as well as quality. By then it was too late to provide enough tanks to equip the armoured formations that were now accepted as necessary. On September 3, 1939, the army possessed only 146 cruiser and "I" tanks. In the

"The most ubiquitous tracked vehicle. . . ." Bren Carriers of the B.E.F. in France, 1940. (Imperial War Museum)

Armoured cars in the desert—Rolls-Royce 1924 pattern of A Squadron 11th Hussars on a reconnaissance to Baharia Oasis, 200 miles south-west of Cairo, January 1935.

eight months between then and Dunkirk 437 were produced, but of these 210 were lost in France. Even so, it was not until July 9, 1941, that tank production became a 1A production priority.

The second point, the trend to heavier armour, was no less symptomatic. While the Germans concentrated on speed and manoeuvrability at the expense of armour, and the French reversed the process, the British could not make up their minds what they wanted. Some had visions of formations of tanks operating like battle-fleets; others saw only a line of trenches from Switzerland to the coast and infantry trying to advance against the barrier of machine-gun fire. When the war began these latter still had the more powerful voices. Their obsession with "Somme mud" resulted in the development of tanks to break through the West Wall. One of these developments, TOG, came to nothing; but the other resulted in the Churchill, Infantry Tank Mark IV. TOG is described in this Volume, the Churchill in Volume Three.

As well as the three classes of tank—light for reconnaissance, medium or cruiser for exploitation, and heavily armoured tanks for close support of infantry in the assault—which studies had suggested were necessary, there was also developed a lightly armoured tracked machine-gun carrier. This was the second design path that came from the early Carden-Loyds, the light tank being the other. Unlike the light tank, however, this carrier was not intended to be used as a fighting vehicle but was to be a means of transporting crew and fire power—originally a Vickers medium machine-gun and then a Bren light MG—which was dismounted for action. Two other specialized versions of the carrier—the Cavalry and the Scout—were produced, to be followed in 1940 by a Universal carrier which was suitable for all purposes, any special requirements being met by minor modifications. Bren and Scout carriers, despite the intention for which they were designed, frequently had to be used as close contact fighting vehicles during the 1940 campaign in France. The carrier later became the most ubiquitous tracked vehicle in the British and Commonwealth armies.

As well as the light tank and the carrier the third type of vehicle used for reconnaissance was the armoured car. In the '20s and early '30s this was virtually the only type, and the armoured car was popular both because of its capabilities in policing operations and co-operation with horsed cavalry, and on account of its cheapness. But as the light tank and carrier were developed—especially the light tank—the armoured car's popularity began to wane in the British army, unlike the German and French armies which still attached importance to the wheeled armoured vehicle. The war reversed the armoured car's fortunes yet again. The success of the Panzer divisions which used armoured cars as the main vehicles for their reconnaissance units, and then the experience of the British and Commonwealth forces in the Libyan desert put armoured cars in the ascendent once more with the result that at the time of second Alamein in October 1942 British forces in the Middle East had as many as 1,473 armoured cars compared with 2,671 tanks.

Throughout the 21-year period covered in this Volume the use of armour and the extent to which the army should be mechanized were the main points of debate in military circles. The debate was conducted, in many instances, with bitterness and disdain. Ironically, those who benefitted most from this debate, which was conducted for the most part in public, were the Germans. While the French went the whole hog in regarding the tank as a supporting arm for infantry, the Germans under the inspiration of Guderian listened to the teachings of Fuller, Lindsay, Martel, Hobart, Liddell Hart and others and made the tank the queen of the battlefield.

As late as November 1939 General Keller, Inspector-General of Tanks in the French army, wrote: "Even supposing that the present fortified line were breached or out-flanked, it does not appear that our opponents will find a combination of circumstances as favourable for a *Blitzkrieg* as in Poland. One can see, then, that in future operations the primary rôle of the tank will be the same as in the past: to assist the infantry in reaching successive objectives."

As early as 1929 Guderian in planning for the future was convinced that "tanks must play the primary rôle, the other weapons being subordinated to the requirements of the armour. . . . What was needed were armoured divisions which would include all the supporting arms needed to allow the tanks to fight with full effect."

The British were unable to make up their minds who was right. They tried to implement both beliefs simultaneously and, initially at any rate, with inadequate resources implemented neither effectively.

Infantry Tanks Mark II—Matildas in the desert.   (Imperial War Museum)

Vickers Medium Tank Mark III. Front view shows armament, gunner's telescope in its aperture, and lack of protection over the observation slot in the command post. (R.A.C. Tank Museum)

Mediums Marks I-III by Maj.-Gen. N. W. Duncan

AFTER the First World War there was a widespread feeling of hope that no longer would it be necessary to reckon with the long lines of trenches, covered by machine-guns and wire that had proved insuperable obstacles to so many attempts to break out into open country. This happy state had been foreshadowed in Colonel Fuller's "Plan 1919" which required large numbers of fast-moving tanks to exploit success after an armoured breakthrough. To a greater or lesser extent this fired everyone's imagination and military thought was concentrated on open warfare with static operations tucked far away in the background.

To meet the 1919 plan, tanks of higher speed had been developed: Mediums A, B and C with a speed between 8 and 12 m.p.h., and the Medium D which was designed to do 25 m.p.h. However the latter was discarded because it proved unreliable and a poor fighting chamber so that the army was left with no fast-moving tank except for a few Medium Cs which had been completed after the Armistice and in any case were not really the type of light speedy vehicle that was vaguely envisaged. Therein lay the trouble: no one could make up their mind exactly what the tank was to do in the post-war army. Tanks were both disliked and feared and it is important to realize the depth of feeling against them for it holds the key to much of the muddled thought and procrastination that followed. Prejudice was rife: in 1920 it was stated in print "the cavalry will never be scrapped to make room for tanks" and a senior officer in a lecture held that tanks could never do what horse and man had accomplished in Palestine and ended by saying "we must rely on the man and the horse for really decisive results". Despite the terrible lessons taught by machine-

guns in France, these views were endorsed by the majority of the Army and Corps commanders who had been in France and who helped to increase the prejudice against the tank.

Clear long-range thought on armoured problems was fraught with difficulty. The British Army never attempted to produce a tactical doctrine for the use of armour or even to define its requirements from manufacturers, which accounts to some extent for the original appearance of the Vickers tank as a Light machine in 1923 and its subsequent reclassification as a Medium in 1924. Across the North Sea, defeated Germany had reached her theoretical tank requirements as a result of tactical studies, even defining class weights: the British eventually blundered into a rough definition that anything under ten tons was a light tank with medium types above that figure.

The army had another problem to face over tank construction: fast movement across country brought a crop of new engineering problems and very few firms were either sufficiently interested or had enough experience to undertake development work of this nature. Vickers-Armstrong for years were the only civilian firm who would do tank work and their only competitor was the Royal Ordnance Factory at Woolwich. The experimental budget was a small one and production orders for tanks were on such a diminutive scale as to afford little inducement for concentrated effort. Despite all these difficulties a great deal of experimental work was carried out from 1926 to 1937 under the continually renewed Cabinet statement that no war was likely for ten years. Continued reiteration inhibited any sense of urgency and virtually meant that all designs remained experimental and were

During development of Johnson's Light "D" Tank, experimental tracks were fitted to an Overland chassis. (Imperial War Museum)

never finalized for production. It was not until 1938 when war was declared to be imminent that tank production, as opposed to tank development, assumed a position of overriding importance.

PART ONE 1921—1926

The story of the post-war Medium tank really begins with the closure of the Tank Design Department, on the grounds of economy, in 1923. The Department had evolved a light infantry tank from the Medium D and although it proved unreliable, despite promising features, it stimulated Vickers-Armstrong to produce a light infantry tank which was running in 1921—not, incidentally, a tank for light infantry but a light tank for use with infantry.

VICKERS LIGHT TANK, 1921

It may seem anomalous to commence an account of Medium tanks with the description of a light tank: the reason lies in nomenclature, for the Medium tanks were originally known as Light tanks. Vickers built two prototypes of their Light tank which appeared in 1921. These looked rather like a Medium B as far as the general outline: the track form was the same and the side doors were retained although the bulge in them to allow the side of the tank to be covered by revolver fire was eliminated. The squat ugly superstructure was replaced by a hemispherical revolving turret with 360° traverse and a turret ring 67 in. in diameter. The commander had a cupola, which could be opened, in the centre of the turret.

The tank weighed $8\frac{1}{2}$ tons and carried $\frac{1}{4}$ in. armour. An 86 h.p. engine drove through cross shafts Williams-Janney infinitely variable hydraulic units which also provided the means of steering the tank. All the power train was housed in a separate compartment at the back of the tank. The track was sprung by articulated bogies controlled by vertical helical springs working in enclosed guides.

The two tanks, Nos. 1 and 2 differed in their armament: No. 1 appeared with three ball mountings for Hotchkiss MGs in the turret sides while No. 2, which was completed in the remarkably short time of five and a half months, carried a 3-pdr. gun and also had three Hotchkiss mountings for ground work and an additional position in the back of the turret roof for AA work. 50 rounds of 3-pdr. ammunition were carried and 6,000 rounds of SAA.

The Vickers Light Tank, 1921, was commendably low, standing about 7 ft. from the ground but it proved unreliable mechanically and the project was abandoned in 1922.

VICKERS MEDIUM TANK MARK I

(originally Vickers Light Tank Mk. I)

Following the failure of their first tank, Vickers-Armstrong designed and built the Vickers Light Tank Mark I and sent the first models to the Central Schools at Bovington for trial in 1923. Some trouble was experienced with the brake bands owing to faulty lining—there was a hideous moment when one of the experimental models suffered steering failure in the middle of a long and very narrow bridge—but this was soon overcome and about 200 Mark Is and IIs were built. They remained in service with the Royal Tank Corps until 1938/39, a record for longevity only equalled by the Rolls Royce armoured car. They could have been replaced earlier for there were a variety of designs and prototypes from which to choose, but no one in the War Office could make up their mind about the future rôle of the tank: consequently no design was ever finalized for production and the Tank Corps had to train with machines which were blatantly unfit for battle. British tank design was probably better than any other in the world at the time but the shortage of orders and money, and the lack of a clear decision on requirements, never gave tank production a chance.

In the '20s the technique of welding armour plate had not been perfected and armour plates were secured by rivets to a frame or chassis of angle iron which was stiffened by gussets and corner plates to resist the strains imposed on the structure by cross-country movement. Mark I's chassis was a box, rectangular in shape, with a smaller box in front of this to contain the engine and the driver alongside it. Between the engine and the driver was a double asbestos and steel partition. Seven plates on each side and six on the floor, made from homogeneous armour ·25 in. thick were attached to the chassis. On top of the main superstructure was a revolving turret carrying a 3-pdr. gun with geared traverse and elevation and four Hotchkiss MGs in ball mountings: one of these, at the back of the turret, which was cylindrical in shape, was intended for use against aircraft. The sides of the turret were bevelled and a circular opening in the centre protected by a hinged lid was provided for the commander who was expected to control his crew by word of mouth. The 3-pdr. was fired by pressing the elevating hand wheel.

Two Vickers MGs in armoured jackets were carried in big ball mountings on either side of the tank just behind the escape doors. These VMG gunners only had limited observation and their firing position, kneeling on one knee, was uncomfortable in the extreme.

The Vickers Mediums, as they were renamed in 1924, were powered by an Armstrong Siddeley engine of 90 b.h.p., air-cooled and developed from contemporary aircraft engines. The drive was taken from the engine by a multiple dry-plate clutch to a four-speed gearbox without synchromesh which provided any driver with a real challenge if it was to be handled silently. A propeller shaft ran to the bevel box at the back of the tank which carried at either end of its cross shafts a two-speed epicyclic gear providing both emergency low ratios on the 1st and 2nd gears and also a means of steering the tank. The whole of the mechanism was scattered about the tank: gone was the rear power compartment, pioneered by the Medium Bs and Cs of war-time days. The engine was perched in front alongside the driver, the gearbox was under the commander's feet and the bevel box and epicylics were at the back underneath the petrol tanks which were attached to the rear wall inside the

machine, an unbelievably retrograde step in view of war-time experience.

The Armstrong Siddeley engine had steel cylinders, an innovation for land use, shrouded by an aluminium casing. Air was drawn through the casing by a fan running in a circular chamber carrying oil cooling pipes on its inside circumference. A clutch allowing limited slip was incorporated in the drive to absorb shocks from sudden changes in engine revolutions. Oil, which played a considerable part in cooling the engine, was carried in a separate four-gallon tank, later increased to one of $13\frac{1}{2}$ gallons, and circulated by the pressure side of a combined pressure and scavenging pump. Bearings were lubricated by pressure through drilled passages and considerable reliance was also placed on splash. Oil consumption was heavy.

Petrol was supplied to the two Claudel Hobson carburettors by gravity from a petrol-feed tank in the driver's compartment: this was kept filled by a special Briggs fuel pump, driven from the engine, the surplus being returned to the main tanks.

Two 4-cylinder magnetos were mounted on a bracket on the front engine cover and flexibly coupled through spur gears to a bevel drive from the crankshaft. Each magneto fired one bank of cylinders and a hand magneto was provided to assist starting. Mark I tank could only be started from the inside by hand but an aperture in the front plate was provided in Mark IA and Mark II tanks which allowed them to be started from the outside. An electric starter motor was fitted as part of a complete 12-volt system but the motor was not notably efficient and could only be used when the engine was warm. All Mark Is and IAs were difficult to start and there was one notable occasion after a fortnight's Christmas leave when a battalion took six hours to start three tanks out of 30 following a period of severe frost!

On either side of the tank there were five suspension units, each housing two helical springs, one three times as long as the other, the differing differential rates being designed to absorb varying shocks. The bogie casing was bolted on to the tank and enclosed a connecting trunk pivoted to the bogie frame. At either end of this was a short axle which carried two small suspension wheels, each bearing on the inside of the track astride the guiding horns. The suspension wheels cantilevered out from the bogie frames were a perpetual nuisance. The axles were continually breaking and the path of the Mark I tanks was littered with discarded wheels. In 1931 a box bogie which

Vickers Light Tank 1921 No. 1, showing the mountings for the Hotchkiss guns. Note superficial resemblance to Medium Mark B, except that side door is no longer bulged and hemispherical turret has replaced angular superstructure. (R.A.C. Tank Museum)

Vickers Light Tank 1921 with commander's cupola open. (R.A.C. Tank Museum)

3

Vickers Light Tank 1921 No. 2 during trials with 3-pdr. gun mounted. (R.A.C. Tank Museum)

were replaced by the No. 3 track which had both sole and connecting link formed in one nickel steel stamping. Each plate had a recessed hollow in it but as there was no means of cleaning out the mud which lodged in its interior it was not particularly effective. Track plates were 13 inches wide and were joined by headed hollow track pins secured in place by a spring washer and nut on the threaded end. Ground pressure was very high—between 30 and 40 lbs. per sq. in.—and the 132 plates, 66 each side, weighed 2,604 lbs. for the No. 3 pattern.

MARK IA MEDIUM TANK

The first thirty Mark I tanks were followed by fifty Mark IAs. Externally there was little difference between the two. The Mark IA had slightly thicker armour, using both ·25 in. and 8 mm. (approximately ·33 in.) plates, and the driver's hood was split vertically down the centre allowing each half to swing back: the top plate folded back on to the superstructure in contrast to the Mark I where the driver's hood was hinged to fold back as a complete unit.

The back plate of the turret was bevelled in the Mark IA which gave the Hotchkiss a better chance in its AA rôle and an opening was provided in the front plate to allow the engine to be started from the outside. Inside the tank, brow and chin pads for the gunners were of improved pattern and a primitive locking plunger in the hand traversing gear for the 3-pdr. which had never been satisfactory was abandoned.

gave support to the outboard ends of the wheel axles was introduced and as a result trouble virtually ceased. Inclined single-wheel suspension units bore against the inclined portions of the track and an adjustable idler wheel at the front end took care of track tension. No shock absorbers were fitted and the ride was apt to be very rough at speed.

The upper run of the track was supported by four return rollers attached to the suspension units. The Mark I wheels with metal rims were later changed for the Mark II type with rubber tyres which proved far more satisfactory. The tracks were originally built by rivetting a sole plate to a connecting link but these

Vickers Medium Mark I showing driver's hood hinging back as one unit. (Imperial War Museum)

Vickers Medium Mark I CS with a 15-pdr. mortar in place of the 3-pdr. for close support. The box on the side of the turret is for signal flags. The bogies are the early open type.
(R.A.C. Tank Museum)

MARK IA★ MEDIUM TANK

The Mark IA★ can be distinguished by the coaxial VMG mounted alongside the 3-pdr. in the turret and by the absence of the Hotchkiss MG mountings. A lead counterweight was bolted to the back of the turret to compensate for the weight of the armoured jacket and a command post (officially described as a "Bishop's Mitre" from its shape when opened) was fitted above the circular opening in the top of the turret; this had independent traverse and could be opened at need; no bullet-proof glass was fitted.

The difficulties which the side VMG gunners faced in handling their weapons were paralleled by the problems confronting the 3-pdr. gunner. No seat was provided for him and he had to crouch over his handles, his right hand working in the horizontal plane controlling the traversing wheel, and his left in the vertical plane operating the elevating gear which also carried the firing handle. A telescope of 1/1 magnification carried cross wires and elevation was put on the sighting drum to alter the angle of sight relative to the bore. Co-ordination of hands was particularly difficult owing to the wide spacing of the handles and before the annual gunnery camp Vickers Medium tank commanders and gunners were to be seen stalking about barracks waving their hands in mystic circles to achieve automatic co-ordination of hand and eye.

MARK II MEDIUM TANK

100 Vickers Medium Mark II tanks were supplied to the British Army from 1925 onwards and they were in service until 1938/39 and were then used in Training regiments for initial instruction in tracked vehicle driving during the early days of World War II. The same chassis, engine and transmission were used but the exterior shape was changed, the Mark IIs appearing much bulkier. The hull superstructure was a little higher and the driver's hood stood proud of this; the driver's vizor was divided in two and the top hinged back as in the Mark IA. Skirting plates were fitted over the suspension, and the box bogies, still controlled by vertical springs, were located by slipper blocks moving in external guides.

The epicyclic gears for steering and emergency low ratios were operated by Rackham clutches which were a form of servo control, mechanically operated.

This Mark I, the only one to be so modified, was fitted with a Ricardo diesel 90-h.p. engine. Note cooler beside number plate and also box bogies in place of early open type.
(R.A.C. Tank Museum)

Mark IA* with coaxial Vickers machine-gun and absence of Hotchkiss mountings. Note also command post and box bogies. The lead counterweight can be seen at the back of the turret.
(R.A.C. Tank Museum)

Mark 1A of 1924 with open suspension bogies. Two of the turret Hotchkiss guns can be seen and one of the side Vickers machine-guns, as well as the 3-pdr. (R.A.C. Tank Museum)

Rollers on a floating brake drum were forced up inclined planes cut on the circumference of the epicyclic gear carrier: in so doing they released the pressure on the compressor levers and so allowed the epicyclic gear to revolve idly on itself—the tank then turned towards the side on which there was no drive to the tracks.

Mark II appeared with the 3-pdr. and 4 Hotchkiss MGs in the turret, the fourth in a bevelled back plate for AA work. The two side VMGs were also retained in this Mark, which weighed ¾ ton more than Mark IA with a consequent reduction in speed to 13 m.p.h. The additional weight coupled with the jerkiness of the Rackham clutches made them appear sluggish in comparison with the Mark Is and IAs whose designed road speed was 15 m.p.h. A properly maintained tank in the hands of a good driver could comfortably exceed this speed and the fastest Mark I, the C.O.'s tank of the 2nd Battalion, RTC, was on many occasions timed at 25 m.p.h. on good going.

MARK II★ MEDIUM TANK

This was the Mark II modified by the addition of a coaxial VMG in the turret, the abolition of all Hotchkiss MGs, and the addition of a commander's post situated further back than in the Mark IA★ which thus removed the commander's stomach from too close a proximity for comfort to the shells ejected from the semi-automatic breech block of the 3-pdr.

MARK IIA MEDIUM TANK

This version was produced in 1930 and 20 were built by Vickers. The 3-pdr. and the Vickers machine-gun were coaxial, and there was a command post cupola as in the Mark II★. But the bevel was removed from the rear of the turret, and on the port side, just forward of the side door, an electrically operated ventilating fan was protected by an armoured box whose top rose above the superstructure.

MARK II★★ MEDIUM TANK

During 1932 work was begun on converting 44 Medium Mark IIs by fitting coaxial mountings, a command post cupola on the turret roof, and an armoured container for a wireless set at the back of the turret. With this wireless bulge attached the tanks were designated Mark II★★—the wireless bulge being indicated by the second star.†

MEDIUM MARK II TROPICAL

Five Mark II tanks which had been specially modified and fitted to meet tropical conditions were sent to Egypt in 1928. The chief modifications were sun screens of woven asbestos fitted outside the upper surfaces and sides of the tank with an air gap of an inch to an inch and a half between the sheeting and the armour plate, and insulation of the Rackham steering clutches and control levers.

MARK IIA CS MEDIUM TANK

As the possibilities of independent tank action revealed themselves, a need arose for cover by smoke and possibly for the assistance of shells to cover the advance of the assaulting tanks. To provide this the main armament in Mark IIA Medium tanks was replaced by a 3·7 in. mortar firing a 15-lb. shell. This was principally used to provide smoke cover behind which manoeuvre could take place unobserved by the enemy. The range of smoke shell was about 1,000 yards. A certain number of HE shells were also carried although there was no means of ensuring the accurate application of HE fire to the target other than the time-honoured formula of "cock her up a bit more and you should be about right"! These Close Support tanks were provided on a scale of two for each company headquarters.

†There is evidence to show that there was also a Mark IIA★ which was a Mark IIA with an armoured wireless container fitted to the back of the turret. A photograph of one in difficulties in a tank trap appears on a later page—Editor.

VICKERS MEDIUM TANK VARIATIONS

The Vickers Medium tank was widely used: it was the first practical tank in production in 1923 and it offered reasonable offensive power and protection at the time it appeared. Vickers were prepared to make almost any variation the purchaser required and both the Medium IA and II appeared in many differing guises. It is not possible to list them all but among the more interesting are the following varieties:

Medium I Wheel and Track, 1926

To overcome track wear rubber-tyred wheels, the front pair steerable, were mounted on sub-frames at the front and back of the tank. These frames could be forced down by power driven jacks so that the wheels took the load and the track was clear of the ground. The rear wheels could be driven and although the tank was in a state of unstable equilibrium, it could move on roads looking, as one observer described it, "rather like a house perched on a very inadequate roller skate". After trials the wheels were removed and the tank was used in its normal state.

Medium II Bridgecarrier, 1927/1928

Bridge girders to construct an 18 foot bridge capable of carrying a medium tank were attached to the sides of a Mark II. A series of experiments to devise a method of launching the completed bridge, which was to be assembled by the crew near the scene of action, were instituted but never achieved success.

Medium II Female, 1927

Two of these tanks were built for the Indian Government following successful trials of Medium IIs carried out under the command of (the then) Lieut. J. T. Crocker. No main armament was mounted but ball mountings were provided for four VMGs in the turret, a lay-out closely resembling that of the Crossley armoured car turret.†

Medium II Box Tank, 1928

This vehicle was built as an experiment to give a battalion commander better facilities for exercising command in the field than he normally had in a tank. A box body was fitted on a Medium Mark II chassis without any armament save for one machine-gun which was also available, if needed, for dismounted use. It was much appreciated by battalion commanders but really came into its own with the Tank Brigade in 1931: fitted with two wireless sets it was used by the Brigade Commander and was really the predecessor of the wheeled Armoured Command Vehicles which were used so much during World War II.

Medium Mark II★ Special, 1929

Australia ordered four of these machines which had the coaxial VMG on the left of the 3-pdr. and a

†Although generally known as Medium Mark II Female their correct designation is Tank Light Mark IA Special (L) India because they were never actually re-classified as Medium.—Editor.

Mark II* with coaxial Vickers machine-gun and armoured command post on turret roof. The cupola was officially described as a "Bishop's Mitre", from its shape when open—as in this photograph. Note base for wireless aerial at corner of turret. Tracks are No. 3 pattern with recesses in the plate.
(Imperial War Museum)

Mark II. Note driver's hood proud of superstructure, one of the recognition points of all Mark IIs and variants. This vehicle was later converted to a Mark II*. The tracks are No. 1 pattern without recesses in the plates. (R.A.C. Tank Museum)

Driver's compartment in Medium Marks II, IIA, and II*. (Imperial War Museum)

separate VMG in a ball mounting on the right hand side of the turret.

Medium Mark II★ Command Tank, 1931
This was a Mark II tank with the 3-pdr. removed and replaced with a dummy gun made of wood. The alteration was carried out to provide a command tank for the Tank Brigade in 1931. Two wireless sets were mounted in the turret which could not be revolved.

VICKERS MEDIUM C TANK

This was a post-war prototype and bears no relation to the Medium C built in 1918–1919 by Messrs. Foster of Lincoln. This tank was based on the Medium II chassis and weighed 11 tons. It was powered by a

110 h.p. water-cooled engine, a striking departure from current thought, and used the normal transmission of the standard medium tank. The turret was considerably larger than usual and was extended to the rear to accommodate a VMG in a ball mounting firing at 180 degrees to the main armament which had

Side view of Mark II* with cupola closed. Note skirting protecting bogies, a feature common to all Mark IIs and variants. In the background a Light Tank Mark IV. (Imperial War Museum)

been increased to a 6-pdr. gun. The tank had a bow VMG and also carried one in each side, better positioned than in the standard mediums. This interesting modification was only produced in prototype form. The increase in calibre and the change to a water-cooled engine differentiate it sharply from the current run of tanks.

THE MEDIUM TANK CHASSIS AND THE ARTILLERY

The medium tank chassis was also used as a basis for a series of vehicles intended to tow guns of varying calibres. They proved fairly satisfactory, having a good performance across country and a satisfactory draw bar pull. They were never produced on a lavish scale but were followed successively by the Light Dragons which were evolved from the light tank chassis and later by the four-wheeled towing vehicle used so extensively from 1939 onwards. Three Birch guns with an 18-pdr. mounted on a tank chassis were also produced between 1926 and 1929 but never developed beyond the prototype stage. It was a great pity that it was not possible to overcome the radical change in the handling of artillery that their use would have involved. Self-propelled guns as such did not come into general use until American tank chassis were available for the purpose.

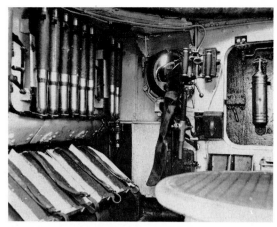

Interior of Medium Mark II showing left side Vickers machine-gun aft of door and 3-pdr. rounds. (Imperial War Museum)

BRITISH MAIN AND SECONDARY ARMAMENTS

All the Medium tanks so far described bristled with machine-guns—heavy ones at that, for the Hotchkiss light machine-gun which had been used by the Tank Corps in the war disappeared in favour of the water-cooled version which became the standard tank gun and was later specially adapted for tank use. Comparatively little attention was paid to the main armament

Mark IIA, showing the armoured box which protected the electrically operated ventilating fan on the port side just forward of the side door. Mark IIA had the ''Bishop's Mitre'' and coaxial Vickers machine-gun like the Mark II.* (R.A.C. Tank Museum)

Above Mark IA

Below Mark II**

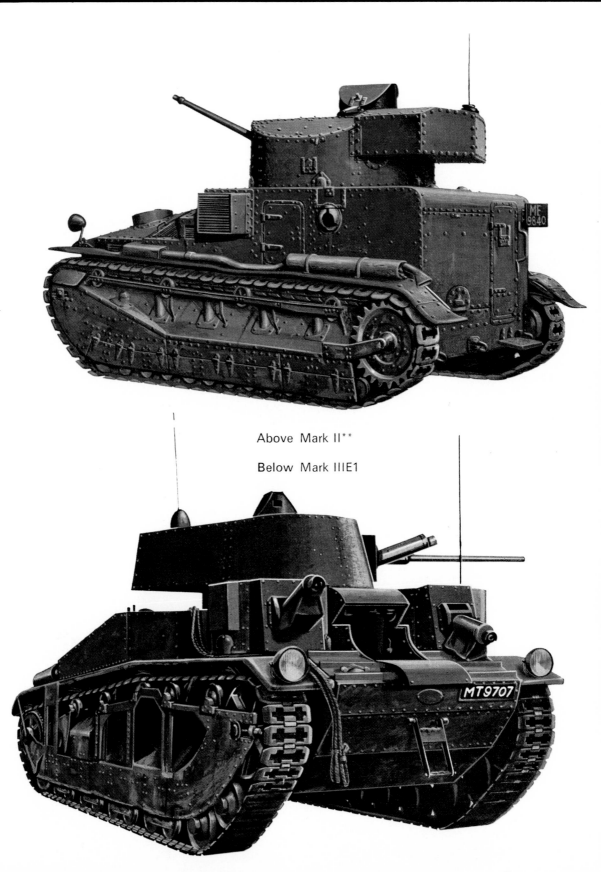

Above Mark II**

Below Mark IIIE1

Interior of Mark IIA showing coaxial mountings and ventilating fan. (Imperial War Museum)

upset all the range drum figures. This lamentable state of affairs was due to the failure to realize that hostile tanks must be a tank's primary target and that until they are destroyed or driven off unarmoured troops are particularly vulnerable. In current military thought at the time, outside the RTC, the tank's principal task was considered to be the destruction of hostile MG and anti-tank gun crews by fire—hence the insistence upon the machine-gun which was considered enough for this task and could also cover the infantry on to their objective. The main armament of British tanks was increased in size and weight very slowly during the War and there was never a period in which the British tank gun was definitely superior to the guns of the tanks that it was opposing. It was not until 1951 that the 20-pdr. in the Sherman assured a British tank of gun superiority over any comparable tank in the world both in the AP and HE rôle.

PART TWO 1926—1937

The medium tanks built during this period were experimental and none ever went into service. They are interesting because they indicate the general trend of tank design at the time and they were all, to a greater or lesser degree, influenced by the Independent tank. This was a heavy machine and only one was ever built: it incorporated some very good features, notably the fighting chamber with its provision for the observation of fire and the machine-gun turrets which were arranged at the four corners of the main turret; in addition the power train was again relegated to a separate compartment at the back of the tank with the fuel stored outside the hull.

Four classes of medium tanks come into this story and the table on a later page sets out their identifying numbers.

which was a 3-pdr. from 1923 to 1939 when it was replaced by a 2-pdr. with the sole exception of the prototype Vickers Medium C which would have had a 6-pdr.

Admittedly the 2-pdr. had a higher muzzle velocity than the 3-pdr. but it was only a shot-firing weapon backed up to some degree by a very few low velocity mortars whose primary function was to fire smoke. In theory the 3-pdr. was supposed to fire both an AP round and also an HE shell, whose explosive content would have been very small. In practice, and for practice, tank crews fired a flat-headed sand-filled shot with a reduced charge to minimize barrel wear, which

Mark IIA CS with mortar in place of 3-pdr. (R.A.C. Tank Museum)

Mark IIA CS. Note driver's hood open, with vizor divided in two and top hinged back—an arrangement common to all Mark IIs and variants. Because of Britain's tank shortage in 1940, especially after the fall of France, Mediums were brought back into service with operational units for a time. The tanks in this photograph, taken in England in autumn 1940, are probably of C Squadron, 3rd. Royal Tanks, part of 1st. Armoured Brigade, 2nd. Armoured Division, which sailed for the Middle East in November of that year.
(Imperial War Museum)

A6—THE 16 TONNER

The procedure for the procurement of a tank shows its evolution from an idea to a running machine, and although the A6s never went into service they did play a considerable part in the development of later machines especially as far as suspension was concerned.

In May 1926 when the Vickers Mediums had been in service for some time, the Royal Tank Corps Centre were asked to forward their views on the improvements required to increase the mechanical and fighting efficiency in a new medium tank. The user was not normally given the chance to express his views in detail before the construction of a new machine but where this procedure was adopted, as for the A6 and the Independent, the results were most satisfactory. The RTCC report, which was completed by July 1926, and the general specification for the new tank which

was based on it, listed the following points: Two machine-gun turrets were needed and the weight was not to exceed $15\frac{1}{2}$ tons. The tank was to be capable of transport by rail and was to be as simple in design and as accessible as possible. The radius of action for lubricating oil was to equal that for fuel—the Vickers Mediums were notorious offenders in this respect even after larger oil tanks had been installed. Wireless was to be developed and installed and the main armament should penetrate comparable hostile tanks at a range of 1,000 yards. Fuel tanks were to be outside the hull, and front and belly armour must provide protection when crests were crossed. Particular emphasis was laid on silence—experiments with rubber tracks and wheel rims had shown promise.

This outline specification was forwarded to Vickers-Armstrong who were also given instructions to build A6, a tank which should incorporate the points laid

*Side view of Mark II** showing wireless bulge at back of turret.*
(R.A.C. Tank Museum)

*Three-quarter rear view of Mark II** with wireless bulge.*
(R.A.C. Tank Museum)

Mark IIA* in difficulties—caught in a pit dug by sappers to test tank stopping techniques. (Imperial War Museum)

VICKERS MEDIUM TANKS 1921–26

Type	Weight tons	Length	Width	Height	Engine	Max speed m.p.h.	Radius Miles	Armament Main	Machine-guns	Armour mm. max/min	Crew	Remarks
Vickers Light Infantry								1 ×3-pdr.	3 × ·303 Hotchkiss			
Medium Mk I	11·7	17'6"	9'1½"	9'3"	Armstrong Siddeley V8 90 b.h.p. air-cooled	15	120	1 ×3-pdr.	4 × ·303 Hotchkiss 2 × ·303 Vickers	6·25/–	5	
Medium Mk IA	11·9	17'6"	9'1½"	8'10½"	Armstrong Siddeley V8 90 b.h.p. air-cooled	15	120	1 ×3-pdr.	4 × ·303 Hotchkiss 2 × ·303 Vickers	8/6·25	5	Bevelled back plate to turret for AA Hotchkiss
Medium Mk IA*	11·9 12·1	17'6"	9'1½"	9'10½"	Armstrong Siddeley V8 90 b.h.p. air-cooled	15	120	1 ×3-pdr.	3 × ·303 Vickers	6·25/– 8/6·25	5	One Vickers machine-gun mounted coaxially with 3-pdr.
Medium Mk II	13·2	17'6"	9'1½"	8'10"	Armstrong Siddeley V8 90 b.h.p. air-cooled	15	120	1 ×3-pdr.	4 × ·303 Hotchkiss 2 × ·303 Vickers	8/6·25	5	
Medium Mk II*	13·5	17'6"	9'1½"	10'0"	Armstrong Siddeley V8 90 b.h.p. air-cooled	15	120	1 ×3-pdr.	3 × ·303 Vickers	8/6·25	5	One Vickers mounted coaxially with 3-pdr. Mk II** had a wireless bulge fitted to turret
Medium Mk II ACS	14·0	17'6"	9'1½"	10'0"	Armstrong Siddeley V8 90 b.h.p. air-cooled	15	120	1 ×3·7 Howitzer	3 × Vickers machine-guns	8/6·25	5	Mk IIA* had a wireless bulge fitted to turret
Vickers Medium C	11·6	18'4"	8'4"	8'0"	6-cyl. 110 b.h.p. water-cooled	20	125	1 ×6-pdr.	4 × Vickers machine-guns	6·5/–	5	Prototype only. No coaxial machine-gun

Experimental Wheel and Track Medium Mark I. Three-quarter front view showing wheels raised. Turret is reversed. This tank has an experimental driver's hood.
(Imperial War Museum)

down. The firm were given a free hand over the lay-out although preference was expressed for a separate rear engine compartment: also an improvement in steering by comparison with the Medium tanks was required and owing to the limitations imposed by bridging equipment the frontal armour could not exceed 13 mm. with 9 mm. elsewhere on the tank.

These instructions to Vickers were followed by another most interesting letter from the War Office which set out three classes of tanks as possible future requirements,

a. The Big Tank—a battle tank.
b. A light tank—to protect troops going into battle and for exploitation.
c. A two-man tank—possibly on the lines of the Morris Martel for reconnaissance duties.

By September 1926 Vickers Armstrong had pro-

Experimental Wheel and Track Medium Mark I with wheels lowered and tracks clear of the ground.
(R.A.C. Tank Museum)

duced an outline of their proposals: the new tank was to be built on the lines of the Independent with a fighting chamber in front and the power train housed separately in rear. The main turret with the 3-pdr. and a coaxial MG would have all round traverse with special facilities for the commander and the observer for observation. (The observer appears in both the Independent and the A6s and Medium IIIs: he would have been valuable even in those days of little obscuration and much more so had it been possible to include him as muzzle velocities became higher: on the other hand the cost, in terms of weight of the additional armour needed to house him, would have upset other factors, weight, power etc, and reduced the tank's performance.) The new tank was to have two machine-gun turrets, each with twin Vickers, and a third MG turret behind the main one was to house an AA MG. Armour was to be on a 13 and $6\frac{1}{2}$ mm. basis and the estimated weight would be about 14 tons. 120 gallons of fuel were to be carried, 110 in outside tanks on the running boards and the rest in a gravity tank inside the tank. At the estimated weight a 120 h.p. engine would give 14 m.p.h. and 180 would be needed to attain 20 m.p.h.

A mock-up was ready for inspection by March 1927 and was approved, Vickers being given orders for a second A6 which was to be fitted with a different gearbox, hydraulically operated and incorporating epicyclic gears. The two tanks were completed and sent to the Mechanized Warfare Experimental Establishment for trials by June 1928, a remarkably short time for the building of a new vehicle. An interesting point arose over the insistence on skirting plates. Vickers felt that they would be unable to provide

Mark II Bridgecarrier fitted with girders.
(R.A.C. Tank Museum)

appeared with an AS 180 h.p. air-cooled engine was later re-engined with a 500 h.p. Thorneycroft 6-cylinder unit: this was a slow speed motor originally intended for nautical use but it performed well under trial as a tank engine and ran a total distance of 500 miles.

A suggestion was put forward that the AS engine on A6E1 should be replaced by two Rolls-Royce/Phantom engines, coupled as one unit. A Wilson hydraulic gearbox and Wilson epicyclic steering units were also specified, but since this virtually involved a complete rebuild of the tank the proposal was abandoned on account of cost. In retrospect it is a pity that the idea came to nothing: it might have solved the problem of adequate horse power for tank engines which has always bedevilled our tank designers. The comparison with contemporary American tanks which were then using aircraft engines adapted for ground work is an interesting one.

these within the weight limitation but they were told that they must be provided even at the cost of an adjustment of armour elsewhere on the tank.

Power units
The Armstrong Siddeley V8 180 h.p. engine was substantially the same as that fitted to the Vickers Mediums. It was an air-cooled unit with steel cylinders and shrouded in similar fashion for cooling. A6E2 was fitted with a Ricardo CI engine of nominal 180 h.p., but it proved unsatisfactory and the original AS engine was replaced in the tank. A6E3 which originally

Gunnery
In July 1928 an A6 was sent to Lulworth for gunnery trials: the machine-gun turrets proved unsatisfactory in use and a new pattern based on the Independent MG turret was designed and approved. This was fitted to A6E3, then building at Sheffield. Quite apart from the MG turrets, the general gunnery installation on the A6 was not considered satisfactory, not even as good as that on the Medium II. To bring the A6s up to date with current gunnery practice would have in-

Brigadier (later Lieut-General Sir Charles) Broad commanding "1st. Brigade, Royal Tank Corps" from the Mark II Command Box Tank during brigade exercises on Salisbury Plain, September 1931.
(R.A.C. Tank Museum)

Mark II special model built for Russia in 1931 with independently mounted Vickers machine-guns in the turret. Basically this "English Workman" was a Mark IIA, but without command post on turret. (R.A.C. Tank Museum)

Vickers Medium C, pilot model built for Japan, with 6-pdr. as main armament and bow machine-gun as well as side machine-guns and another in rear of turret. Engine was in rear. Bulkheads and outside fuel tanks were to reduce fire risk. Eire also bought Medium C. (R.A.C. Tank Museum)

volved a considerable amount of redesign: it was therefore decided to keep the A6s for automotive trials and experiments and to concentrate attention on the gunnery installation in the Medium IIIs which were building at the time.

Suspension

Accurate firing on the move was a tactical requirement for tanks in the early '30s and a stable gun platform was therefore a prime necessity. The Medium II suspension had proved unsatisfactory in this respect and the A6s were considered even worse after the gunnery trials at Lulworth. In 1929 Vickers-Armstrong produced three new alternative designs, two of which could be exchanged with existing suspension units, but the third, which weighed 5 cwt, involved structural alterations to the vehicle. It was decided that A6E3 should be modified to take this last pattern, the others being fitted to E1 and E2. None proved satisfactory and all were subject to excessive bumping on the front bogies. Various modifications, including shock absorbers, both single and double acting, and stronger springs to both main and inclined bogies, were suggested and tried with only partial success. In 1934 entirely new suspension units, built by a firm specialising in this type of work, proved satisfactory. The contrast between the time taken to build the tank and the time needed to finalise modifications is striking, even allowing for financial stringency and the lack of urgency over completion, and vividly illustrates the lengthy nature of development trials.

THE MEDIUM MARK III

In 1928 it was decided to build a new medium tank based on the A6. The general lay-out and external appearance were the same except for the turrets which

Birch gun, Mark I, 1929 pattern, mounting an 18-pdr. After the Gun Carrier tanks of the First World War the Birch was the first SP gun. (Imperial War Museum)

The Independent, which had considerable influence on tank design in several countries. Four of its five turrets can be seen in this view. (Vickers-Armstrong)

curiously close parallel with the NbFz of the Germans which looked very like the Medium III and was never issued to troops or brought into production. The significant point of difference between the two lies in the armament—a 3-pdr (47 mm.) as against a 75 or a 105-mm. gun.

A7—THE 14 TONNER

In external appearance these tanks are a complete departure from their predecessors. They were conceived as a cheaper machine, carrying the same armament but without the complications of the separate MG turrets. Design began in 1928 and by the end of 1929 A7E1 and A7E2 had been completed by the Royal Ordnance Factory at Woolwich. Externally the top run of the track was straight, with no less than seven return rollers: a continuous mud chute was provided all along the upper part of the track, and the two separate machine-gun turrets had disappeared and been replaced by a single Vickers MG in the vertical front plate, housed in a gimbal mounting alongside the driver. Both tanks were powered by the Armstrong Siddeley 120 h.p. V8 air-cooled engine. E1 had a normal Armstrong Siddeley indirect drive 4-speed gearbox of the pattern fitted to the Medium IIIs, E2 had a Wilson hydraulically operated epicyclic box. Both tanks were fitted with modified epicyclic steering of the pattern fitted to the Medium III and these proved completely satisfactory once some minor trouble over brake-band linings had been overcome.

Suspension problems were still to the fore. E1 appeared with a compensated leaf springing assembly while E2 used single bogies with vertical volute springs. Comparative trials of suspensions were held in 1934 when A7E2 came off best but damaged all assemblies to a considerable extent in so doing. Sanction for the construction of A7E3 was given this same year and she appeared with trailing single wheel bogies fitted with helical coil springing. E3 was commissioned as a fast tank of medium weight and to obtain the necessary power twin AEC CI engines, coupled as one unit and giving 280 h.p., were used. This proved very satisfactory and was eventually adopted as the power unit for A12—the Matilda. The most unsatisfactory feature of the tank was the suspension which bumped badly at anything over 15 m.p.h., a fact confirmed on the Churchill which used the same type of suspension. Further work on these tanks was stopped in 1937 but the turret design was used in A9 and A10 with a redesigned front plate, incorporating an external mantlet.

A8—EXPERIMENTAL MEDIUM TANK

This tank never got beyond the drawing-board mock-up stage. It was the last experimental tank in the vital inter-war medium tank series and was conceived by Vickers-Armstrong as a successor to the Medium III. A wooden mock-up was built by July 1933 on the lines of the A7. It had virtually the same fighting chamber and the turret ring could take the A7 turret with the new 2-pdr. gun. Water-cooled engines were specified for this tank because it was felt that the problems of manufacturing an air-cooled engine of a pattern not in general use might prejudice supply in

were quite different. A6 appeared with a conical turret, having two mushroom-shaped cupolas perched at the back, one for the commander and one for the observer. By the time that A6E3 appeared these had been changed to a single cupola. No wireless bulge was fitted to any of these tanks. The Medium III turret retained the sloping sides of the A6 but there resemblance ceased. The front plate was flattened for the gun mantlet and the rear of the turret was extended to form a wireless bulge big enough to take a No. 9 set. Single-gun MG turrets were fitted and the front of these turrets was again flatter than in the A6, presenting an unbroken front with the driver's visor right across the front of the tank. A command post was located at the back of the turret. The MG turrets had a 36 in. ring with geared traverse and shoulder control for elevation. They were set a little further forward than in the A6 in order to get the centre of gravity of the whole tank further forward. In the A6 it had been only just in front of the centre of length, which was considered likely to affect cross-country performance.

The mechanical layout of the Medium III was like that of the A6 and the same 180 h.p. Armstrong Siddeley engine was used. To improve the steering performance larger diameter brakes had been designed: to accommodate them it had been necessary to move the whole of the back end further forward than in the earlier tanks but this change was not noticeable externally.

By 1933 trials had been completed on two of the Medium IIIs which had performed well on roads and on good going. The automotive performance was up to design specification and the gunnery trials had proved satisfactory. On rough going the story was not so good: the suspension was still unsatisfactory with the bogies "bottoming" over obstacles or rough going. The third Medium III was fitted with a modified suspension which showed some improvement over the other patterns.

On the whole the Medium IIIs proved satisfactory: they were used by HQ The Tank Brigade in 1934 and were easy to handle, reliable, and considerably better than the Medium Mark II both for comfort and for ease of maintenance. Little further use was made of them but with the A6 they had provided the answer to a lot of design problems and considerably facilitated the production of later high speed tanks. There is a

Vickers Medium Mark III with altered turret, command post, wireless bulge, and the two single machine-gun sub-turrets brought forward in line with the driver's visor.
(R.A.C. Tank Museum)

A6 E2 (the 16-tonner) showing twin Vickers machine-guns in sub-turrets which are set back from the front of the tank, and the twin cupolas on the turret. (R.A.C. Tank Museum)

BRITISH MEDIUM TANKS 1926–37

Type	Weight tons	Length	Width	Height	Engine	Max speed m.p.h.	Radius Miles	Armament Main	Machine-guns	Armour mm. max/min	Crew	Remarks
A6 E1	16	21′6″	8′9″	9′2″	Armstrong Siddeley V8 180 h.p./1800 r.p.m. air-cooled	26	120	1 × 3-pdr.	6 × ·303 Vickers	14/9	7	Sub turrets originally 2 machine-guns each: later changed to single guns 1928. 6th AA Machine-gun removed
A6 E2	16	21′6″	8′9″	9′2″	Armstrong Siddeley V8 180 h.p./1800 r.p.m. air-cooled	26	120	1 × 3-pdr.	3 × ·303 Vickers	14/9	7	E2 fitted with Ricardo CI engine later replaced by Armstrong Siddeley 180 h.p. V8. Oil operated gearbox SLM (Winterthur) pattern. A6 E1 E2 delivered for trial June 1928
A6 E3	16¼	21′6″	8′9″	9′2″	Armstrong Siddeley V8 180 h.p./1800 r.p.m. air-cooled	26	120	1 × 3-pdr.	3 × ·303 Vickers	14/9	7	Fiited with new machine-gun turrets based on Independent tank pattern later fitted with 500 h.p. Thorneycroft 6-cyl. engine
Medium III E1	16	21′6″	8′10″	9′8″	Armstrong Siddeley V8 180 h.p./1800 r.p.m. air-cooled	30	120	1 × 3-pdr.	3 × ·303 Vickers	14/9	7	
E2, E3	16	21′6″	8′10″	9′8″	Armstrong Siddeley V8 180 h.p./1800 r.p.m. air-cooled	30	120	1 × 3-pdr.	3 × ·303 Vickers	14/9	7	E2 destroyed by fire
A7 E1 E2	14	—	—	—	Armstrong Siddeley 120 h.p. air-cooled	25	120	1 × 3-pdr.	2 × ·303 Vickers	14/9	5	A7 E2 turret modified to take 2-pdr gun. This pattern was to be fitted to A8
A7 E3	18·2	—	—	—	Twin AEC CI 6-cyl.: coupled to give 252 h.p.	25	—	—	—	14	5	A 12 Matilda infantry tank developed from this machine. Wilson epicyclic steering. Built of mild steel
A8	17·5	—	—	—	Twin Rolls Royce 6-cyl. engines. Wilson gearbox	—	—	—	—	—	—	Drawings and mock-up. Never completed in steel

A6E3 showing single Vickers machine-guns in the sub-turrets and the modified suspension.

(R.A.C. Tank Museum)

time of war. Vickers suggested twin Rolls-Royce engines coupled as a unit and driving a Wilson epicyclic gearbox and steering units.

Considerable doubts were expressed on the possibility of supplying Rolls-Royce car engines without interfering with the production of aero engines, even though the former were to be built in a separate factory. However in 1937 after parts of the drawings and the mock-up had been completed the project was abandoned because, except for the engine arrangement, A8 showed no significant advance over any of its predecessors.

A.F.V. Series Editor: DUNCAN CROW

The Author particularly wishes to acknowledge the generous help and information received from the Royal Armoured Corps Tank Museum without which this Profile *could not have been written.*

Medium Tank A7E2. Development work on the A7 14-tonners was stopped in 1937 but they contributed different points to the A12 (Matilda), the Churchill, the A9 and the A10.

(R.A.C. Tank Museum)

	Development No.	W.D. No.	Registration No.	M.E.E. No.	Maker and year*	Remarks
A6s or 16 Tonners	A6E1	T404	ML8698	MEE97	VA. Sep. 1927	Mild steel
	A6E2	T405	ML8699	MEE123	VA. Sep. 1927	Mild steel
	A6E3	T732	MT9637	MEE225	VA. Oct. 1928	Mild steel
Medium Mark IIIs	Mark III E1	T870	MT9707	MEE742	ROF. May 1929	Armour plate
	Mark III E2	T871	MT9708	—	ROF. May 1929	Armour plate
	Mark III E3	T907	MT9709	—	VA. Feb. 1931	Armour plate
A7s or 14 Tonners	A7E1	T816	MT9639	MEE383	ROF. May 1929	Mild steel
	A7E2	T817	MT9640	MEE493	ROF. May 1929	Mild steel
	A7E3	T1340	BMM117	MEE961	ROF. May 1934	Mild steel
A8	A8E1	T1341	BMM118	—	VA. —	Never completed

*VA—Vickers-Armstrong.   ROF—Royal-Ordnance Factory, Woolwich

The A6 (left) and A1E1 Independent. Designed in 1926, the year the Independent was finished, the A6 was built on the lines of the Independent.
(Imperial War Museum)

A1E1—The Independent
by Major-General N. W. Duncan

AFTER the First World War a revulsion against trench warfare occurred, a revulsion against the slow and deliberate preparations before any attack could be mounted, against the barrenness of success, indeed against the close nature of warfare as waged during the preceding four years. Men's minds glimpsed a new horizon with open warfare as the key of the soldier's training and light mobile operations in which long-range flanking movements would bring victory. Thought turned to lightly equipped infantry soldiers, with perhaps lorries to lift them to the battlefield. In Mesopotamia an infantry brigade had marched 35 miles a day for six days across the desert and then fought a three-day battle, which they won in handsome fashion. But it was felt desirable to conserve human energy. Armour would be needed, and so attention turned to fast light quick-moving tanks, of which the Medium D and the Light Infantry tank were examples. They proved unreliable and would have required development before they were efficient weapons of war, but none the less the germ of speed in warfare had been sown and began to bear fruit.

Suddenly, in the midst of this "mobile" thinking, came a requirement from the War Office for a heavy tank. No one knows what led to this *volte-face*, but in December 1922 Vickers were asked to investigate the possibilities of a heavy tank with the following characteristics:

Speed—7 m.p.h. Ground pressure—12 lb. per sq. in.
Clearance—18 in. Crossing capacity—9 ft.
Armament—one 3-pdr. and two Vickers machine-guns.

The upper run of the tank was to be a straight line and the driver's head cover was to be the highest point. The 3-pdr., firing between the horns, was to have 30 degrees of traverse, and a machine-gun sponson mounted either side was to cover a 180-degree arc of fire. A rear engine was required and in the interests of height Vickers were asked to consider using a horizontally opposed version.

Under the direction of Sir George Buckham the firm went ahead on this curious specification, working on a 1½-in. armour basis, and by March 1923 had produced two sets of drawings setting out alternative versions. The first adhered to War Office requirement: at an overall weight of 24¼ tons it mounted the 3-pdr. in a casement and used four machine-guns to cover all sides by fire. The second had the 3-pdr. in a turret with all-round traverse, and four MGs in sub-turrets; it was estimated to weigh 25 tons 7 cwt. on the same armour basis.

After considerable delay the turretted alternative was selected and a provisional order was placed in December 1923, although it was not clear at the time either what the tank was intended to do or how it should carry out its task.

It was not until 1925 that the detailed specification was finally decided and financial sanction for building was obtained. A V12 air-cooled Armstrong-Siddeley engine on the lines of those used in the Vickers Medium tank was to be used. This should develop 350 b.h.p. at 1,500 r.p.m. and was estimated to give a top speed of 20 m.p.h.

The armament installation was the subject of much discussion: the MG turrets were altered in the final drawings to improve both traverse and observation.

Side view of main turret with flash of 1st Bn. R.T.C. painted on side.
(Duncan Crow)

View from above showing main turret, left forward sub-turret, left rear sub-turret with MG in AA position.
(R.A.C. Tank Museum)

Rear view showing exhausts, engine room decking with air inlets, and the two rear sub-turrets. Note difference of height between them—the one on the right is the same as the two front sub-turrets and is for the ground rôle only; the left-hand one is higher overall to accept the dual AA/ground rôle.
(R.A.C. Tank Museum)

The gun mounting in its highest position. The gunner would be crouching on the floor of the tank holding the spade-grips. This sub-turret was probably the first permanent provision for AA fire in a tank. Turret traverse, as for other sub-turrets, is by hand wheel and toothed turret-ring, with clutch to disengage for free traverse. (Left, above.) (Duncan Crow)

All three pieces of the top hatch are opened up, and the front hatch (hinged to the right front top hatch) is swung back. Holes in arc for positioning mounting are shown. Mounting has been lifted two holes from its lowest position. (Left.)
(Col. P. H. Hordern)

Side view of Independent from the rear showing side-door open. This was designed to admit a standard army stretcher.
(R.A.C. Tank Museum)

At the same time the opportunity was taken to give the left-hand rear machine-gun a high angle line of fire for AA work by an ingenious adaptation of the armoured turret and the gun-mounting—probably the first permanent provision for AA fire in a tank.

Keeping track of all the guns faced the commander with a formidable task and the provision of an indicator to show the direction of all the weapons relative to the tank's centre-line was considered necessary. To control the volume of fire it was proposed that two men should be in the cupola—the commander and an observer. They were provided with a platform which went round with the turret. This was traversed by hand by the gunner who must have had to work very hard although a 2-speed gear was provided.

By November 1926 the Independent was finished, roughly three years after approval of the specification: this is a remarkably short time for the construction of a big machine embodying many new ideas. The designers relied heavily on the experience and suggestions of a committee of Tank Corps officers with battle experience over the internal lay-out and general arrangement of the fighting chamber. As an example, the side doors were designed to admit a standard army stretcher in order to make the task of evacuating wounded men easier.

Trials commenced on delivery and trouble was immediately experienced with the bottom rollers. These were mounted in box bogies and rubber-tyred. The rubber failed to stand up to the weight, and steel rims were substituted which cured the wear on the roller but increased that on the track. By June 1927 trouble was being experienced with the final drive. Engine power was taken through a single dry plate clutch to a 4-speed gearbox. Two were provided: one a standard lorry pattern with sliding pinions, the other an epicyclic box with brake bands operated hydraulically, of Swiss origin. It is probable that this box was used throughout the trials since there is reference to the troubles experienced with the hydraulic operating pump.

From the gearbox output shaft the drive was taken to cross shafts with normal clutch and brake steering. Considerable trouble was experienced with the original design: with the brake fabrics which were subsequently changed and proved fairly satisfactory, and also with the drums which warped badly under the high stresses and temperatures involved. Ultimately new brake drums were turned from the breech ends of worn-out 15-in. naval guns and they stood up satisfactorily.

By 1928 the back end had been completely redesigned by Major Wilson and re-engined by Vickers. Epicyclic steering units with an additional reduction gear on each final drive input shaft were incorporated. These were servo-operated but hydraulically controlled by the driver's steering wheel.

These modifications were completed by October 1928 by which time a considerable amount of knowledge had been acquired. However, the Tank Testing Committee who were responsible for the overall direction of the trials which were carried out by the Mechanisation Experimental Establishment at Farnborough did not, at that time, know if the Independent was a "one off" experiment or a prototype for future models. No clear guidance on this point was ever given, despite the fact that it was of great importance both to the test organization and to the manufacturers.

Interior of main turret with sight left centre and gun equipped with guard for gunner on left of breech. Clips set vertically for 3-pdr. ammunition restricted crew movement from one compartment to another; once in your sub-turret space, there you were!

(Imperial War Museum)

By 1930 a lot of experimental running had been accomplished. Trouble was again experienced with the engine, principally over loss of oil pressure and with burnt-out manifolds, both arising from the unforeseen and unsuspected problems connected with an air-cooled unit of such a size. In retrospect it seems a pity that further work was not done on the problem in view of the advantages of air-cooling. The Independent's engine was overhauled in August and the tank was back on the road in December.

Two years later, 1932, trouble was being experienced with the gearbox hydraulic operating pump. It had to be replaced since no other pattern would fit the available space. Trials continued until 1933 when the tracks were reported as badly worn. From that date little use was made of the machine until on the outbreak of war in 1939 it was used to guard the approaches to Bovington Camp in a stationary rôle. In all the A1E1 did 630 miles in its time, having cost the taxpayer £77,400—a running cost of £120 per mile. It is now in the R.A.C. Tank Museum at Bovington.

As mentioned on page 12, the Independent influenced the design of the medium tanks built in Britain in the period from 1926 to 1937. But it also aroused much, if not more, interest abroad. The French and the Russians both produced tanks that were influenced by the Independent—the French *Char de Rupture* and the Russian T-28 and heavier T-35. The Germans too showed a close interest and it was the Independent which figured in the Baillie-Stewart "Officer in the Tower" case and was reflected in the multi-turretted *Neubaufahrzeug*.

Driver's position. Toothed segments fixed to the white uprights are for driver's seat backrest. Disc on the steering column below the wheel shows the angular position of the wheel and what effect it is having. Wheel at top left is 3-pdr. elevating gear wheel. Ammo clips have been removed. (Col. P. H. Hordern.)
(Below): Influence of the Independent can be seen in the Soviet T-35 with its sub-turrets fore and aft. In the foreground is a T-27 tankette, the Russian-built version of the Carden-Loyd Mark VI with armoured head covers (see p. 102). (Col. R. J. Icks)

The Independent, designed with the advice and assistance of a representative body of user opinion, was a very good fighting machine and probably at the time of its construction the best and most powerful tank in the world. Its fighting chamber was almost spacious and it was possible for the commander to talk to and touch every member of the crew. Adequate provision had been made for fire control which could easily have been developed into a precision lay-out.

Oddly enough, despite the length of track in contact with the ground, the Independent was never difficult to steer and in general was quite manoeuvrable. Those who drove it liked the steering wheel control: rotation gave successively, on either side (1) an easy turn using a track brake; (2) clutch out, resulting in a slightly sharper turn; (3) epicyclic brakes on, track movement arrested and a sharp turn.

The suspension left a good deal to be desired against the requirement for a stable platform for moving fire. This may have been partly due to the absence of shock absorbers but is probably inherent in the use of box bogies controlled by vertical coil springs. An inertia starter was fitted to the engine which took some time and hard turning before the necessary revolutions were attained. By this time the starter had reached a high-pitched whine, rather like a modern jet engine, and at this point its spinning flywheel was engaged by a dog clutch with the big air-cooled engine of the tank. The result was almost always an instantaneous start—very galling to the drivers of Vickers Medium Mark IIs who were turning their engines over with a starting handle.

It is easy with hindsight to condemn the stupidity which built and tested a tank over 11 years without deciding if it was an experimental on its own or a class prototype. Out of it came, almost by chance, the Sixteen Tonners and the Medium IIIs. How much better it would have been had these evolved directly from the Independent and what a lead Britain would have established over the rest of the world in tank construction. Engines and transmissions would have increased in reliability. But the great question will always remain unanswered: would we have increased the striking power of the main armament in step with the increased potential of the machine?

SPECIFICATION: A1E1 VICKERS "INDEPENDENT" HEAVY TANK

Crew	Eight.
Weight	32 tons.
Length	24 ft. 11 in.
Width	8 ft. 9 in.
Height	8 ft. 11 in.
Track plate width	16 in.
Armament	
Main	One 3-pdr. QF gun (47 mm.).
Secondary	Four Vickers machine-guns, one in each of four subsidiary turrets.
Ammunition	
Main	200 rounds.
Secondary	7,000 rounds.
Armour	28–13–8 mm.
Engine	Armstrong-Siddeley 370 b.h.p./1,500 r.p.m V.12 air-cooled. An inertia starter was fitted to supplement the inadequate electric motor.
Fuel	180 gallons.
Transmission	SLM or lorry pattern gearbox.
Suspension	Four double bogies (four wheels 15 in. diameter) each side plus one single bogie (two wheels 24 in. diameter) fore and aft. Coil springs in trunked guide.
Speed	20 m.p.h.

The heyday of the light tank—a Light Mk. VI (right) followed by four Mk. VIBs leads the light and medium tanks of the Tank Brigade on summer manoeuvres, Salisbury Plain, August 23, 1938.
(RAC Tank Museum)

Light Tanks Marks I-VI

By Major-General
N. W. Duncan

THE ORIGIN OF THE LIGHT TANK

THE ancestors of the British light tanks Marks I to VI are the medium tanks of World War I although the reasons which called them into being are not those that brought the later versions to light. British medium tanks A, B and C were intended to take advantage of the opportunities created by the heavy tanks for the dislocation and exploitation of a defeated or partially defeated enemy. Only one of these tanks, the Medium A, was ever in action and, despite many brilliant actions on their own, they failed to live up to expectations since their speed of 8 mph was insufficient on good going to keep up with the cavalry on the few occasions when they were able to advance mounted; equally 8 mph was too fast in face of enemy opposition for horses to take advantage of the opportunities which armour could create. Only the prototype Medium D was intended to carry out the duties which light tanks were later called on to perform. It was fast enough to pursue a retreating enemy, to carry out independent actions in the form of raids, and to undertake reconnaissance duties for the main mass of heavy tanks which it was intended to use in independent operations in 1919.

After the Armistice in 1918 tank development was in a state of flux: tanks were built under various designations to fill differing roles and as the military mind changed its thinking on the subject—which was pretty often in those days—so tank nomenclature changed too: tanks which started life as mediums found themselves successively light and heavy before reverting again to the medium category.

In 1925, Major G. le Q. Martel, an engineer officer who had been on the staff of Tank HQ in France, electrified the military world by building in his garden a one-man tank, which worked. Demonstrating it he suggested that a mass of these machines could materially help the infantry in an advance. On further reflection it was considered that one man would have his hands too full to carry out his duties effectively and

in 1926 a two-man version appeared. Eight of this model were built by Morris Motors for the Experimental Mechanised Force in 1927 while eight of another version of the two-man machine built by Carden and Loyd were also ordered at the same time.

No clear General Staff requirement for a light tank was ever issued but after the 1927 trials it was decided that two types of light armoured vehicle were needed; an open one for use with the infantry as a machine-gun carrier, and one with a turret for use by the battalions of the Royal Tank Corps. As an infantry weapon the Carden-Loyd Machine-gun Carrier was produced, weighing a ton and a half, capable of a speed of 25 mph and able to convey two men and a machine-gun in extreme discomfort. It was used as a light tank pending the arrival of the proper vehicles and from it was descended the Bren gun carrier of World War II.

To meet the RTC requirement, Carden-Loyd produced a series of experimental light tanks with turrets and their Mark VIII became the prototype Light Tank Mark I. These experimental vehicles were produced by Sir John Carden, one of the most talented tank design-

Morris-Martel one-man tank. The steering-wheel is visible through the loop-holes. This picture emphasises the height of the engine compartment and turret compared to the narrow track.
(RAC Tank Museum)

Left: *The Morris-Martel two-man tank, shown from the rear to reveal the mode of steering via the back wheel. This is the experimental version. The production model had two rear wheels for steering.* (Imperial War Museum)
Right: *Martel-Crossley two-man tank with Kegresse pattern track.* (RAC Tank Museum)

ers the U.K. has ever had, as a private venture. It could almost be said that light tank design evolved itself. No military specification had been drawn up but the product of evolution appealed to the General Staff: it was a tank, it was cheap, it was easily produced and did little damage. However as no clear conception of light tank duties existed outside the Royal Tank Corps British light tanks were undergunned by comparison with those of other countries whose equivalent machines were better armed and more thickly armoured than British contemporary medium tanks. The likelihood of tank having to fight tank was outside the official view: at worst light tank would only ever have to fight light tank and powerful anti-tank weapons were not needed because the destruction of hostile tanks was primarily the task of the anti-tank gun. The melee and confusion of an armoured battle was not appreciated except in armoured circles: in consequence many casualties were later sustained by British light tanks against a more heavily armed and better protected enemy.

On the credit side it must be said that in overseas operations against a lightly armed enemy they more than proved their worth in India and Palestine before World War II, and that they were excellent training machines. It was only when they came up against the mass of German tanks in France in 1940 that they finally disposed of the idea that it was not the task of a tank to fight another tank and disproved the fallacious idea that numbers of undergunned vehicles could successfully oppose fewer enemy tanks of superior gun power—an idea that was to cost us very dear in all our tanks until the 17-pdr. Sherman could face its enemies on virtually equal gun terms in 1944.

THE EVOLUTION OF THE LIGHT TANK

The Morris Martel two-man light tank was dropped after the disbandment of the Armoured Force in 1929. While these vehicles had proved their tactical value, continual trouble was experienced with their light construction and particularly with the rear wheel steering mechanism which was often damaged in rough going. The centre of gravity was too high and the cross-country performance was indifferent.

Carden-Loyd developed their machine-gun carriers and a range of light tanks from their version of a one-man tracked vehicle which was produced about the same time as the Martel machine. This turned into a

two-man version which first appeared in 1926/27: it was small and light, giving only cramped accommodation for its crew but it did provide quick and speedy transport across reasonable going for a machine-gun and ammunition. A later version had overhead cover, two non-rotating turrets for the crew, and although this was discarded in favour of an open version for infantry use it probably played some part in the tank development. It is interesting to note that some of the Carden-Loyd carriers made provision for travel on either wheels or tracks in an endeavour to reduce track wear which was always such a bugbear and led in World War II to the extensive use of tank transporters.

By 1929 Carden-Loyd, who early in 1928 were taken over by Vickers-Armstrong, had produced their Mark VII light tank: this was a two-man machine armed with a .303 ins. Vickers machine-gun mounted in a low bevel-sided rotating turret which was cramped and difficult to operate from. A 59 hp Meadows engine gave it a top speed of 35 mph. Four suspension wheels either side, grouped in two leaf-sprung bogies, were used with an external girder connecting the outside bogie pivots. The outside girder has been used by almost all tank designers in all countries in early versions of comparatively speedy tanks. It has always been rapidly discarded probably due to the additional drag imposed by unfavourable going, bogie pivots and hull supports being increased in strength to take the additional load caused by the absence of external support.

The Carden-Loyd Mk. I one-man tank, or "tankette", earliest stage of Vickers light tank development.*
(Imperial War Museum)

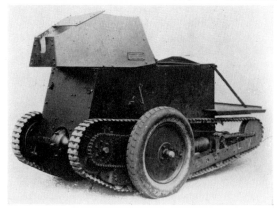

Four Morris-Martels followed by a Carden-Loyd marching past, Salisbury Plain, 1929. The Carden-Loyd is an original two-man vehicle, very low in build and thus inconspicuous, and armed with a light machine rifle. (RAC Tank Museum)

The Carden-Loyd Mark VIII light tank which followed was accepted as the prototype vehicle for the Mark I light tank. Very few Mark I's were built and they never became a general issue to troops. However they and the Mark IA's provided valuable data for the design of subsequent light tanks.

THE LIGHT TANKS DESCRIBED
LIGHT TANK MARK I AND MARK IA

This was a two-man vehicle with a cylindrical turret mounting one .303 VMG. Suspension was by two pairs of two-wheeled leaf-sprung bogies on either side with no external girder: three return rollers mounted on the hull took the top run of the track and track adjustment was effected by the rear idler which was raised above the ground at the same height as the front driving sprocket, itself an innovation in British tank design. The idler was mounted on an eccentric bush located by a ratchet which allowed the track to be tightened when necessary.

Armour was on a 14mm basis which increased the weight to $3\frac{1}{4}$ tons: a 59 hp Meadows engine gave it a top speed of 30 mph. Steering was effected by breaking the drive to either track through a clutch with subsequent application of a brake to steepen the turn if required. A normal four-speed crash gear box was used.

Light Tank Mark IA followed: compared with Mark I the superstructure had been built up and the cylindrical turret had been slightly enlarged to facilitate handling the VMG which was of standard infantry pattern. These guns were enclosed in armoured jackets and considerable trouble was experienced over cooling them in the earlier light tanks. A header tank for the water jacket to reduce overheating was built into the Mark IV light tank while the Mark VI had a circulating pump in addition.

Mark IA had Horstmann suspension using two horizontal coil springs in place of the leaf pattern used on the Mark I's. These coil springs bore on a ball and socket joint at the top of the quarter circle shrouds on each wheel. The shrouds were pivoted at their other corners on the hull pivot pin. This was the best suspension that had been devised for tank work up to that date although the uncontrolled springs were liable to bounce to such an extent that the tank could become almost uncontrollable. At medium speeds over reasonably good going it gave a very easy smooth ride. Three return rollers on the hull took the top run of the track.

Four of these tanks were sent to India in 1931 to undergo tropical trials. They were fitted with cupolas,

The Carden-Loyd Mk. VI Machine-Gun Carrier marked the point where the design concept it represented diverged into two lines of development, the machine-gun carrier and the light tank. (RAC Tank Museum)

Carden-Loyd Mk. VII—prototype light tank (A4), 1929, the first to incorporate a traversing turret. (Imperial War Museum)

square, bevel sided and non-rotating by Base Work-shops Chaklala who also carried out other modifica-tions principally connected with engine cooling. To reduce the temperature inside the tank experiments were carried out with various linings to absorb the heat and satisfactory results were obtained with an asbestos fabric. Modifications arising from these Indian trials were incorporated in later tanks intended for service overseas.

LIGHT TANK MARK II

This appeared in 1930: it was the pattern on which all subsequent light tanks were based up to Mark VI. The

Left: *The Light Tank Mk. I (A4E4) of 1930 which saw limited service. This picture shows it mounted on a specially built recovery trailer (designed at M.W.E.E. Kidbrooke) which was tested in 1931. It will be noted that the trailer features standard Carden-Loyd road wheels as used on the tank itself.* (Imperial War Museum) Right: *Prototype Light Tank Mk. IA (A4E8).* (RAC Tank Museum)

Left: *Prototype Light Tank Mk. IA (A4E10) with double machine-gun turret. A .303 Vickers machine-gun superimposed on a .5 VMG.* (RAC Tank Museum.) Right: *The Vickers Light Tank Mk. II which was the first major production model.* (Imperial War Museum)

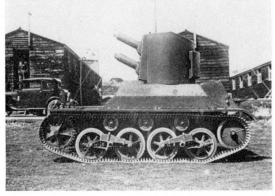 

Left: *Light Tank Mk. IIA (A4E18). Note bullet-proofed air louvres on turret and air hatch to engine beyond driver's loop-hole.* (RAC Tank Museum). Right: *Light Tank Mk. IIB—Indian pattern with cupola, 21 of these (T964-984) were built for India. They had a Meadows engine.*
(RAC Tank Museum)

engine, gearbox and transmission were on the right-hand side of the vehicle driving forward to a cross shaft, through a bevel drive, which carried on either end a clutch by which the drive to the track could be broken. The left-hand side of the tank accommodated the driver and the commander in his turret with a machine-gun and a wireless set in the turret bulge behind him. This general arrangement varies in detail with different Marks, especially when the three-man is introduced but the basic pattern remains unchanged.

Mark II had a Rolls Royce engine developing 66 bhp. This was coupled to a Wilson pre-selector gearbox, driving forward to the cross shaft. The Wilson box was very handy for cross-country work but it was more complicated than the usual pattern. Mark IIs intended for service in India had a Meadows engine and a normal gearbox. These Indian service vehicles were also fitted with a square bevel sided non-rotating cupola.

Light Tank Mark II was fitted with a No 1 Mark I turret: this was rectangular in shape with sloping sides and mounted a .303 VMG, which had been specially adapted for tank use by the addition of a pistol grip incorporating a trigger and an ejector tube through which spent cases were passed into another tube in the gun mantlet and so into a cartridge bag which hung below the jackets outside the tank. The turret had no air louvres and a small aperture for the commander in the roof was closed by a sliding door. The No 1 Mark II turret fitted to Marks IIA and B was similar in construction but had unguarded air louvres fitted at the top of the side plates. These two turrets were subsequently reconstructed as Mark I* and Mark II* with anti-bullet splash baffles fitted into the louvres that now covered the air intakes in the turret sides. The unsatisfactory small sliding door was replaced by a larger pair of folding doors which could be locked from either inside or outside the tank.

Light Tank Mk. II (T880 MT9679) with experimental 4½t. Vickers "slow motion" suspension. This was originally fitted with Horstmann suspension (as in the illustrations above). Its hull had "close" rivets to facilitate waterproofing (compare hull nose plate rivet spacing with the Mk. II opposite). A flotation unit on either side and an outboard motor on the rear hull plate gave the tank swim capability.
(RAC Tank Museum)

The bulge at the back of the turret housed a No 1 Wireless set, an instrument of uncertain behaviour and widely varying range. Designed for voice communication up to three miles, it was sometimes mute at 400 yards, occasionally gave ten miles, and with an outside aerial enabled voice communication to be established between Tidworth and Cairo until the International Board of Wireless Control put a stop to that practice!!

LIGHT TANK MARK III

This tank was similar in shape to the Mark II except that the hull superstructure was carried further to the rear. A modified Horstmann suspension with inclined double springs, one to absorb shock and the other to check rebound, were fitted either side of the suspension wheels. The quarter circle shrouds of the Mark II's were abandoned. Production models had two return rollers either side on the hull, although the prototype models appeared with three.

The Mark III was originally fitted with a Rolls Royce engine and a Wilson gearbox. 36 of the Mark were built and were sent to Egypt where they were used by the 6th Bn Royal Tank Corps.

The engine fitted to Mark II and Mark III can be distinguished by the silencer. The Rolls Royce pattern is about half the length of the off side track guard, from level with the driver to the rear of the turret and has a final exhaust pipe with a fish tail protruding above the silencer. The Meadows engine used a short silencer with a tail pipe protruding straight to the rear with no fish tail.

Mark III was fitted with either a Mark I or a Mark II turret. The only difference between these two patterns lay in the top plate. In the Mark II this was higher to incorporate a header tank for gun cooling. No cupolas were fitted.

Light Tank Mk. IIB Indian pattern of the 2nd Light Tank Company, R.T.C., crossing the Nahakki Pass by mule track, Mohmand Operations, North-West Frontier, September 1935. This was the first British operational use of tanks after 1920 in south Russia. (RAC Tank Museum)

Up to and including Mark III all light tanks had a rear idler wheel clear of the ground which also served as a means of adjusting track tension. The top run of the track was horizontal with the ground and the whole suspension gave a very comfortable ride, especially in the Mark III where the modified Horstmann springing greatly reduced the tendency to bounce which had been noticeable in the Mark II's.

LIGHT TANK MARK IV

This was the first light tank to use the hull as a chassis and to mount automotive components directly

Light Tank Mk. III which was the production model introducing the revised type of Horstmann suspension. (RAC Tank Museum)

Light Tank Mk. IIA, with revised Horstmann suspension, forms part of the motley equipment of the 6th Australian Divisional Cavalry Regiment in training in Egypt in summer 1940.
(Imperial War Museum)

on to it. Earlier models had their armour-plate attached to a chassis. The new construction saved weight and gave a more rigid structure which was less liable to distortion over bad going. Considerable changes had been made in the external appearance of the tank: the superstructure was higher than in earlier models and the turret was set further back. There was no rear idler although the modified Horstmann suspension using the two springs either side of the bogie was retained. In the Mark III the angle of the springs was opposed, that of the front bogie pointing forward, that of the rear one pointing aft. In the Mark IV both springs pointed forwards. Track adjustment was effected by moving the rear wheel of the back bogie forwards or back in its housing. Lacking a rear idler wheel clear of the ground the suspension was not so smooth as on

An umpire leaves the turret of a Light Tank Mk. IV after hitching a lift in the 1938 summer manoeuvres on Salisbury Plain.
(RAC Tank Museum)

previous Marks—a matter of considerable importance where firing on the move was concerned.

A 90 h.p. Meadows EST engine with a four speed synchromesh gearbox was used and armour was on a 12 mm basis.

The turret mounted the usual tank pattern machine-gun: this was located by two bevel sided slides on the bottom of the breech casing which fitted into two bevelled grooves machined in the gun jacket. These guns were very satisfactory and the cooling problem had been largely overcome with the header tank in the turret roof. Turret rotation had provided many problems and in Marks I and II a circular roller path had been formed on the upper side of the traversing rack. Six traversing rollers mounted on ball bearings were secured to the turret base and side thrust was taken by a vertical flange on the traversing ring bearing against a roller fitted ring on the underside of the turret. Six "L" shaped clamps on the turret, bearing against the traversing rack, prevented the turret coming off. Raising gear, an eccentric cam, was fitted at four points on the turret and was always to be used when there was no likelihood of turret rotation being required. This was to avoid "pitting" the surface of the traversing rack or forming "flats" on it which would have hindered the traverse.

A different system was adopted on the Mark IV. A turret ring on the underside of the turret rested on nine ball bearing rollers secured to brackets on the traversing ring. These rollers had a double profile; part at a slight inclination to take the weight of the turret, the rest at an acuter angle to locate the turret in its ring. Clips to prevent the turret coming off were secured to six of the roller brackets.

One revolution of the traverse wheel gave a movement of 5 degrees: an adjustable brake was fitted which prevented rotation until released by pressing the hand grip.

Wireless batteries were housed in a box, pivoted on the bottom of the tank and moved with the turret

Light Tank Mk. IV in use for training in summer 1940. Note hand-grips for commander (also fitted in Mks. II and III).
(RAC Tank Museum)

through an arm joining the two. In the Mark IV this was elaborated, the battery box being mounted on roller bearings which considerably reduced friction.

The Mark IV light tank's centre of gravity was too high in relation to tank length. Its cross-country performance was poor although its maximum speed had been increased and it was still only armed with one .303 VMG. It was to be the last of the two-man tanks for by the time it appeared it had been realised that the demands made on the commander were more than one man could possibly carry out. He had to:

  i Control his driver
 ii Find his way and read a map
 iii Control other tanks under his command
 iv Acquire and fire on targets, controlling the fire of his other tanks meanwhile
  v Operate a wireless set

—and, much worse, he often had to carry out several of these duties at the same time. The stage was set for the three-man light tank for which the Royal Tank Corps had been clamouring.

LIGHT TANK MARK V

This was the first British three-man light tank. It too was built by Vickers-Armstrong who were to build so many tanks for the British Army. Twelve prototype Mark V's were sent to the 1st (Light) Bn RTC in 1934 and with them came a team of Vickers-Armstrong mechanics who lived with the battalion during user trials. This was a complete innovation, almost the first direct contact between manufacturer and user, and it paid an excellent dividend. User faults were immediately rectified, internal stowage for the first time met user needs and the trials materially shortened the time into service after the first appearance of the prototypes. It was a great pity that it was so rarely possible to repeat the practice with later tanks because it did create a very valuable fund of goodwill, mutual trust and understanding between the user and the manufacturer.

One of the two men in the turret was the tank commander. The other was the gunner who was also responsible for operating the wireless set. A new trade category was instituted for these men which caused many lengthy discussions with the trades unions in order to fit a man with these qualifications into existing trade categories. However this was eventually achieved and the gunner-operator more than proved his worth in the light tank world. He made an immense difference not only when the tank was on the move or in action but also when maintenance had to be carried out and for guard duties when the tanks halted at night.

Apart from the third man the other innovation in

Light Tank Mk. V (with another just behind it) was the model which introduced the longer, deeper hull and a two-man turret with twin machine-gun armament. Only 22 production Mk. Vs were built.
(RAC Tank Museum)

Light Tank Mk. V showing the sloping back turret plate. The return roller on the front bogie (see also the Mk. IVs illustrated) gave continual track trouble, accentuated no doubt by having the rear suspension wheel on the ground which seemed to transmit "shakes" in the top run of the track and make it come off. This tank is being used for training at Catterick, October 1940. (Chamberlain Collection)

this Mark was the addition of a .5 VMG to its armament in addition to the normal .303. The recognition of the need for a light tank to have some anti-tank capacity was revolutionary in its concept as far as British military thought was concerned. The .5 at the time of its introduction was a match for any comparable light tank in Europe since their armour basis was the same as that of the Mark V—12mm. However, United States tanks, which the Americans classified as light, were at that time mounting a 37mm gun and were carrying an inch of armour on the front plate. None the less the anti-tank potential was more than welcome:

the tragedy is that no-one outside the armoured world recognised the need for upgunning in order to keep abreast of other nations.

The Mark V was a little better balanced than its predecessors and its cross-country performance was distinctly better than that of the Mark IV. It had the same engine as the Mark IV and although the weight had risen by half a ton to 4.8 the radius of action of the two tanks remained approximately the same. But the top speed had been reduced to 32 mph in place of the 37 mph which the Mark IV would attain.

The turret of the Mark V was basically circular in

Light Tank Mk. VI, with a two-man turret and twin machine-guns. (RAC Tank Museum)

1

2

2
A.T.C.
T 273

WALLABY

C
273

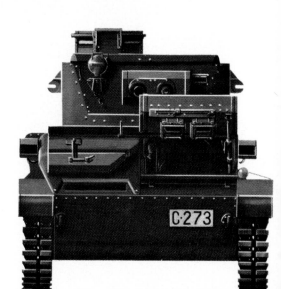

C·273

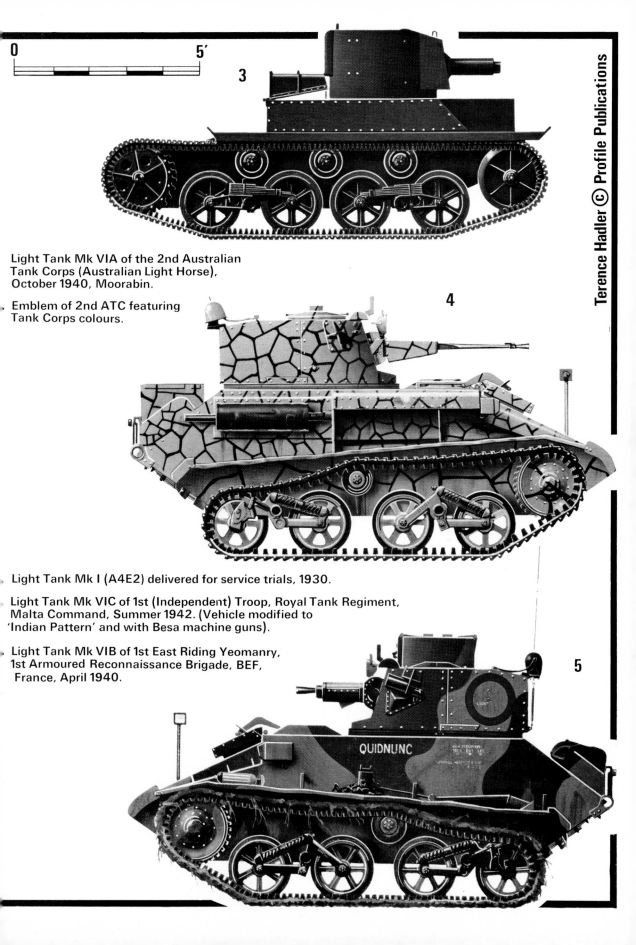

0   **5′**

3

Terence Hadler © Profile Publications

Light Tank Mk VIA of the 2nd Australian
Tank Corps (Australian Light Horse),
October 1940, Moorabin.

Emblem of 2nd ATC featuring
Tank Corps colours.

4

Light Tank Mk I (A4E2) delivered for service trials, 1930.

Light Tank Mk VIC of 1st (Independent) Troop, Royal Tank Regiment,
Malta Command, Summer 1942. (Vehicle modified to
'Indian Pattern' and with Besa machine guns).

Light Tank Mk VIB of 1st East Riding Yeomanry,
1st Armoured Reconnaissance Brigade, BEF,
France, April 1940.

5

QUIDNUNC

Left: *Based on the Mk. V, this experimental "tank destroyer" model with 2 pdr. gun developed by Vickers was tested by the army in 1938 but never went into production.* (Imperial War Museum.) Right: *A fine view of a Light Tank Mk. VIB showing all the standard fittings of the 1939 period, including spotlight on turret, smoke discharger, and headlights in armoured housings.*

(Imperial War Museum)

Light Tank Mk. VIA distinguished from the VIB by the twin louvres over the engine. (RAC Tank Museum)

shape with vertical sides. It was interrupted both front and back by sloping plates, one of which carried the gun mantlet pierced in two places for the ejector tubes for the guns. The back plate came down at such an angle that it was difficult to get a wireless set of any power to fit in the space provided. The two machine-guns lay side by side in an armoured jacket which was so counterweighted as to make elevation and depression by shoulder-piece easy. A sighting telescope was provided with fixed graticules; range was put on the sighting drum in the sight gear assembly which raised the rear end of the telescope relative to the line of fire. Compared to later installations it was unbelievably simple, only two scales—one for each gun. The commander had a small circular revolving cupola which gave him observation of fire.

A new method of mounting the turret came in with this tank. A ball-race was machined on the under side of the turret and another on the upper side of the traverse ring. The two were separated by a "crowded" ball-race of 213 balls, and six clips were provided to avoid any danger of the turret coming off. The usual geared hand traverse was used, but one revolution of the wheel only traversed the turret 3 degrees, and the normal turret braking device was used.

A floor-mounted revolving pedestal carrying the wireless batteries, ammunition bins and a seat for the gunner was attached to the turret by a stay.

Modified Horstmann suspension like that of the Mark IV was used in Mark V, and one return roller was mounted in forks on the leading suspension bogie. Track adjustment was effected by moving the rear suspension wheel in its brackets.

LIGHT TANK MARK VI

This tank had a maximum armour thickness of 14 mm and its weight had risen to 5 tons. The engine transmission and general layout were as for the Mark V, the only major change being in the engine clutch which gave a great deal of trouble when first installed: this was rectified in due course and the machine, apart from its fighting value, proved itself reliable, easily maintained and speedy.

The turret mounting was on a crowded ball-race as in the Mark V: the turret shape was basically circular, flattened in front to take the gun mantlet and with the sides extended at the back to house a No 7 wireless set, a very much better affair than the No 1, with a range of

A training turret for crews on the pellet range at the 56th Training Regt., RAC, Catterick, October 1940. This view shows the position of the commander and gunner inside the turret. Radio on the actual Mk. VI fitted in the turret rear where the pellet range equipment is here. (Imperial War Museum)

Light Tank Mk. VIB negotiating an obstacle with a crew of officer cadets at the OCTU, R.M.C., Sandhurst, late in 1940. (Imperial War Museum)

Light Tank Mk. VIB Indian pattern was distinguished from the standard VIB by the absence of the cupola. Some VIBs in Britain were later modified to this standard. (Imperial War Museum)

ten miles using a rod aerial. It was a precision instrument whose assembly, like all other pre-war sets, demanded a high proportion of skilled labour. It was not until the greatly increased demands of the war required quicker production that the 19 set, requiring only 5% skilled labour in its manufacture, was designed for use in tanks.

The geared traverse gave a movement of 3 degrees for each revolution of the wheel; quite enough because this Mark had a revolving platform on which both commander and gunner stood and which housed beneath the floor boards ammunition boxes and wireless batteries. A rotary connection in the centre of the floor brought current from the dynamo to the wireless batteries and also provided voice-pipe connection between the commander and the driver—in theory. No satisfactory means of communication between the members of a tank crew had been evolved up to that date. Every kind of device had been tried, reins attached to the driver's arms, flashing lights and hose-pipes with funnels at each end. All these had failed because of turret rotation, and while the Mark VI had the germ of success in it, voices were so distorted by the long passage and abrupt bends in the voice-tube that little benefit resulted from it. Again it was not until the advent of the 19 set that clear and satisfactory communication between all members of the crew was achieved.

Horstmann suspension with the inclined springs of the Mark V was also used on the Mark VI with a return roller on the front bogie assembly. In spite of its increased weight, the power/weight ratio of 16:1 was better than that of any British medium or heavy tank. The centre of gravity had been brought further forward and the tank was a better ride than any of its predecessors although it was distinctly uncomfortable at speed on rough going.

If an attempt was made to steer a light tank down hill on the engine "overrun", "reverse steering" was experienced. Once the drive to a track had been broken by the steering clutch, the tank's weight swung the free track round the one still connected to the engine and the tank went the opposite way to that intended by the operation of the steering lever. The phenomenon could be dangerous: the remedy was always to steer with the engine pulling.

LIGHT TANK MARK VIA

An octagonal commander's cupola was substituted for the circular pattern of the Mark VI. One return roller was positioned on the hull instead of on the suspension bogie. A Meadows ESTB engine was used in place of the Meadows ESTL on the Mark VI: both were of the same hp.

LIGHT TANK MARK VIB

This model reverted to the circular cupola of the Mark VI but it had only one cooling louvre on the inclined plate that covered the radiator instead of the two used on Mark VI and VIA.

Mark VIB's for India had no cupola but were provided with a single periscope for the commander which was located in one half of the hinged conical-shaped hatch.

An experimental Mark VIB appeared in 1940 with a rear idler similar to those on the Mark II and III. It was a great success and gave a very smooth ride together with a better cross-country performance but the modification was never adopted for service use.

LIGHT TANK MARK VIC

This was a Mark VIB with wider suspension wheels and a broader track. No cupola was fitted but the commander had a periscope as for the Indian pattern Mark VIB. Otherwise the turret was the same but the armament had completely changed and Besa air-cooled machine-guns of 7.92 and 15 mm respectively replaced the Vickers pattern used in earlier tanks. These guns, adapted from a Czech design, had been standardized for the Royal Armoured Corps: they used, for the first time in the British Army, rimless cases in place of rimmed cartridges. The Besa was a

A few Mk. VIs were modified by the provision of larger diameter sprocket wheels of the twin ring type as shown on this VIB at 102nd OCTU, Blackdown, August 1940. The badge painted on the turret below the wireless aerial is of the Westminster Dragoons.
(Imperial War Museum)

good gun but the earlier varieties were liable to many stoppages. The 7.92 was used on all British tanks up to 1958 but the 15 mm gun was dropped very early on in World War II.

LIGHT TANK AA MARK I

In action the Mark VI's, undergunned and under-armoured, soon showed their inferiority to their opponents. They were withdrawn from service as the Stuart tanks arrived in the Middle East from America and were then converted into AA tanks mounting either quadruple Besa 7.92 mm guns or two Besa 15 mm. The crew was reduced to two men but the vehicle, lacking any form of power traverse for the turret, was never particularly effective.

2-PDR. LIGHT TANK

One Mark VI light tank chassis was modified to take a

Line up at 102nd OCTU in August 1940 shows some of the external differences between Vickers light tank models. Mk. IV is nearest, then come two Mk. VIBs, then a Mk. V. Note the trays in each case for empty shell cases. (Imperial War Museum)

A picture taken at the same OCTU which clearly illustrates how much smaller the Mk. IV was compared with the Mk. VI. Mk. IV is second in the line of Mk. VIs.
(Imperial War Museum)

2-pdr. gun in an open topped turret in 1938. This most interesting innovation, (illustrated on p.36) which would have made the British light tank superior to any of its kind in the world, was never developed. No records of its performance are available and it is probable that had it been adopted some lengthening of the tank would have been required. Failure to realise that the best anti-tank weapon is another tank was probably responsible for the abandonment of the idea.

EXPERIMENTAL MARK V(L4E1)

A much modified Mark V was designed by the Superintendent of Design during the latter half of 1935. It was to be superior to the Mark V in armour and silhouette but still within the $5\frac{1}{2}$ ton limit. Built by the Royal Ordnance Factory it appeared as a prototype in 1937. The tank was longer, giving a better ride. The superstructure had been carried further to the rear to give a vertical face in which there was a door for use as an emergency exit. The centre of gravity had been shifted further forward so that cross-country performance was improved. Armour was on a 14 mm basis and for the first time the tracks were protected by shields of thin armour plate like the sand shields fitted to the Mark VI's in the Desert campaigns. All this had to be paid for and the weight had risen to $7\frac{1}{2}$ tons:

Last of the Vickers light tank models stemming from the Carden-Loyd was the Mk. VIC which had a 15 mm. Besa and 7.92 mm. Besa armament.
(RAC Tank Museum)

engine power remained the same and in consequence this tank was slow especially across country.

This tank came to the 1st Tank Brigade for inspection and users' comments in 1937 on Salisbury Plain. Its trials finished on June 20, 1938, after which it was abandoned. Designated L4E1 its WD number was T1725 and its registered number CMM 881.

LIGHT TANKS IN PEACE AND WAR

As a result of trials carried out by the 1st Tank Brigade in 1931 and 1932, the medium tank battalions of the Royal Tank Corps were reorganised on a mixed basis. Each had three mixed companies with a section of seven light tanks and one of five mediums: they also had one light company of four sections each of three light tanks. In 1934 the three light companies were grouped together to form the 1st (Light) Bn RTC.

In 1938 cavalry regiments began to be converted to light tanks. On completion of their preliminary training they were either grouped in Light Armoured Brigades each of three light regiments or else they were allotted to infantry divisions as divisional cavalry regiments, providing an armoured reconnaissance element with each. Towards the end of 1938 the Mobile Division was formed with a Heavy Tank Brigade of medium tank battalions on a mixed basis and two Light Armoured Brigades of light tank regiments. In 1939 this was changed to the 1st Armoured Division with one Heavy and one Light Armoured Brigade and with this basic organisation the division went to France in May 1940. Considerable doubts had been expressed about the fighting qualities of the Mark VIB's and just before the division sailed it was reorganised with one cruiser tank squadron in each light armoured regiment and correspondingly one light tank squadron in each of the heavy armoured units which by that time were on an all cruiser tank basis. The division arrived in France and came into action against the Germans after they had broken through, and with its high proportion of light tanks (108 out of a total of 321) found the lack of gun power a considerable handicap in its withdrawal to Cherbourg.

Four Regular and three Territorial divisional cavalry regiments were in France when the Germans broke

Light Tank AA Mk. I. (RAC Tank Museum)

through. They found the Mark VI lacking in gun power and too lightly armoured for its duties. All regiments suffered severely in their withdrawals to Dunkirk or St Valery.*

INDIA

In 1933 approval was given for the conversion to light tanks of two of the eight armoured car companies of the Royal Tank Corps then serving in India. 7 Light Tank Company first attracted attention by the invaluable work that it did with its tanks in patrolling the area of the Quetta earthquake in 1935 and in rescue

operations in the stricken town. The ground was in such a condition that nothing except tracked vehicles could have traversed it.

2 Light Tank Company, the other unit to be converted initially, were stationed in Peshawar. They took part in the suppression of civil disturbances, the most unpleasant duty that could fall to an armoured unit. It was constantly allotted to them between 1921 and 1939 and it always posed a most difficult question to any commander detailed for the task. Armoured vehicles are not suited for mob control. Their offensive power is limited to the gun or the track: either can mean heavy casualties which may not achieve their end. If the mob rush the car or tank and surround it, the crew may be placed in a most dangerous situation and usually a show of force by armoured troops is not of itself enough to make the crowds disperse. Despite all these difficulties armoured troops were used constantly in aid of the civil power, willingly and cheerfully but with their commanders well knowing that whatever action they took, they were bound to be wrong!

*They were the 4th/7th Dragoon Guards, the 5th Royal Inniskilling Dragoon Guards, the 13th/18th Hussars, the 15th/19th Hussars, the 1st Lothians and Border Horse, the Fife and Forfar Yeomanry, and the East Riding Yeomanry. The 1st Armoured Division's two brigades were the 2nd Armoured Brigade (consisting of the Queen's Bays, the 10th Hussars, and the 9th Lancers) and the 3rd Armoured Brigade, the Heavy Brigade (consisting of the 2nd, 3rd, and 5th battalions of the Royal Tank Regiment as the Royal Tank Corps had by then been re-designated).

Another view of light tanks, Mk. VIBs in this case, being "re-manufactured" at the MG works, showing the simple lines of the Vickers design. The twin coil springs of the "four pair" Horstmann suspension are clearly shown. (Imperial War Museum)

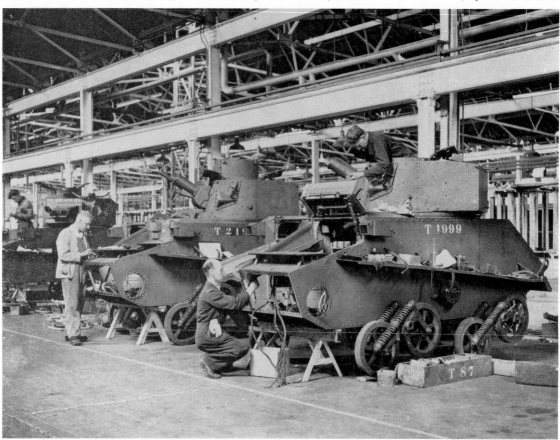

The MG Car Co., Abingdon, Berks., part of the Nuffield Organisation, was responsible for the "re-manufacture" of over 100 light tanks from mid-1940 onwards, refurbished vehicles going initially to armoured divisions in Britain and the Libyan desert and latterly to training units. This general view of the MG assembly shed, summer 1940, shows ex-1st Armoured Division vehicles salvaged from France being stripped and overhauled.
(Imperial War Museum)

Having got themselves clear of civil duties 2 Light Tank Company went to the Frontier in 1935 where they took part in the Mohmand campaign against rebellious tribes of the district, stirred up by the Fakir of Ipi. In the course of this campaign the light tanks demonstrated their ability to go where no armoured vehicles had ever been able to go before their advent. The operation—campaign is perhaps an overstatement —lasted several months with the light tanks proving so effective in their role that the Indian Government decided to convert the remaining armoured car companies as machines became available. A third company (9) was converted to the light tank rôle in the autumn of 1935 and by 1936 all eight companies in India had been converted to tracks.

Working on the turret of a Mk. VIB at the MG works.
(Imperial War Museum)

The Indianisation of the Indian Army had been adopted as official policy in 1935 and conversion of Indian cavalry regiments to armour was commenced in 1937. By 1938/39 it had been completed and the light tank companies left India, having more than proved their worth in country that had been considered impossible and impassable for any tracked

Refubished vehicles were thoroughly tested before being re-issued "as new" to units. Stowage of the tow rope and tools on the track cover is here shown.
(Imperial War Museum)

Left: *L4E1 Experimental modified Mk. V* (RAC Tank Museum). Right: *Experimental Light Tank Mk. I in AA role. Armament is two .5 in. Vickers machine-guns. This is A4E2 modified.*
(RAC Tank Museum)

vehicle. Light tanks were often in action against an enemy but his arms were inferior and he had no anti-tank potential. Under these circumstances both two- and three-man tanks performed satisfactorily: the tale of their performance against anti-tank guns is a very different one despite the bravery of their crews: personal courage is not the answer to inferiority in armament—at any rate in these days.

EGYPT AND THE WESTERN DESERT

The 6th Bn Royal Tank Corps was reorganised on a mixed basis in 1932/33 and was equipped with Mark III light tanks. The light company of this unit took part in operations in Palestine in 1936. That same year 1st (Light) Bn with Mark V's came out from England but returned home in December. It again returned to Egypt in 1938 with Mark VIB's and together with the 6th Bn formed the Heavy Brigade of the Mobile (later to become the 7th Armoured) Division (The Desert Rats) in 1939. Two of the cavalry regiments which had been converted to light tanks, the 7th and 8th Hussars, became part of the division's Light Brigade. The brigades were subsequently reorganised with one heavy and one light regiment in each. But even in the so-called heavy regiments more than half the tanks were light. In September 1940 the division (now the 7th Armoured) was reinforced by the arrival in Egypt of

A Light Tank Mk. IV (left) passed by a line of Mk. VIs at the 102nd OCTU, August 1940. (Imperial War Museum)

Mk. VIBs in the Western Desert, 1940. Sandshields have been fitted over front of tracks. (RAC Tank Museum)

the 2nd Bn Royal Tank Regiment and the 3rd Hussars. The reorganised brigades now consisted of: 4th Armoured Brigade—2 RTR, 6 RTR, 7 Hussars; 7th Armoured Brigade—1 RTR, 3 Hussars, 8 Hussars.

Light tanks Mark VI of various models were in action with all armoured regiments of the 7th Armoured Division throughout 1940. Lacking gun power and adequate armour they proved a death trap and no tears were shed when they were replaced by Stuart tanks in 1941.

A.F.V. Series Editor: DUNCAN CROW

Errata: P.35 No. 4. The use of the words 'modified to "Indian Pattern" (and)' gives a wrong impression and they should be deleted. Mk. VICs did not have cupolas and thus although this gave them an "Indian Pattern" look it was their "natural" state. Equally all Mk. VICs had Besas. The words 'with Besa machine-guns' were added only to emphasise the fact.

P.36. The caption of the top left-hand picture is incorrect. It should read: Based on a Mk. VI hull this experimental 'tank destroyer' with 2-pdr gun was tested by the army in 1938 but never went into production. Officially designated Carrier Anti-Tank Mk. II it was modified from a Mk. VI Light Tank by Ruston & Hornsby Ltd. (Mk. I was based on a Bren Carrier hull). The Mk. II was T1667 CMM823.

A battered Light Tank Mk. VIB still in use for training seen in company with a Grant in August 1942 at Catterick. The light tank, fitted with No. 19 set, is probably from 51st Training Regiment. (RAC Tank Museum)

PROTOTYPE LIGHT TANKS

Experimental No.	Vehicle	Builder	Engine/BHP	Suspension	WD Number	Reg'd. Number	Remarks
A4 E1	Carden-Loyd Mk VII	CSOF	Meadows EOC/60	Leaf spring	T 1022	ML 8726	
A4 E2	Light	CSOF	Meadows EOC/60	Leaf spring	T 491 .	ML 8784	3 return rollers
A4 E3	Tank Mk I	CSOF	Meadows EOC/60	Leaf spring	T 492	ML 8785	3 return rollers
A4 E4	Prototypes	CSOF	Meadows EOC/60	Leaf spring	T 493	ML 8786	3 return rollers
A4 E5		CSOF	Meadows EOC/60	Leaf spring	T 494	ML 8787	
A4 E6	Light	Vickers	Meadows EOC/60	Leaf spring	T 855	MT 9652	Some Mk I A prototypes later
A4 E7	Tank Mk IA	Vickers	Meadows EOC/60	Leaf spring	T 856	MT 9653	converted to Horstmann
A4 E8	prototypes	Vickers	Meadows EOC/60	Horstmann	T 857	MT 9654	suspension.
A4 E9		Vickers	Meadows EOC/60	Leaf spring	T 858	MT 9655	
A4 E10		Vickers	Meadows EOC/60	Leaf spring	T 859	MT 9656	Double turret: superimposed ·303 and ·5 V.MGs—latter lowest.
A4 E11	Amphibious	Vickers-	Meadows EST/100	Leaf spring	T 985	MT 9779	L1 E1
A4 E12	Light tanks*	Armstrong	Meadows EST/100	Leaf spring	T 986	MT 9780	L1 E2
A4 E13	Light	V-A	Rolls Royce/66	Horstmann	T 873	MT 9684	3 return rollers
A4 E14	Tank Mk II	V-A	Rolls Royce/66	Horstmann	T 874	MT 9685	3 return rollers
A4 E15	prototypes	CSOF	Rolls Royce/66	Horstmann	T 885	MT 9686	3 return rollers
A4 E16	Light tank Mk IIA	CSOF	Rolls Royce/66	Horstmann	T 931	MT 9725	3 return rollers
A4 E17	Light tank Mk IIB	V-A	Rolls Royce/66	Horstmann	T 967	MT 9762	3 return rollers
A4 E18	Light tank Mk IIA	CSOF	Rolls Royce/66	Horstmann	T 954	MT 9748	2 return rollers
A4 E19	Light tank	V-A	Meadows EST/90	Modified	T 992	MT 9783	Indian pattern No. 1 (L2 E1)
A4 E20	Mk IV prototypes	V-A	Meadows EST/90	Horstmann	T 993	MT 9784	Indian pattern No. 2 (L2 E2)
A5 E1	Carden-Loyd 3-man Light Tank				T 834	MT 9648	Built in 1930 it resembled a Mk II hull with a larger diameter turret like A4 E4 and A4 E8 but with co-axial ·5 and ·303 VMGs.
L3 E1	Light Tank Mk V	Experimental (3-man 1933 No. 1) V-A			T 1097	HX 6858	Bishop's Mitre cupola fitted Return roller on bogie
L3 E2	Light Tank Mk V Second pilot, similar to production Mk V				T 1159	HX 6916	
—	Light Tank Mark V	V-A	Meadows EST/90	Modified Horstmann	T 1203	HX 6960	This was the first official Mk V, March 1935 (22 production Mk Vs built; T1203–1224 HX 6960–6981
L4 E1	Light Tank Experimental R.O.F. design to improve on Mk V				T 1725	CMM 881	

*L1 E3 (T2430 FME 985) was another amphibious light tank.

COMPARATIVE TABLE OF LIGHT TANKS

Light Tank (Crew)	Wt. (Tons)	L.	W.	H.	Engine BHP/RPM	HP/ton	Suspension	Max Spd mph	Rad mls	Armament M.G's Vickers M.G's	Amn. No of rounds	Armour Max/Min mm	Remarks
Mark I (2)	4·8	13'2"	6'1"	5'7"	Meadows 6 cylinder 58/2400	12·1	Two wheel bogies leaf spring. Rear idler wheel. 3 return rollers on hull.	32	160	1×·303	2,500	14/4	
Mark I A (2)	4·8	13'2"	6'1"	5'7"	Meadows 6 cylinder 58/2400	12·1	Horstmann suspension horizontal coil spring.	32	160	1×·303	2,500	14/4	4 sent to India for trials and fitted with non-revolving square cupolas.
Mark II (2)	4·25	11'8"	6'1"	6'9"	Rolls Royce 6 cylinder 66/—	15·5	Horstmann-horizontal springs. Fitted Wilson pre-selector gear box.	30	125	1×·303	4,000	10/4	Mark II for India Meadows 58 bhp engine and mesh gearbox. Mark II A & B as Mark II but with reconstructed turrets, Mark I* and II*.
Mark III (2)	4·5	11'10"	6'1"	7'0"	Rolls Royce 6 cylinder 66/—	14·6	Horstmann with opposed inclined springs.	30	150	1×·303	4,000	10/4	36 of these tanks sent to Egypt to 6 Bn RTC.
Mark IV (2)	4·3	11'6"	6'10"	7'1"	Meadows 6 cylinder 88/2800	20·7	Horstmann-inclined springs parallel in bogies. No return roller or one on leading bogie.	36	125	1×·303	4,000	12/4	No rear idler was fitted.
Mark V (3)	4·8	13'0"	6'10"	7'4"	Meadows 6 cylinder 88/2800	18·3	Horstmann-inclined springs parallel in bogies. Return roller on leading bogie.	32	125	1×·303 1×·5	2,500 400	12/4	Circular cupola.
Mark VI (3)	4·8	13'2"	6'10"	7'5"	Meadows 6 cylinder 88/2800	18·3	Horstmann-inclined springs, parallel in bogies. Return roller on leading bogie.	35	125	1×·303 1×·5	2,500 400	15/4	All Mark VI's–Mark VI C were fitted with 2 one shot 4" smoke dischargers either side of the turret. Range 50 yds. Mark VI had a circular cupola.
Mk VI A (3)	4·8	13'2"	6'10"	7'5"	Meadows 6 cylinder 88/2800	18·3	Return roller on hull.	35	125	1×·303 1×·5	2,500 400	15/4	An octagonal cupola was fitted.
Mk VI B (3)	5·2	13'2"	6'10"	7'5"	Meadows 6 cylinder 88/2800	16·9	Return roller on hull.	35	125	1×·303 1×·5	2,500 400	15/4	A circular cupola was fitted.* Only one cooling louvre on radiator cover plate.
Mk VI C (3)	5·2	13'2"	6'10"	7'5"	Meadows 6 cylinder 88/2800	16·9	Return roller on hull.	35	125	Besa M.G's 1× 7·92mm & 1 ×15mm	2,500 400	15/4	No cupola. Periscope in conical shaped hatch.

*Mark VI Bs for India had no cupola. A periscope was provided for the commander in a conical shaped hatch.

Tetrarch is remembered as the first airborne tank. Lashed in the nose of the huge Hamilcar gliders they swooped down on the Normandy battlefield on D-Day, June 6, 1944. (Imperial War Museum)

Light Tanks
Mk VII Tetrarch and Mk VIII Harry Hopkins
by Peter Chamberlain and Chris Ellis

D-DAY, June 6, 1944, holds memories for millions of men, but for the relatively few who were near enough to the landing zone in the fields of Normandy to see it, including the men of the 21st Panzer Division, counterattacking on the right flank of the 6th Airborne Division, one of the most indelible impressions must have been the sight of hundreds of gliders, Horsas and Hamilcars, swooping in, dead on time at 8 p.m. that evening to reinforce the parachute brigades which had dropped at dawn.

Yet another chapter was being written in the story of the tank. For this was the occasion when, for the first time, tanks were being flown into the battle zone in the massive Hamilcars. They bounced and crashed their way on to a grass strip already festooned with discarded parachutes and the wreckage of other gliders. As they skidded to a halt, the doors swung open and each of the Hamilcars lurched forward on to its nose and spawned either a tracked Universal carrier or a tank—the Tetrarch—from its cavernous interior. The 6th Airborne Reconnaissance Regiment, Royal Armoured Corps, had arrived on the scene of battle . . .

THE P.R. PROJECT

Although Tetrarch is now remembered as Britain's first airborne tank, it was not initially conceived for this rôle. Like all previous British light tanks, it was a Vickers design and had been started as a "private

venture" in 1937 to follow the Light Tank Mark VI which Vickers then had in production for the War Office. The Mark VI was, in turn, the latest of a series of light tanks and tankettes which Vickers had commenced producing in the 'twenties for the British Army and for commercial sale to a number of foreign countries: Japan, Thailand, China, Germany, Italy and Russia had been among the customers for variations on earlier models. The new design, designated P.R., was radically different from the Light Tank Mark VI and was a notable advance over anything Vickers had made before in this field. It carried heavier calibre main armament than previous light tanks. The suspension was also quite different. Instead of Horstmann type sprung bogies, characteristic of Vickers light tanks, the P.R. had four large road wheels with the drive to the rear pair. Steering was effected by warping the tracks, a similar system to that which Vickers had developed for the machine-gun carrier which they were already building for the British Army.

Because of the close liaison which existed between Vickers and the War Office, existence of the P.R. design was known to the Mechanisation Board from the early stages. To the War Office it was known by the nickname of "Purdah". Legend attributes the name to a remark by the Director of Mechanisation that Vickers had had the design "in purdah for so long". The prototype was completed in December 1937. It was originally unarmed but later fitted with

TETRARCH ICS, T9353 "Ritz", of Headquarters Squadron, 6th Airborne Reconnaissance Regiment, 6th Airborne Division. This unit was flown into Normandy in the second airborne wave on the evening of **D-Day**, 6th June 1944, to help secure the River Orne crossings.

© JAMES LEECH

0   5'

Left: *The unarmed P.R. prototype as completed in December 1937. The turret shape differs from the production version.*
(Imperial War Museum)

Right: *First public appearance of the new Light Mark VII was early in January 1941 when two vehicles under test by 1st Armoured Division appeared at a demonstration at the Army Staff College, Camberley. General Sir Alan Brooke, C.-in-C. Home Forces, and staff officers talk to the crews.*
(Imperial War Museum)

a standard 2-pdr. gun and a co-axial Vickers ·303 in. machine-gun. As a private venture design, Vickers could have offered the P.R. for sale on the open market but, following their usual procedure, they gave first refusal to the War Office. The Mechanisation Board received the offer in early May 1938 and instructed the Mechanisation Experimental Establishment (M.E.E.) at Aldershot to test the prototype and report on its suitability for adoption as a standard light tank.

THE INSIDE STORY

Immediately following these trials, on June 8, 1938, a meeting was called at the War Office by the Director General of Mechanisation Policy (D.G.M.P.) attended by representatives of the General Staff and the Royal Tank Corps. Since the existing light tank programme was proving satisfactory discussion turned to the suitability of Purdah as a "light cruiser" tank if it was to be adopted at all. War Office policy at that time stipulated that all cruiser tanks should be armed with the 2-pdr. gun, which Purdah did not have at that stage. Also the trials had shown it to be slower than the A.13 cruiser and its obstacle crossing performance was inferior. The deputy Chief of the Imperial General Staff therefore felt that it was not worth accepting in the light cruiser rôle. But he did agree that a small number "might be worth having" and the meeting decided that 70 vehicles could be ordered from Vickers at the tail end of the existing light tank programme. This led to a further meeting on June 15, 1938, also at the

A production Light Mark VII. Note the addition of stowage boxes, revised turret, and bracket for a smoke discharger on the turret side.
(Imperial War Museum)

Front view of a standard Tetrarch used at the AFV School, Lulworth, in 1944. (Imperial War Museum)

Side view of the same vehicle shows smoke dischargers in place. (Imperial War Museum)

Aerial view of a Tetrarch I with Littlejohn adaptor fitted to the gun. The turret roof opens in two flaps. Note also the rear external fuel tanks, smoke dischargers on turret, and Bren gun stowage. (Imperial War Museum)

War Office, which was attended by representatives of Vickers, D.G.M.P. and his staff. At this significant meeting Vickers were told that the Army would place an order—subject to a guarantee of delivery by 1940, no hindrance to existing light tank output, and some design changes.

No final decisions were taken at this stage, however, for a special meeting had been arranged for June 20 by the Mechanisation Board at which the results of the M.E.E. trials would be evaluated in the light of General Staff requirements. Among changes called for in the basic design were better engine cooling and adoption of hardened steel for track shoes and suspension ball pins. Larger access doors for the engine compartment were also required, a ventilator in the turret roof and larger hatch doors. Following this meeting, the type designation A.17 was allocated to Purdah and on June 23 the Director of Mechanisation sent an officially revised specification to Vickers.

SPECIFICATION A.17

"**General:** To be generally in conformity with the pilot model machine submitted for tests during May 1938. Adapted for service as a three man light tank.

Armour: To full 4-mm. basis. All plates to be to IT Specification 70C, unless the contractor finds it easier to use plates of IT 60B. Thickness will be accordance with the lower limits of the graph "A" handed to Vickers on 22nd June 1938—i.e. 14-mm. standard, as with A.9 and A.13 machines, revised 1937.

Armament: One 7·92-mm. 2B machine-gun and one 15-mm. 2B anti-tank machine-gun in dual mounting in the turret. Two smoke discharger generators mounted on the turret.

Performance requirement: 200 miles radius on the 22 mile circuit at Farnborough, a fuel capacity of 42 gallons and a maximum road speed of not less than 40 m.p.h. Average cross-country speed of not less than 22 m.p.h. on the two mile circuit at Farnborough. Trench crossing 5 ft. Fording 2 ft. Slope 35 degrees."

The Mechanisation Board were worried by the lack of range of the Purdah prototype and the location of the main fuel tanks in the nose which indicated a grave fire risk from any frontal strikes. A compromise was reached by placing a 14-mm. bulkhead of armour plate inside the hull immediately aft of the fuel tanks. Drain holes were also provided in the floor of the fuel tank compartment so that any petrol from punctured tanks would flow out through the bottom of the vehicle. The addition of the armoured bulkhead inside the vehicle meant that any shell would now have to pass through two thicknesses of armour plate to penetrate the fighting compartment, and at this period only an armour piercing shell equivalent in performance to a 2-pdr. would have been capable of this. To increase the range a cylindrical external fuel tank was mounted on the hull rear.

Tests continued at M.E.E. with A.17 and at the end of July 1938 the Mechanisation Board compiled a full report which stated:

"This vehicle is provided with a new type of steering whereby the bogie wheels are tilted and turn in a manner which constrains the tracks to take a path of concentric circles. The diameter of the turning circle at full lock is 80 feet. A steering wheel is provided for normal purposes but provision has been made for skid steering by means of brakes and a differential control which are operated from a lever and selector gate mechanism. The experimental type of Meadows engine is installed in the rear of the vehicle. It has 12 cylinders in two horizontally opposed banks of six and develops 175 b.h.p. at 2,800 r.p.m. This provides the vehicle with a power-to-weight ratio of 27·2 b.h.p. per ton. The armament consists of a Vickers 2-pdr. gun and a ·303-in. machine-gun mounted co-axially in the turret. Protection is to 14-mm. standard and a crew of three is carried . . . the steadiness of the vehicle on roads and cross-country was very good and implies the achievement of a steady gun platform . . . Hydro-pneumatic suspension is employed, the weight of the tank being supported by air with a cushion of oil to absorb rebound. The committee recommend that the Vickers P.R. tank be purchased and subjected to extended reliability trials at M.E.E."

INTO PRODUCTION

At this stage Vickers were not keen to sell the prototype outright, mainly because they needed it to complete their production drawings and to work the various changes that had been called for. Also they were working on a true "light cruiser" tank (the still-born A.18 project) which was based very closely on the P.R. design. But by October 10, 1938, Vickers had submitted the final hull drawings to the War Office for approval and on November 11 these were followed by new turret drawings which incorporated the features asked for after the first trials. Some criticisms which remained were now overlooked probably because the period of approval coincided exactly with the Munich crisis. The Director of Mechanisation had already approved the official designation "Tank, Light, Mk. VII" for the P.R. project on September 4 and the prototype was re-designated A.17 E1 to distinguish it from production vehicles (subsequently designated A.17 E2). Trials at M.E.E. had meanwhile shown a tendency for the vehicle to shed its tracks when subjected to extreme, but not violent, manoeuvring at low speed and Vickers took the prototype back for further modifications to its suspension.

A three day conference on tank production was held at the War Office in November 1938 and, by agreement with Vickers, Metropolitan-Cammell Carriage and Wagon Co. were asked to undertake manufacture of the Light Mk. VII. An order for 120 vehicles was made for delivery in 1940. By this time it had also been decided to drop the machine-gun armament originally specified and adopt instead the 2-pdr. main armament fitted to the prototype by Vickers. The ·303-in. co-axial Vickers gun was replaced by the 7·92-mm. Besa machine-gun. Tooling up and preparation of components took up the whole of 1939. Production was just beginning at the Metro-Cammell works in July 1940 when the order was cut by half to only 70 as a result of the General Staff's re-assessment of tank requirements following the B.E.F.'s withdrawal from Dunkirk. To counter the expected invasion, cruiser and infantry tanks were urgently needed. The ineffectiveness of light tanks against the German panzers in the short Flanders

The Tetrarch ICS fitted with a 3-in. howitzer. These were conversions from 2-pdr. Tetrarchs. (Imperial War Museum)

Left: A rare and historic view of the Tetrarch DD tank at Hendon Reservoir in June 1941. The propeller and folding flotation screen remained virtually unaltered on later DD tanks. (Imperial War Museum)

Right: A.25 Harry Hopkins, showing the new turret and revised hull. (Imperial War Museum)

campaign had also brought about a marked switch of interest to armoured cars for the reconnaissance rôle. Metro-Cammel, however, had already ordered armour plate for 235 Mk. VIIs and persuaded the War Office that it would take very little extra trouble to complete 100 vehicles. The Ministry of Supply agreed and confirmed the revised figure of 100 production Mk. VIIs on July 30, 1940. Subsequently a further 120 were ordered but only 177 vehicles eventually were built, numbered T5185–T5254 and T9266–T9365. The shortfall was mainly due to extensive bombing of the Metro-Cammell factory in April 1941.

First deliveries of Light Mk. VIIs were made in November 1940. Two vehicles each went to 1st and 6th Armoured Divisions and one vehicle each to the AFV School at Lulworth and M.E.E. at Aldershot. The first production vehicle went to M.E.E. who used it for extensive trials. Apart from a few minor modifications which M.E.E. suggested for added crew comfort, it was found to be quite satisfactory. The AFV School reported on their trial vehicle in January 1941, and concluded that the Light Mk. VII was excellent as a gun platform and mechanically reliable, but they were critical of the suspension and the noisy transmission. They also considered that command problems might arise in action due to the tank commander having to act as loader for the 2-pdr. gun.

LIGHT TANK MK. VII DESCRIBED

The Tetrarch was divided internally into three compartments: the driving position, the fighting compartment, and the engine room. Taking these in order, the driving position housed the driver's seat centrally, flanked each side with a 22½-gallon fuel tank. The driver controlled the steering by means of a car-type steering wheel which acted through a steering connector rod to the steering head on each suspension unit.

The fighting compartment housed the turret and the other two crew members, the commander and the gunner. A rotary platform formed the turret floor and was carried on six Bakelite rollers mounted on a support ring attached to the hull floor. The turret floor was rotated by the commander's seat pillar, the upper end of which was attached to the turret inner ball race, the lower end engaging with a ball pin attached to the floor. A hatch in the turret floor gave access to the rotary connections.

The two-man turret was of hexagonal flat plate construction, the front plate carrying a co-axial mounting for 2-pdr. QFSA gun and 7·92-mm. Besa machine-gun. The shield supporting the cradles for the co-axial mount and the telescope carrier had protections on each side which formed trunnions, free to pivot in bushed housings attached to the front plate. An external shield plate was bolted to the turret front with end covers riveted to it. It also had an armoured liner for the 2-pdr. gun, a mantlet for the Besa machine-gun, and a sight aperture bush bolted to its outer face. Traverse was effected by a two-speed hand gear giving 7·06 degrees per revolution in high gear and 2·6 degrees in low gear.

The rear compartment housed the 12-cylinder flat Meadows engine mounted above the gearbox and bevel drive longitudinally with the flywheel end towards the front. All accessories except the fans were mounted on top of the engine for easy access through the two detachable inspection hatches on the hull top. The radiator was placed vertically across the engine rear.

There were eight independently sprung, steerable, rubber-tyred wheels, four each side, with springing of the "Airdraulic" type—air springing with oil damping. All wheels were detachable from their hubs which ran on spindles bolted to the steering head of each suspension unit. The steering heads were attached to the hull by a short top link and longer bottom link and the steering head was connected to the steering connector rod. Length of the link arms was so arranged that in rising and falling during movement over uneven ground, the bottom point of the wheel remained approximately in line with the other wheels. Suspension springs were mounted between brackets on the hull sides, and a track adjuster and shock absorbing spring was incorporated in each front steering head.

Wheels consisted of steel disc centres with channel section rims which held the tyres. The second and third wheels on each side were interchangeable and the tyres were reversible, but the leading wheel tyres on each side differed, being narrower at the top than the bottom with the top slightly offset from the base. The inner wheel rim reached nearly to the top of the tyre. The reason for the special tyre and rim arrangement at the front was to obviate the possibility of track guide lugs climbing up the side of the tyre and so causing the track to run off when the wheels were turned to full lock. The rear wheel on each side was also the driving or sprocket wheel. It had identical centres but included a bullet-proof pressing riveted to the outside to provide additional protection for the gears in the final drives. The rear tyre was held by clincher rims and holes were moulded through the centre line to take the 30 sprocket teeth.

Track was of case-hardened malleable cast-iron links joined by case-hardened steel pins. The cored holes for the pins were ·30 inches larger in diameter than the pins themselves to give adequate side play when the tracks were curved. Inverted U-section rubber seals in the pin boss prevented the ingress of mud and water. There were 99 links to each track.

IN SERVICE

The first "public" appearance of the Light Mk. VII was in January 1941 when the vehicles issued to 1st Armoured Division, in the hands of the 9th Lancers, were included in a demonstration for General Sir Alan Brooke, C-in-C Home Forces, and other senior officers at the Army Staff College, Camberley. A small number were issued for training in the months ahead when tanks generally were in short supply. The 9th Lancers had 17 on strength by summer 1941 among a motley assortment of A.9s, A.13s, Covenanters, Crusaders, and Light Mk. VIs. In July 1941 consideration was given to sending some to the 8th Army in the Western Desert, who at that time were

in desperate need of tank reinforcements. However, the original, prototype engine cooling system had been simplified for production vehicles and this made it unsuitable for tropical use and the scheme was abandoned.

As the supply of cruiser tanks increased, light tanks were dropped altogether from the establishment of armoured divisions, and the Light Mk. VII was virtually redundant. In the spring of 1942, a batch was sent to Russia in a consignment of British tanks which also included Matildas, and Valentines. The first employment of the Light Mk. VII in offensive operations was in Operation "Ironclad"—the invasion of Madagascar—on May 5, 1942 when 12 vehicles manned by "B" Special Service Squadron (an *ad hoc* unit formed for the purpose) landed under command of 29th Independent Brigade Group in Ambararata Bay. Little opposition was met from the Vichy French in the drive on Antisirane and the tanks were hardly tested in action. Choice of the Light Mk. VII for this operation was almost certainly dictated by its light weight and small size, as all equipment carried by the invading force had to be ferried to shore from the troop transports which brought them from Durban.

TETRARCH AIRBORNE

Meanwhile, the development of an airborne forces command and the means of delivering troops from the air, either by parachute or glider, had been proceeding in Britain, following the Germans' effective use of this method of attack in Norway, Holland and Crete. The possibility of landing tanks from the air by glider was considered, and the Light Mk. VII, now surplus to requirements elsewhere, was thought to be light and compact enough for the purpose. General Aircraft Ltd. were asked to design a glider for this mission and early in 1942 the remaining Light Mk. VIIs were earmarked for airborne use. At this time also, the name Tetrarch, by which the vehicle is best known, was adopted.

The new glider, the Hamilcar, was the largest ever

The Alecto self-propelled 95-mm. howitzer was built on the Harry Hopkins chassis.
(Imperial War Museum)

New turret, driver's escape hatches and revised hull shape are apparent in these views of Harry Hopkins.
(Imperial War Museum)

built in Britain. It weighed 16 tons, spanned 150 ft., and had nose doors for loading and unloading. The fuselage was tailored very closely to take the width and height of the Tetrarch stowed in the front on specially reinforced track ways. It was lashed down by quick-release spring clips. Carrying a 7½ ton tank posed problems with loading and unloading, and the method adopted was to remove the Hamilcar wheels and lower the aircraft on to its belly skids to allow the tank to be driven aboard and secured. The aircraft was then jacked-up and the undercarriage replaced for the towed take-off. On landing, the undercarriage either collapsed and the Hamilcar was brought to a halt on its belly skids or, failing this, the crew let the oil from the oleo legs and the air from the tyres to bring the aircraft onto its belly. The tank engines were started during the landing run and the nose doors released so that the tank simply drove out as the glider came to rest. This caused the glider to tip forward, but as it did not have to take off again, any damage at this stage could be overlooked, The Hamilcar, incidentally, could also carry a Universal Carrier or a Bofors-Quad.

Hamilcars did not enter service until November 1943 and the first trial landings with Tetrarchs were carried out at Tarrant Rushton in April 1944. It was on this occasion that a famous incident occurred when a Hamilcar pilot misjudged his landing, bounced and crashed into a couple of Nissen huts. The Tetrarch tank inside broke loose and shot forward 50 yards from the nose of the aircraft, through the remains of the Nissen hut at about 90 m.p.h. The crew inside the tank were uninjured.

For their new rôle, some Tetrarchs were fitted with a 3-in. howitzer in place of the 2-pdr. and these vehicles were designated Tetrarch ICS (i.e. infantry close support). For the Normandy landing by 6th Air Landing Brigade, as part of the overall airborne assault by 6th Airborne Division, the 6th Airborne Reconnaissance Regiment was equipped with a mixture of Tetrarchs and Universal Carriers manned by Royal Tank Regiment personnel. Eight Tetrarchs —half the Regiment's tank squadron—were included in the second wave air assault on the evening of D-Day to reinforce the two parachute brigades which had landed earlier to secure the River Orne crossing. Most of the Tetrarchs fouled their tracks

Rear view of the Alecto I.
(Imperial War Museum)

53

Modified muzzle-brake installed experimentally on the howitzer of this Alecto I.
(Imperial War Museum)

as they raced out on to the landing ground which was littered with abandoned parachute silks and lines. They were virtually out of action until the balance of the squadron arrived later by sea. But they were only intended for the initial assault and a few days later the crews changed them for Cromwells.

Airborne tanks were not used again until the 6th Airborne Division's drop across the Rhine on March 24, 1945. A few Tetrarchs were used in this operation, but most of the small number of tanks employed were American M.22 Locusts which had become available since the Normandy landing.

Tetrarch remained in service with the airborne forces until well into post-war years. A Hamilcar flight was based at Fairford until 1948 and the 3rd Hussars maintained a troop of Tetrarchs which made periodic glider-borne landings on Salisbury Plain and Netheravon for training and demonstration purposes until the Hamilcars, and subsequently the Tetrarchs, were withdrawn from service, thus ending the brief but fascinating epoch of the tanks that flew into battle.

HARRY HOPKINS AND ALECTO

The Harry Hopkins or A.25 E1 was derived very closely from the A.17: in fact, it was originally designated "Tank, Light Mk. VII, revised" and three prototypes were authorised in April 1941 utilising components which were available from the cancelled A.17. While incorporating wheels, chassis components and many other Tetrarch parts, Harry Hopkins had a completely redesigned hull with thicker armour protection (38 mm.), more room and comfort for the crew, hydraulically assisted steering, a faceted turret to give better shot deflection and large escape hatches for the driver. This was another Vickers design, but Metro-Cammell carried out production, following on from Tetrarch and another 99 Harry Hopkins tanks were built, the order being completed in 1944. These vehicles all went into reserve and none were used operationally. The Harry Hopkins chassis served as a basis for the Alecto, or A.25 E2, which was a self-propelled 95-mm. howitzer, originally called Harry Hopkins ICS. Though never used operationally, this interesting design was an attempt to produce a fast, heavily armed, air-portable vehicle. The gun was mounted low in the hull, the original turret removed and accommodation provided for a crew of five. A

traverse of 30 degrees each side was possible with the gun, and up to 48 rounds of HE or smoke ammunition could be carried. A variant produced as a pilot model only was the Alecto Recce. (or Mk. II) which was similar to the basic Alecto but carried a 6-pdr. gun instead of the 95-mm. howitzer. Two further Alecto variants projected, but never built, were Alecto III, which would have mounted a 25-pdr. howitzer, and Alecto IV, which would have had a 32-pdr. The War ended before any of these vehicles could be developed and all work on Alecto was abandoned in 1945. At least one Alecto was used until about 1955, however, as a general towing vehicle and "hack" by artillery units on Salisbury Plain.

Alecto was also used experimentally to tow the Centipede anti-mine rollers which had been developed for use with the Sherman Crab. The final version, and most important of all, was Alecto Dozer, which had the gun and mounting removed and replaced by a two-edged dozer blade with hydraulic lift mechanism operated from the hull top. Only a small number of these were made, also with an air-portable rôle in mind.

The abandonment of Alecto in 1945 marked the end of an era of U.K. light tank development which began in the mid-twenties with the work of Major G. le Q. Martel and John Valentine Carden. It was not simply that the light tank was discredited—its usefulness in reconnaissance remained—but that the British Army was now embarked on a standard "Capital Tank" policy exemplified by Centurion.

LITTLEJOHN

A few Tetrarchs were fitted with Littlejohn bore reducers on their 2-pdr. guns, and were the only tanks —as opposed to armoured cars—to feature this equipment. The Littlejohn was an adaptation of an idea first put up by a refugee Czech designer in the summer of 1940. A tapered bore liner built up pressure in the barrel when the gun was fired, giving increased muzzle velocity. Development was given a very low priority until the capture of similar German equipment in the winter of 1941–42 gave impetus to the development. Production began in 1943. By this time, however, the main interest was in 6-pdr. gun tanks. The promising Littlejohn idea was taken up too late to have much influence on tank warfare.

Tetrarch in Russia. These rare war pictures wired to London by the Russian Tass News Agency in 1942 show Tetrarchs in action on the Russian Southern Front. The front tank of the mountain column still carries the U.K. War Department number—W.D. No. T.9267 —with which it left the depot in England. The open formation, led by a T-34, graphically illustrates the Russian technique of taking infantry into action on tanks.   (Imperial War Museum)

Rare view of the prototype Alecto II at speed. This had a 6-pdr. gun. Note the suspension adjusting to the rough ground.
(Imperial War Museum)
The Alecto Dozer showing the control box on the top.
(Imperial War Museum)

TETRARCH IN PERSPECTIVE

Tetrarch was the first of the British airborne tanks and also the last to see service. Its importance in the history of armoured warfare was to demonstrate the limitations of the tank in the airborne rôle. The conclusion must be that other than proving that tanks could be flown into the heart of a battlefield—if only at great expense and effort—the tactical value, even in Normandy, one of the greatest battles in history, was negligible. Even in 1942, when the Tetrarch was first proposed for airborne use, the light tank was obsolescent as a type. Its reconnaissance and limited offensive rôle could be undertaken just as effectively by the armoured car. This was already true in 1944, and is even more so today when even the lightest main battle tank weighs over 30 tons, and the most expensively equipped air forces with purpose-built freighters would be hard-pressed to transport a dozen such vehicles strategically in one lift, let alone tactically into a battle zone. For most situations today in which the tactical use of airborne armour can be envisaged, the armoured car remains the optimum air-portable vehicle in terms of cost-effectiveness.

As an airborne tank Tetrarch remains an interesting memory, and its greatest contribution to the development of the tank is probably one of the least known parts of its story. This dates back to one morning in June 1941 when a little band of scientists stood on the bank of the Hendon Reservoir and watched a diminutive Tetrarch tank—one of the early test vehicles which had gone to 1st Armoured Division— crawl to the water's edge, pause to erect a boat-shaped canvas screen around its hull, and then launch itself like a duck. The first DD (Duplex-Drive) "swimming" tank had arrived. Ironically enough, this paved the way for one of the most important contributions to the Normandy landing, the DD Shermans which swam ashore to make the first touch down on enemy soil while the Tetrarchs were left to their glider-borne sideshow.

TETRARCH SPECIFICATION

Vehicle
Tank Light Mk. VII, Tetrarch Mk. 1.
Designation: A.17 E1.
Combat weight: 7½ tons.
Ground pressure: 7·9 lb./sq. in.
Bridge classification: 8.

Dimensions
Length overall: 14 ft. 1½ in. (gun to front).
Length over hull: 13 ft. 6 in.
Height: 6 ft. 11½ in.
Ground contact: 108 in.
Width: 7 ft. 7 in.
Track width: 9½ in.
Track centres: 6 ft. 6 in.

Armament
One 2-pdr. (40 mm.) QFSA in turret.
One 7·92 mm. Besa machine-gun (co-axially mounted).
Two 4-in. smoke dischargers.
(One 3-in. tank howitzer in place of 2-pdr. in Tetrarch Mk. ICS).

Fire Control
Hand traverse and elevation; percussion or electric firing.

Ammunition
50 rounds 2-pdr. AP.
2,025 rounds 7·92 mm.
Eight smoke generators.

Sighting and Vision
Driver: Bullet-proof glass forward look-out and slit type side look-outs.
Commander: Vickers tank periscope and side look-outs.
Gunner: Vickers tank episcope and side look-outs.

Communications
One telephone set, AFV, with microphone, headset, and jack plug for each crew member (internal communications).
One wireless set No. 19.

Armour
Hull—Front: 6-10 mm.; sides: 6 mm./90°; roof: 4 mm.; floor: 14 mm.

Engine
One Meadows, type MAT.
12 cylinders in two horizontally-opposed banks.
165 b.h.p. at 2,700 r.p.m.
Fuel capacity: 45 gallons in two 22½-gallon tanks in driving compartment.
Oil capacity: Four gallons.

Transmission
Gearbox: Sliding pinion type, five speeds and reverse, direct on 4th gear.
Ratios: (1) 6·48 to 1, (2) 3·24 to 1, (3) 1·8 to 1 ,(4) 1 to 1, (5) ·726 to 1, (reverse) 7·952 to 1.
Steering: Curving track with auxiliary steering by brakes.
Turning circle: 87 feet with curving tracks (turns in own length with brakes).
Brakes: Girling internal expanding type, in drums on bevel drive shaft.

Suspension
Three road wheels and combined road wheel/sprocket wheel each side. Solid rubber tyres.
Track: Case-hardened malleable iron links with case-hardened nickel steel pins. 99 track links each side. Pitch 3·1 in.

Performance
Maximum road speed: 40 m.p.h.
Maximum cross country speed: 28 m.p.h.
Maximum trench width: 5 ft.
Wading depth: 3 ft. (unprepared).

Special Features
Littlejohn adaptor fitted to 2-pdr. gun on some vehicles.
Detachable external fuel tank transversely across hull rear.

Securing a Tetrarch inside a Hamilcar after loading. Crew remained in the vehicle while the glider was in flight since there was not room to move around once airborne. (Imperial War Museum)

1919, Mark IX with "camels" lashed alongside ready to take to the water. The box gives access to the interior and the pipes are for engine exhaust. (R.A.C. Tank Museum)

Mark IX afloat. The top of the "camel" is visible along the side of the tank. (R.A.C. Tank Museum)

Amphibious Tanks

by Major General N. W. Duncan

THE critical factor in any opposed landing over a water obstacle, whether sea or inland water, is the rate at which the attacking force can be built up in relation to the speed of reinforcement of the threatened area by the defenders. Any substantial increase in the power of the attacking force makes the establishment of a secure bridgehead so much the more certain. The tank, with its inherent mobility and offensive power, is an obvious answer provided that it can be got across the water in such a way that its offensive powers are not inhibited by the means employed to make it float.

The tank's weight is the principal difficulty and this is irreducible if it is to face hostile armour, having crossed the water, with any chance of success. It presented such a problem in World War I that the proposed Nieuport landing scheduled for 1917 was to be carried out from long pontoons, carrying tanks, infantry and artillery: motive power for the pontoons was provided by two monitors lashed alongside and the pontoon would be driven ashore so that the assault troops could land dry-shod. The equivalent for inland waters was the raft, but both were unwieldy and vulnerable and the search for a true amphibious armoured fighting vehicle continued without remission.

The problem of making individual vehicles float could be solved in three different ways:

(i) by a basic redesign of the tank hull to provide the necessary buoyancy, or

(ii) by the provision of exterior pontoons to provide the necessary buoyancy. It was desirable that these should be quickly detachable to facilitate manoeuvre, or

(iii) by the provision of a tube or screen round the tank whose volume was sufficient to displace enough water to counteract the tank's weight. This is the principle of the DD tank which was only invented in World War II. A large enough tube will make anything float, but the problem of staying the tube against the motion of the vehicle in water may prove insurmountable.

The first recorded individual amphibious tank was a Mark IX, the supply tank of the First World War. "Camels," usually employed in salvage operations,

were borrowed from the Royal Navy and were attached to the sides of the tank. These provided the necessary buoyancy to make the tank float and the whole contraption was propelled by its tracks and by an outboard motor mounted at the rear of the tank hull. It was reasonably handy in the water but the "camels" were bulky and heavy and restricted manoeuvre on land, while the process of attaching and detaching them took some time.

The Medium D which appeared in prototype form in 1918 was made to swim successfully two years later. In its amphibious form it was called the Medium D**. Propulsion was by the tank's tracks, a method which, although inefficient, did propel the tank in the water. This tank was to have carried a 6-pdr. gun and would have been invaluable in the early stages of an assault across a water obstacle, but the armour was very thin even for the anti-tank weapons of those days.

In 1930-31 Vickers-Carden-Loyd built two amphibious tanks, A4E11 and 12: they were larger than contemporary light tanks intended for land use in order to give their hulls the volume needed to make them float. However, their inherent buoyancy was only achieved by making the machines very light: armour was thin and weight was cut to the bone everywhere, to such an extent that if the tank encountered really rough going the suspension bogie pivots on the hull were liable to twist, throwing the wheels out of line and the track off. They had a two-man crew and only mounted one ·303 Vickers MG in a circular turret on the left of the tank. The internal layout, with engine, gearbox and transmission on the right-hand side of the vehicle followed contemporary light tank practice. When water-borne the tank was steered by a movable shroud round the single propeller which was driven by an auxiliary shaft off the gearbox. Ground clearance had been reduced by additional buoyancy tanks under the hull while even the track guards were hollow boxes, filled with Kapok to give a little extra lift. The tanks proved manoeuvrable afloat and when water-borne had a speed of 6 m.p.h. They could do 40 m.p.h. on land provided that the going imposed no great strain on the suspension. Although the machines are interesting and represent a brave attempt to solve a difficult

1931, Vickers-Carden-Loyd amphibious tank. Note box track guards and buoyancy tank which shapes the front of the hull. (Below right) Rear view showing single propeller and movable shroud by which water flow could be diverted to steer the tank afloat. (R.A.C. Tank Museum)

(Left above) *1939, Vickers amphibious light tank—L1E3—showing side and bow sponsons. This prototype was built in mild steel.*
(R.A.C. Tank Museum)

Rear view of Medium D** showing the tank under propulsion by its tracks at Christchurch, Hants. A front view of this tank afloat appears on page 105 of Volume One. Johnson's Light Infantry Tank was also amphibious (see Vol. One p. 107).
(R.A.C. Tank Museum)

(Left below) *Vickers amphibious tank, 1931, going ashore.*
(R.A.C. Tank Museum)

(Below) *Sherman DD tank with float screen erected.*

Type	Vickers-Carden-Loyd 1931	Vickers 1939
Length	13 ft. 2 in.	14 ft. 0 in.
Width	6 ft. 11 in.	7 ft. 7 in. (over sponsons), 6 ft 10 in. (over tracks)
Height	6 ft. 0 in.	7 ft. 0 in.
Weight—tons	3·1	4·67
Engine	Meadows 6 cylinder 100 h.p.	Meadows 6 cylinder 85 h.p.
Transmission	Four forward 1R sliding pinion and single propeller.	Four forward 1R, sliding pinion with optional drive to twin propellers.
Steering	Clutch and Brake: steerable shroud afloat.	Clutch and brake and steerable shrouds afloat.
Suspension	¼ elliptic leaf spring	Horstmann coil spring.
Speed, land, m.p.h.	40	30
Speed, water, m.p.h.	6	3·7
Radius of action land-miles	150	120
Armament	1 × ·303 in. VMG	1 × ·303 in. or ·5 in. VMG
Armour—mm.	9	9
Crew	2	2

problem, their military value was questionable and their mechanical performance insufficiently reliable to make the experiment worth continuing. They were stripped of their amphibious fittings and sent to 2nd Bn. R.T.C. in 1933 for use as ordinary light tanks. The whole conception of these amphibious vehicles aroused considerable interest in foreign countries and specimens were purchased by Japan, U.S.S.R., Holland and China, the first two using them as a basis for their own developments.

A Vickers amphibious light tank was built in 1939 and was a marked improvement on the earlier versions. However, the armour at 9 mm. was thinner than that used on normal machines of the period which carried up to 14 mm. Only one machine-gun, which could be either a ·303 in. or a ·5 in., was mounted, but the turret was of better design than the earlier round pattern. While a three-man crew was regarded as the minimum for land work, this machine had to be handled by two men and the commander had to face the additional problems raised by water-borne operations.

Buoyancy in this tank was assured by exterior sponsons, filled with Kapok or balsa wood and shaped to give the whole assembly a boat form. In theory the sponsons could be detached from inside the tank once the water had been crossed but in practice, for some obscure reason, the sponsons were always very hard to get rid of: this was not a matter of tremendous importance because they were not unduly bulky. The tank was driven by twin propellers through a shaft from the gearbox, a somewhat complicated business with the front drive sprockets then in use. Five years later this particular problem was much more easily solved on the DD Sherman, where the propeller drive was taken directly off the rear idler wheels.

The propellers on the Vickers tanks were enclosed by shrouds, shaped like a truncated cone with its larger diameter facing forward. The shrouds were pivotted and could be moved laterally by cables connected to the driver's steering levers. Movement of the shrouds altered the direction of flow of water from the propellers and made the tank turn. This proved highly effective and manoeuvrability when water-borne was very good. Some trials work was carried out with these tanks but the project was dropped on the outbreak of war.

Both the 1931 and 1939 patterns of amphibious tanks had proved that flotation and movement afloat were feasible—at a price. That price was either a construction so light that the tank was really only suited for reconnaissance duties and was not powerful enough to take its place in the encounter battle, or the use of exterior pontoons or sponsons which could present difficulties in carriage and assembly, were apt to be hard to handle afloat, and could impede manoeuvre ashore. Both the Americans and the Japanese developed pontoons for attachment to medium gun tanks of the 15–30 ton class. They were very difficult to move and very bulky when attached to the tank which was then very hard to handle either ashore or afloat. It was not until the advent of Nicholas Straussler's DD principle that there was any prospect of getting a tank ashore in the early stages of the battle, with sufficient armour and armament to stand any chance of playing a decisive part in the struggle to establish a bridgehead. However, the DD equipment is vulnerable to hostile fire and the problems of providing built-in equipment which will allow a tank to cross even minor water obstacles without any delay has not yet been solved.

One other method of crossing water, currently receiving much attention, is by submerged movement. It is possible by special waterproofing and breathing apparatus to wade in depths up to 20 ft. The Germans were the first to adopt this method with the Tiger tank because of the difficulty experienced with these very heavy tanks crossing normal bridges. Pipes were provided for air intakes for both the engine and crew and another pipe dealt with the exhaust gases. A similar system was developed in 1940 for a British A.9 tank but this never went into Service use. Modern materials, notably fibre-glass, together with better waterproofing have helped the post-war development of submerged movement. The early air pipes have grown into Schnorkel tubes big enough to allow the commander to observe progress from water-level, with a better air supply and means to clear the engine exhaust. The equipment is bulky and takes time to assemble; it can be rapidly discarded on the other side of the water where it can be collected for use again if it is undamaged. Whether the built-in waterproofing will stand up to the stresses imposed by tank fighting remains to be seen.

Vickers Six-Ton Tank Type A with two machine-guns mounted side-by-side in separate turrets.
(Photo: Vickers-Armstrong Ltd.)

Vickers Six-Ton Tank Type B with a single turret mounting a 47-mm. gun and a co-axial machine-gun.
(Photo: Vickers-Armstrong Ltd.)

Vickers Six-Ton Tank

by Duncan Crow

ONE of the most significant British tanks produced in the inter-war period was not adopted by the British army. This tank was the Vickers "Six-Ton", which was produced as a private development venture by Vickers-Armstrong in 1929. Vickers were at the same time also engaged in developing light tanks from the Carden-Loyd prototype as well as producing a replacement for the Medium Mark II. This replacement, the Medium Mark III, which was based on the Vickers A6 "16 Tonners", was excellent in most ways except price; it cost £16,000. In a period of financial stringency a tank that cost as much as that was not likely to be ordered in dozens. In fact only three Mark IIIs were built.

In order to produce something cheaper that would be purchased on a wider scale Vickers built the Six-Ton tank. There were two types: Type A had a crew of three and was armed with two Vickers MGs each mounted in a separate turret, the turrets being placed side by side. This armament was in accordance with dominant thinking about British tank employment, that a light tank's job was to destroy enemy infantry by machine-gun fire. Such a limited rôle was not accepted in Germany where it was recognized that even a light tank would have to fight another tank and that it was not much use if it could not even fight its like.

Vickers, too, recognized the truth of this with their Type B, which had a single turret with a 47-mm. (3-pdr.) gun and a co-axial machine-gun. The duties of the three-man crew were commander, gunner, and driver. The Type B appeared in 1930.

Both Type A and Type B were powered by an Armstrong-Siddeley 4-cylinder, 87 b.h.p., air-cooled engine, which gave a speed of 22 m.p.h. Type A with a 13-mm. armour basis weighed 7·2 tons, and Type B with a 17-mm. basis weighed 7·4 tons. The remarkable thing about the Type B was that it gave the Medium Mark III main turret armament and armour protection at a fraction of the Mark III's cost and weight. Nor was its speed all that less— 22 m.p.h. against 30. Furthermore, its mechanical reliability was high and it set new standards in track life with a manganese steel skeleton type track.

AMERICAN T-2

Despite these advantages, the British army refused to adopt the Six-Ton tank because of doubts about the suspension. Not so other armies, however. A Six-Ton tank was acquired by the United States army for a 30-day trial and several of its features were embodied in a new American light tank, the T2, which was the progenitor of the M1-M5 series, the Stuart/Honeys. The hull form of the T2, its leaf spring suspension, its sponsons which overhung the track, and the long sloping glacis plate—all were copied almost exactly from the Six-Ton tank.

RUSSIAN T-26

The Russians also purchased and copied the Six-Ton tank, which was produced from 1932 on a large scale as the T-26. There were three versions: T-26A weighing 7·7 tons, which was the Type A with two turrets each with a 7·62-mm. machine-gun; and the T-26B and C developed from the Type B with a single 45 mm. gun-armed turret and a co-axial machine-gun.

POLISH 7TP

In Poland the Six-Ton tank was built as the 7TP. Both the 7TP and the T26B and C could be classified as light-medium tanks because of their high velocity gun. In the case of the 7TP this was a 37-mm. Bofors for which 80 rounds were carried, as well as 4,000 rounds for the co-axial MG. The 7TP, which weighed 9·5 tons, had a 25-mm. armour basis and was powered by a 140 b.h.p., 6-cylinder, water-cooled diesel engine Its maximum speed was the same as that of the Six-Ton tank—22 m.p.h. Its suspension, too, was the same—two pairs of twin bogies on rocker with leaf springing. It was 15 ft. long, 7 ft. 11 ins. wide, 7 ft. 2 in. high, and had a belly clearance of 1 ft. 3 in., all dimensions comparable with the Vickers original.

The 7TP was not built in large numbers.

THE GRAN CHACO

Among other countries which bought Six-Ton tanks was Bolivia. Together with some Carden-Loyd Mk. VI Tankettes, Six-Ton tanks of both types took part in the 1932-35 Gran Chaco War between

Bolivia and Paraguay. Only Bolivia had tanks in the Gran Chaco. Its small tank force was commanded by Wim Brandt, a German major, who later served in World War II with the SS.

Tanks were only used in action three times during the Gran Chaco War: in July, August and November 1933. On the second occasion only the Six-Ton tanks were used, but in July and November the Carden-Loyds were in action as well, when they were deployed in ones and twos and proved vulnerable to artillery and AP machine-gun fire.

In *Blackwood's Magazine* of April 1934 appeared an article by George Larden, a British officer who had visited the Gran Chaco while he was on leave the previous year. "The infantryman", he wrote, "backed by the machine-gun . . . once more proved his domination of the field of battle when the latter lies in thick and impenetrable country; for without observation or room to manoeuvre, such arms as artillery, tanks and even air planes can be of little value. Indeed, the Bolivians, who relied to a great extent on these arms to compensate them for their other disadvantages, have been somewhat disillusioned, and it is to their credit that their morale remained unshaken when the results they hoped for failed to materialise."

Commenting on this observation, Colonel Robert Icks wrote: "For students particularly of the new, developing art of armoured warfare, the Gran Chaco War demonstrated not only the limitations of armour facing modern firepower in close country but also, in the comparison between the Vickers 6-Ton and the Carden-Loyd, that the concept of the tankette as a form of mechanized, protected infantry which was a popular theory of the time, was not viable."

Close-up of Type B turret. (Photo: Vickers-Armstrong Ltd.)

Close-up of suspension common to Six-Ton tanks and its derivatives (in this case the T-26C) which was the cause of its rejection by the British army. (Photo: Imperial War Museum)

Russian T-26C copied from the Vickers Six-Ton tank.
(Photo: Imperial War Museum)

Bolivian Carden-Loyd Mk. VI Tankette variant with water-cooled armoured machine-gun and shield in the jungle of the Gran Chaco. The split roof is folded back. Picture of similar vehicle with split roof closed is on page 102. (Photo: Wim Brandt)

Vickers Six-Ton Tank Type B at Pirijayo, Gran Chaco.
(Photo: Wim Brandt)

Vickers Six-Ton Tank Type A at Nanawa in the Gran Chaco.
(Photo: Wim Brandt)

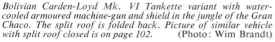

Matildas of 4th Royal Tank Regt. patrolling in the Western Desert, 1941. The pennants, flown for identification purposes, were raised in different positions each day.
(Imperial War Museum)

Infantry Tanks
Mks I and II Matilda
by Major James Bingham

THE first major action in which the Matilda took part was a comparatively minor counter-attack against the German Panzer divisions sweeping through France in May 1940. Yet it was a battle which was to have a profound effect, out of all proportion to the numbers involved. Lord Gort, the British Commander-in-Chief, had ordered withdrawals from Belgium for a counter-attack south of Arras, but the forces eventually available on 21st May consisted of no more than the remnants of 4th and 7th Battalions Royal Tank Regiment and two tired battalions of the Durham Light Infantry. The tank strength amounted to 58 Infantry Tanks Mk. I armed with machine-guns, and 16 Mk. IIs (the future Matilda) armed with 2-Pounder guns. The tanks led the attack at 2.0 p.m. and struck the flank of Rommel's motorized infantry regiments and of the SS Division *Totenkopf* where they created havoc. Anti-tank guns and artillery had little effect on the tanks, but superficial damage, breakdowns and sheer exhaustion under heavy fire brought the attack to a halt as darkness fell. Next day the force withdrew north of Arras.

Small though the material results of the attack appeared to be, it created an impression amongst the German commanders of far superior armoured strength, indicated in Rommel's report of the action:

"Very powerful armoured forces had thrust out of Arras and attacked the advancing 1st Battalion of the 6th Rifle Regiment, inflicting heavy losses in men and material. The anti-tank guns which we quickly deployed showed themselves to be far too light to be effective against the heavily armoured British tanks, and the majority of them were put out of action by gunfire, together with their crews, and then over-run by the enemy tanks. Many of our vehicles were burnt out. SS units close by also had to fall back to the south before the weight of the tank attack. Finally, the divisional artillery and 88-mm. anti-aircraft batteries succeeded in bringing the enemy armour to a halt south of the line Beaurains-Agny."*

The attack had come at a critical moment when some German commanders feared that the Panzer divisions might be cut off in Flanders. Guderian, whose Panzer Corps had already reached the coast near Abbeville, noticed the immediate impression made at von Kleist's Panzer Group Headquarters "which suddenly became remarkably nervous". This anxiety was reflected in Hitler's order to "Halt" after visiting von Runstedt's Headquarters on 24th May.

*"The Rommel Papers", edited by B. H. Liddell Hart.

Guderian's tanks were then only ten miles from Dunkirk. The 48 hours respite given to the British Expeditionary Force by Hitler's "halt order" gave them time to strengthen defences round the port and to prepare for evacuation.

DEVELOPMENT AND PRODUCTION

Throughout the 1930's and until the threat of war in Europe became imminent, the first priority in the production of tanks had been the need to support peace-keeping operations. This was set against a background of severe financial restraint for a small army that was committed to "colonial type" wars and which was beset by uncertainty as to the type of war it would have to fight. The financial restraint was such that in the period up to 1936 the highest annual sum allotted for tank development was £93,750. This was scarcely enough to allow an extensive study and trial of new designs.

Mechanization was generally unpopular and the orthodox soldier could only envisage another European war in terms of 1918, with infantry attacks against wire and trenches, supported by tanks and artillery. The medium tank of the 1920's and early '30's was accepted as a general purpose tank but the independent rôle of mobile forces which was being evolved in the Tank Brigade was viewed with the greatest suspicion by many senior and junior officers. This led to the demand for heavily armoured tanks designed for and committed to the "intimate support of infantry". In April 1934 outline requirements were prepared for two types of "infantry" tank, both with at least 1 in. (25·4 mm.) armour all round and a speed of 10 m.p.h.

 (1) A small tank, mounting a ·303 or ·5 in. machine-gun, inconspicuous and available in large numbers to act as mobile machine-gun posts.

 (2) A heavy tank, mounting the new 2-Pdr. high velocity anti-tank gun to deal with enemy tanks and protected machine-gun positions.

In May 1934 Sir John Carden of Vickers-Armstrong was asked to design a heavy infantry tank to

Infantry Tank Mk. 1—the original Matilda, traditionally so-named by Gen. Elles for its comic duck appearance. D for Demon identifies 4th Bn., Royal Tank Corps. (Imperial War Museum)

Matilda 1. The heavy water cooling jacket on the Vickers ·303 machine-gun has a steam outlet on the right front turret roof. (Imperial War Museum)

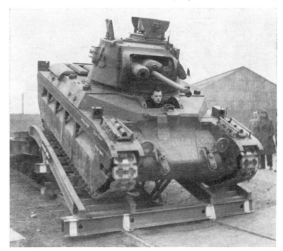

Infantry Tank Mk. II pilot model A 12 E1. Note six mud chutes. Production vehicles had five.   (RAC Tank Museum)

Matilda III CS. In the foreground is the Close Support tank—3 in. Howitzer—in a squadron of Valentines paraded on a U.K. training ground, July 1941. (Imperial War Museum)

Matilda IV with jettisonable auxiliary fuel tank. (RAC Tank Museum)

Matilda IV and Matilda IV CS with box section spudded tracks. The IV has a high cupola and the CS a low one. (Imperial War Museum)

Matilda Scorpion prototype. Note housing for 30 h.p. Bedford engines to drive rotary flail. (Imperial War Museum)

this general specification, based on a similar new "cruiser" tank, the A 9. The proposed infantry tank emerged as the A 10 with 30 mm. armour, but by 1937 it was realised that this was not sufficient armour for the rôle. The A 10 was, however, produced and went into action as a heavy cruiser, and it was later used by Vickers as the basis for the Infantry Tank Mk. III, Valentine.

General Sir Hugh Elles, who had commanded the Tank Corps at the Battle of Cambrai in 1917, was a firm believer in the need for tanks to support infantry in the assault, and when he became Master General of the Ordnance in May 1934 he exercised a predominant influence on the types of tank which were to be produced with the money available. When Sir John Carden said that he could produce a small infantry tank for £5,000–£6,000 if given a free hand, the offer was quickly accepted and in October 1935 the project was started under the security code name "Matilda". Designated A 11, the pilot model appeared in September 1936. This had 60 mm. armour (65 mm. on the front), weighed 11 tons and, powered by a commercial Ford V 8 engine of 70 h.p., had a top speed of 8 m.p.h. There was a two-man crew and it mounted a ·303 Vickers machine-gun in the turret. The tank had the merit of cheapness and it was mechanically very reliable, but it was obviously unsatisfactory with only a two-man crew and orders were given in November 1936 for the design of a successor—more powerful and with a speed of 10–15 m.p.h. At first this was envisaged as an extension of A 11, mounting the 2-Pdr. or, alternatively, two co-axially mounted machine-guns, with a weight of about 14 tons and, preferably, an oil engine.

The design was undertaken by the Mechanization Board in the War Office, in conjunction with the Vulcan Foundry at Warrington, and it was soon apparent that an extension of the A 11 was not practical. Instead, the new design (A 12) was based on an earlier medium tank (A 7) which had not gone beyond pilot stages; the 2-Pdr. turret was agreed upon and the mock-up was ready by April 1937. After various trial engine layouts had been examined, twin-ganged A.E.C. diesels were installed using standard A.E.C. components in production. These were matched to the Wilson epicyclic gearbox which was the only type in commercial production with output at both ends, although it was anticipated that there would be some delay in production of this assembly. The suspension was developed from the Vickers "Japanese type" to take the extra weight which had gone up to 24 tons with 70 mm. armour. The first pilot was ready in April 1938 but already an order had been given in December 1937 for work to start at once on a batch of 65 tanks. In May this was increased to 165.

The A11 was an unsatisfactory tank but it was produced as an interim measure, as the Infantry Tank Mk. I. A total of 140 were built and these were eventually to form the greater part of the two infantry tank battalions in France in 1940. For, although work was concentrated on the A 12—or Infantry Tank Mk. II—the design did not lend itself to mass production. There were only two in service at the outbreak of war on 3rd September 1939. The Mk. II was sometimes known as "Matilda senior", since both

Matilda III entering El Adem, 1941. The blade vane sight shows prominently in front of the cupola.   (Imperial War Museum)

were referred to as Matildas, until the Mk. I went out of service after Dunkirk and the name Matilda was formally adopted.

Matilda proved at that time to be the most powerful tank in operation anywhere. After its successes in the British Army it was taken into service in Australia and was shipped in large numbers to Russia where it was a welcome reinforcement and was reputedly popular with the Russian troops for its reliability and excellent protection. A total of 2,987 were built until production ceased in August 1943. But, the design could not be extended to take the 6-Pdr. gun, although trials were carried out with the Cromwell turret, and Matilda dropped out as the heavier weapons took over on the battlefield.

DESCRIPTION OF MATILDA

The hull was divided into the three usual compartments, with the driver in the nose section, the commander, gunner and loader/wireless operator in the fighting compartment, and the engine housed at the rear. An innovation was made in the construction of this tank by eliminating the conventional frame and by bolting the armoured castings and plates together through tapped holes to form a rigid structure.

Welding was not sufficiently advanced for large scale production. Steel castings were used for the first time in hull structure, with the nose and tool box castings being mainly responsible for hull rigidity; this strength was increased by the top and bottom plates being rebated into the side plates. A bulkhead forward of the engine compartment acted as a stay.

The driver sat in the centre, in the nose, with the gear selector and gate between his knees and steering levers on either side. An armoured hood above his head was rolled back to open by levers on both sides on the roof. When closed down the driver could use either the standard periscope or lookout slits in the front armour, protected by a bullet-proof glass block and an armoured visor. There were only two control pedals—the gearbox clutch pedal on the left and the accelerator on the right. An emergency escape hatch was provided in later models through the floor under the driver's seat, making a hole about 1 ft. 3 in. square.

The turret crew were carried in the turntable which was suspended from the turret and moved on rollers on the floor of the fighting compartment. The commander sat on the left behind the gunner. There were two types of cupola, either of which might be seen on

Matilda Baron III A. The tank turret is removed and two 75 h.p. Bedford flail drive engines fitted, one on either side.
(Imperial War Museum)

Matilda CDL (Canal Defence Light) with special turret for night fighting searchlight. (RAC Tank Museum)

Tobruk, 1941. Matilda III receives a near miss from a German bomb. (Imperial War Museum)

the same Mark. The early one was 12 in. high and incorporated protected lookout slits on one side; the other version was only 6 in. high and had no lookout slits. Both types were rotated by hand and had two upward opening hatches in one of which was fitted a standard rotating periscope. The Lakeman anti-aircraft mounting could be attached to the cupola: a simple device with springs to balance the weight of the Bren LMG suspended from hooks. A tall, single-blade vane sight was at first mounted externally on the turret roof to assist in directing fire but later models sometimes fitted a smaller three-pronged vane sight. For direction keeping, the commander had a magnetic compass mounted on a binnacle immediately behind the rotary base junction on the turret floor, but this needed careful adjustment to be reliable.

The co-axially mounted 2-Pdr. and 7·92-mm. Besa guns moved freely in elevation, controlled by the gunner's right arm round the shoulder piece and holding the trigger grip for each weapon. Firing was mechanically operated. Traverse was by the left hand, either by spade grip on the hydraulic powered traverse system or by handwheel. At fast speed the powered traverse gave complete rotation of the turret in 14 seconds, but it could also be used for fine-laying without moving to the handwheel. This powered traverse was adapted from the Nash and Thompson system which had been fitted by Vickers on the A 9, the first tank to have powered traverse, and this system was to be used in all the cruisers up to Cromwell. An extractor fan was fitted in the roof of all Marks mounting the Besa machine-gun to expel fumes, but this was not fitted in the Matilda I with the Vickers gun; instead, a pump for water cooling was fitted with a steam outlet through the roof.

Besides attending to both guns and the wireless set, the loader/operator would also fire the two smoke generator dischargers mounted externally on the right side of the turret. The generators were projected by ballistite cartridge fired by cable mechanism. The Wireless Set No. 11 in the back of the turret consisted of a single set for communication on squadron or regimental net, having a single aerial on a bracket at the rear of the turret. The No. 19 Set mounted in Matilda IV and V also incorporated a set for communication within the troop ("A" and "B" sets) and also permitted two-way communication between the crew in the tank: these tanks can be identified by the

two separate aerials on the turret roof. Apart from signalling flags available to the commander, the last item of communications equipment was the signalling lamp which could be raised through an armoured hatch on the right side forward of the turret roof.

In the engine compartment, two fuel tanks were mounted outside the engines which were coupled by the cross drive assembly at the front to a central propeller shaft giving power to the Wilson epicyclic pre-selector gearbox. For starting, or to isolate either engine, each engine clutch was disengaged manually by handwheels in the fighting compartment. The cooling system for each engine was separate, with fans and radiators mounted above the gearbox, cooling air being drawn past the engines and exhausted to the rear. The fuel supply for each engine was also separate although up to Matilda III there was a balance pipe between the two tanks. An improved system in Matilda IV and V removed the balance pipe and added connections and pump for using an auxiliary fuel tank carried on the outside; also, ether carburetters for starting in very cold or sub-zero conditions improved performance particularly in Russian service. With the Leyland engines, both exhaust pipes were led upwards through the roof and along each side to the silencers on the rear hull plate; with the A.E.C. engines (Matilda I and II) the exhaust of the right engine was led downwards to come out at the bottom of the rear hull plate. A two-stage Reavell air compressor, driven from the cross drive, was mounted between the engines to deliver air to a reservoir with a capacity of 1,520 cu. in. situated in the fighting compartment. Air pressure was normally adjusted to 110 lb./sq. in. and the reservoir held enough for eight gear changes, without the compressor running, operated by the main gearbox servo between the driver's foot pedal and the gearbox bus bar operating lever. Selection of the gears was carried out mechanically but the gear was not engaged until the foot pedal had been depressed and released, thereby applying a brake to the epicyclic gear train through the bus bar. In Matilda V, a Westinghouse air cylinder situated on top of the gearbox operated direct on the bus bar. The Rackham steering clutches and brakes on each side of the gearbox were operated mechanically from the driver's steering levers.

The suspension on each side consisted of one front jockey wheel and five bogie assemblies of the bell crank, coil spring type mounted between the hull and

Matilda III overrunning an abandoned Italian gun position.   (Imperial War Museum)

the fixed skirting plates. Access to the assemblies was through doors beneath the mud chutes. On top the track was supported by three skids which were easier to produce and more satisfactory than the six rollers which had been fitted to earlier tanks. Track tension was adjusted by the idler wheel moving in slides between the tank horns. Hard rubber mudguards were fitted at front and rear, until broken off.

SPECIALIZED MATILDAS

Matildas were used for development and trials in a number of rôles for breaching or crossing obstacles. In the Middle East they were prepared to carry a fascine on the side ready to drop into the ditch to be crossed, after which the tank operated in its normal rôle. Some of the developments saw action and others led to improvements on later tanks which played an important part as Specialized Armour in Normandy in 1944.

Matilda Scorpion. A rotary flail device for sweeping a path through minefields was suggested by Major A. S. du Toit of the South African Army in the Middle East in 1942. This device, called Scorpion, was first mounted on the Matilda and consisted of a rotary flail mounted on the front of the tank, driven by auxiliary 30 h.p. Bedford engines mounted externally on the right side of the tank. The Scorpion device was later mounted also on the Valentine and Grant tanks, and 32 Scorpions, including Matildas, were used at El Alamein in October 1942 and in the advance to Tunis at the Mareth Line and Wadi Akarit. Scorpion I

had the flail operator in an armoured box beside the right track. Scorpion II was similar to the prototype (see illustration) but with a simplified lattice girder.

Matilda Baron. Similar to the Scorpion but with the turret removed and the flail driven by two 6-cylinder Bedford 73 b.h.p. engines in panniers on each side of the tank. This was the Mk. III A, the final form of the Baron development. Previous Marks retained the tank's turret and were under-powered. The Baron device was also fitted to the Valentine but the power for the flail was insufficient and developments led to the Sherman Crab in which the flail was driven by the main engine.

Matilda CDL. Three hundred special turrets were ordered in 1940 to be mounted on Matildas, incorporating a searchlight with flickering device shining through a narrow slit. Called "Canal Defence Lights" for secrecy, this was the first development of a tank to give light for night action. Although units were equipped and trained in its use in the United Kingdom and the Middle East, the Matilda CDL tank was never used for its real purpose. A few were available at El Alamein but were held in reserve, partly because of the secrecy and desire to retain their surprise effect until they could be used in quantity, and also because of doubts about their tactical value compared with more familiar means. The opportunity did not arise again and the Matilda CDL was replaced for the Normandy invasion by the Grant CDL—which was not used either.

Matilda Frog. Flame-throwing equipment was

Matilda AMRA—Anti-Mine Roller Attachment. 28th August 1942. These are Fowler Rollers originally designed for fitting to the early cruisers. (Imperial War Museum)

mounted in Australia in the gun mantlet of Matilda IV and V. Externally it looked similar to the 3-in. Howitzer. Fuel was carried in the turret and it had a range of 80–100 yds.

Matilda with Anti-mine Roller Attachment (AMRA) Mk. I A. This device consisted of a framework and suspension carried on spring-mounted and castoring rollers positioned in front of the tracks. The rollers were wide enough to cover the track path of the tank and were designed to protect the tank crossing a minefield. Later Marks were fitted to other tanks.

Matilda with Carrot. This demolition device was intended for breaching obstacles; the heavy Carrot was mounted at the front of AMRA and consisted of 600 lb. of high explosive which could be placed and fired without the crew leaving the tank; the light Carrot consisted of a smaller charge carried on a frame without rollers.

Matilda with Inglis Bridge. Trials were carried out with special attachment links welded on the nose of the tank, enabling it to push a span of Inglis bridge on a tracked mount into position over an obstacle whilst under fire. This did not progress further.

Matilda Lobster. This had Crab rotor arms but Baron rotor and flail.

Matilda of 42nd Royal Tank Regt. supporting 4th Indian Div.
carries the white-red-white recognition marks more familiar on
British tanks of World War 1. (Imperial War Museum)

Matilda with 2-in. Anti-Mine Torpedo Mortar.

Matilda with Trench-Crossing Device. Long lattice girders pushed ahead of the tank with front end supported on tracked bogies taken from Bren carrier. This was a Middle East experiment for allowing infantry and "B" vehicles to cross.

Matilda with Experimental Crane.

TACTICAL EMPLOYMENT

The decision was made in November 1934 to provide an infantry tank battalion for each division of the Expeditionary Force. 4th Battalion Royal Tank Corps was designated the first and it was agreed to form others later, but it was not until 1937 and 1938 that the 7th and 8th Battalions were re-formed to fill this rôle. The methods of employment, studied on exercises, all involved close and intimate support of the infantry in attack and defence, varying between use of the tanks as a slow-moving wave in front of the infantry or as a relatively fast element moving from bound to bound and reaching the objective just before the infantry. The organization established in 1938 provided the battalion with three companies, each of five sections of three infantry tanks. At company headquarters there was one infantry tank and one light tank—but the Mk. I was no use as a command tank. The terms "company" and "section" were retained in these units until early 1940 to emphasize their association with the infantry rôle.

In September 1939 the three tank battalions were grouped under H.Q. 1st Army Tank Brigade which became responsible for training, operational control and administration, but which was seldom to command its units in battle since they were normally assigned to divisions as required, with companies allotted to brigades. The 4th Battalion went to France in September 1939 equipped with 50 Infantry Tanks Mk. I, but the 7th was not to follow until May 1940 when it had been built up to strength with 27 Mk. Is (with ·5-in. machine-gun) and 23 Mk. IIs. It was these two units that were to create such an impression on the German commanders at Arras on 21st May.

In August 1940 the 7th Royal Tank Regiment, now fully equipped with Matildas, was sent to Egypt and soon took a leading part in Wavell's offensive against the Italians. As an independent tank unit, it supported the 4th Indian Division by leading the assault into the rear of the forts around Sidi Barrani, where the Matildas created havoc whilst being virtually immune to the Italian weapons. Against the stronger defences around Bardia and Tobruk, the 6th Australian Division made the openings through which the Matildas then passed to provide the spearhead for destruction of the forces within. From then on until mid-1942 the Matildas were in operations in the Western Desert and Cyrenaica; a single squadron of the 4th Royal Tank Regiment went to Eritrea with the 4th Indian Division and a detachment of six Matildas was lost in Crete whilst protecting the airfields. Matilda was a powerful weapon which could defeat any of the German tanks until the arrival of the PzKpfw III (J) "Special" on the desert battlefield in small numbers in early 1942. The 2-Pdr. gun could penetrate their armour almost anywhere at 1,000 yds. and, although Matilda might be put out of action with a jammed turret or damaged suspension, it was impervious to all anti-tank weapons except the 88-mm., the Pak 38 (after May 1941) and the long 50-mm. gun on the PzKpfw III (J).

The regimental organisation was changed early in 1941 to provide two Close Support Matildas with 3 in. Howitzer (76 mm.) at squadron headquarters, in addition to one Matilda for command. The high explosive performance of this gun was poor and it was used mainly to provide protective smoke. Otherwise the organisation was much the same and the rôle had not varied.

Matilda retained its commitment to direct support of the infantry, and in the defence of Tobruk and the many fierce desert battles it was frequently responsible in great part for their successes in attack and defence, even in night operations. Despite this contribution, the piecemeal dispersal of Matildas meant the loss of a weapon that, if concentrated in action with the cruisers, should have been capable of defeating Rommel's Panzer divisions. However, Rommel's successful use of tanks and anti-tank weapons together, and the mishandling of British armour of that period is another story. It was not until the battles of Gazala and Knightsbridge in June 1942 that three regiments of Matildas, brigaded with Valentines, were of necessity used in mobile actions in tank versus tank fighting. But, by then, the 2-Pdr. gun was already inadequate and after a stand at El Alamein in July 1942, the Matilda was withdrawn from operations. The Australian 1st Tank Battalion was later to use Matilda successfully against the Japanese in the New Guinea jungle at Finschhafen in November 1943, but its use was limited and only one squadron was in action there.

Matilda was the first effective British infantry tank and for two years contributed in no small way to the success of British operations. Although the tank could not be developed to mount heavier weapons, it was a vehicle for development of some special devices which were successfully used on later tanks.

SPECIFICATION:
A 12 INFANTRY TANK Mk. IIA*, MATILDA III

General
Crew: Four—commander, gunner, loader/wireless operator, driver.
Battle weight: 26·5 tons.
Bridge classification: 26.
Power/weight ratio: 7·2 to 1 b.h.p./ton.
Ground pressure: 16·2 lb. per sq. in.

Dimensions
Length overall: 18 ft. 5 in.
Height overall (high cupola): 8 ft. 3 in.
Width overall: 8 ft. 6 in.
Width over tracks: 7 ft. 11½ in.
Track centres: 6 ft. 9½ in.
Track width: 14 in.
Length of track on ground: 10 ft. 10 in.

Armament
Main—2-pdr. Mk. IX or X.
Auxiliary—7·92 mm. Besa machine-gun co-axially mounted. Two 4 in. smoke generator dischargers mounted on right side of turret. ·303 Bren LMG, for ground use or with Lakeman AA mounting on cupola.

Fire Control
Shoulder controlled free elevation. (+20° to −15°), (−9° over rear). Traverse by hydraulic power from variable flow pump driven by main engine, with auxiliary hand traverse. Mechanically operated firing gear from trigger grips for each weapon.

Ammunition
2-pdr.—93. Besa—2,925 (13 boxes). Bren—600.

Sighting and Vision
Commander: Two types of cupola fitted, both rotated by hand and mounting one standard Vickers Periscope No. 1 Mk. I. High cupola also had slits with armoured visor and glass block. Sighting vane mounted externally on turret roof.
Gunner: Telescopic Sight No. 30 Mk. I, and standard periscope.
Driver: Standard periscope, and slits in front armour with visor and glass block.

Communications
Wireless Set No. 11. Inter-communication system in one direction only from commander to each crew member through tank telephone. Visual communications provided by signalling lamp raised through right front of turret roof, and by flags. On some tanks a press-button fitted at the rear sounded a gong inside the fighting compartment to attract attention.

Armour
Bolted plates except for cast nose section and turret.

Thickness in mms.:		
Hull—front		78
Glacis		47/67°
Nose tip		78
Upper side		70/30°
Lower side		40
Skirting plates		25
Rear		55/25°
Top		20
Floor front		20/rear 13
Turret—front		75/11°
Sides and rear		75
Top		20
Cupola side		75

Engine
Two engines side by side coupled by cross drive to common propeller shaft.
Type: Leyland E 148 and E 149, or E 164 and E 165, 6-cylinder, vertical, water-cooled, compression ignition.
Cubic capacity: 425·7 cu. in.
B.h.p.: 95 at 2,000 r.p.m.
Fuel consumption: Road, 2·0 m.p.g.; cross-country, 1·0 m.p.g.
Fuel oil capacity: 46·5 gallons in tanks both sides of engine.

Transmission
Gearbox: Wilson epicyclic pre-selector, six forward speeds, and reverse, operated by air servo.
Steering: Rackham type steering clutches and brakes.
Final drive: Reduction 4·86 to 1.

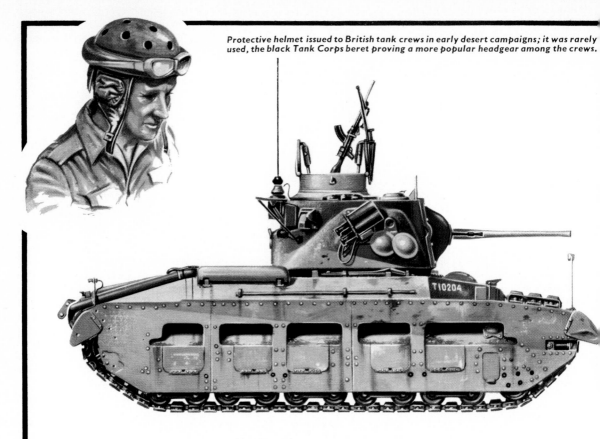

Protective helmet issued to British tank crews in early desert campaigns; it was rarely used, the black Tank Corps beret proving a more popular headgear among the crews.

Note Bren LMG mounted for anti-aircraft use (above) and crew's steel helmets stowed on turret.

0   5Ft.

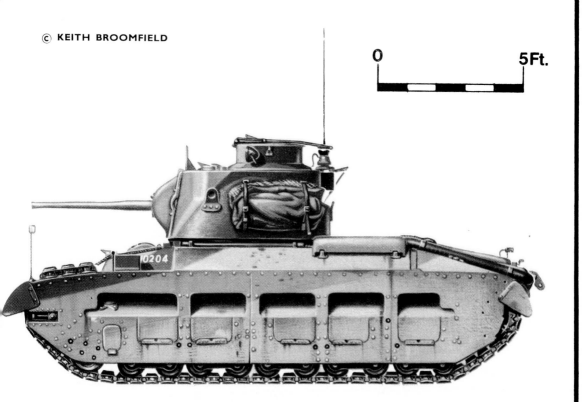

INFANTRY TANK Mk. II A* MATILDA III

The standard camouflage pattern shown here was used on Matildas and cruiser tanks in the Western Desert in 1940-41. Usually, the only form of vehicle identification marking, apart from the number, was the name which always began with the initial **D** in 4th Royal Tank Regiment and **G** in 7th R.T.R. The 1st Army Tank Brigade sign (red diabolo) was carried on Matildas of 42nd and 44th R.T.R. but 32nd Army Tank Brigade had no registered sign before it was captured in Tobruk in 1942.

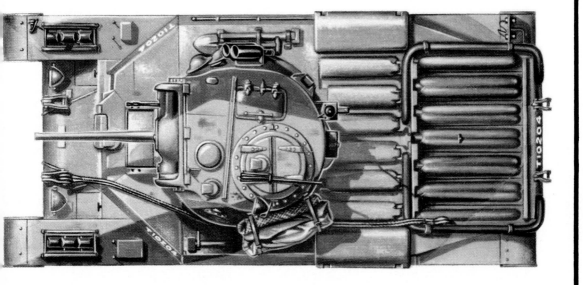

Suspension

Bell crank, coil spring type. Five bogie assemblies (ten pairs of wheels) and front jockey roller each side between hull and fixed skirting plates. Track carried on top by three skids, returning round idler (tensioner) at front. Three types of track were used: stamped, of carbon steel, 6·5 in. pitch, 68 links; webbed and spudded, of manganese steel, 6·4 in. pitch, 69 links; box section spudded, of cast steel, 6·3 in. pitch, 69 links.

Electrical System

12-volt system of "Three Wire Balanced" type supplied by two 12-volt battery sections carried on either side of driver, each section consisting of two 6-volt 130 AH batteries connected in series. Charging from a 12-volt dynamo fitted to each engine. 24-volt starter motors on each engine powered by both battery sections being placed in series through selector switches.

Performance

Maximum speed: 15 m.p.h.

Vertical obstacle: 2 ft.
Trench: 7 ft.
Wading depth: 3 ft. or 3 ft. 6 in. with fording flap closed over rear air outlets.
Radius—road: 160 miles.
　Cross-country: 80 miles.

BRITISH ARMY UNITS IN ACTION WITH MATILDA

Variously under command:
1 Army Tank Brigade—France, Egypt, Cyrenaica.
32 Army Tank Brigade—Tobruk, Cyrenaica.
4th Royal Tank Regiment—Eritrea, Egypt, Tobruk.
7th Royal Tank Regiment—France, Egypt, Tobruk, Crete, Cyrenaica.
42nd Royal Tank Regiment (formerly 23rd Bn., London Regiment)—Egypt, Cyrenaica.
44th Royal Tank Regiment (formerly 6th Bn., Gloucestershire Regiment)—Egypt, Cyrenaica.
Matilda Scorpion detachments from 6th, 42nd and 44th Royal Tank Regiments at second battle of El Alamein, Oct. 1942.

MATILDA MARKS AND VARIATIONS

Original Name	Subsequent Name	Armament	Engines	Remarks
INFANTRY TANK **Mk. I**	"Matilda"	1 Vickers ·5 or ·303 machine-gun	Ford V-8 70 b.h.p.	Mk. I M was soft steel pilot. There was a Mk. I with Coulter plough for anti-mine use
Mk. II	Matilda I	1–2-pdr. 1 Vickers ·303 machine-gun	2 A.E.C. diesel, type A183/184, 87 b.h.p. each	No. 11 Wireless Set Mk. II M: soft steel training tank (10 built)
Mk. IIA	Matilda II	1–2-pdr. 1 Besa	—	Mk. II AM and Mk. II BM: soft steel training tanks
Mk. IIA*	Matilda III	1–2-pdr. 1 Besa	2 Leyland diesel, Type E148/149 or Type E164/165, 95 b.h.p. each	—
	Matilda III C.S. (Close Support)	1–3 in. How. 1 Besa	—	—
Mk. II A**	Matilda IV	1–2-pdr. 1 Besa	2 Leyland diesel, Type E170/171, 95 b.h.p. each	No. 19 wireless set, 2 aerials. Larger fuel tanks, 56 gallons. Fitted for auxiliary fuel tank, 36 gallons
	Matilda IV C.S.	1–3 in. How. 1 Besa	—	
	Matilda V	Same as Matilda IV but with direct operated air servo gearbox control		
	Matilda Scorpion I and II	1–2-pdr. 1 Besa	—	Rotary flail device driven by engines on right side. 2-pdr. gun sometimes removed. Also with Breach Marker
	Matilda Baron III A	—	—	Turret removed. Rotary flail driven by engines on both sides
	Matilda CDL	1 Besa	—	"Canal Defence Light." Special turret with searchlight shining through narrow slit
	Matilda Frog	—	—	Flame-throwing equipment in turret of Matilda IV. Australian development
	Matilda with AMRA Mk. IA	1–2-pdr. 1 Besa	—	Anti-Mine Roller Attachment mounted on front
	Matilda with Carrot	1–2-pdr. 1 Besa	—	Demolition charges carried on AMRA

Matilda in Malta camouflage. (Imperial War Museum)

Valentine II of the 50th Royal Tank Regiment near the Mareth Line, Tunisia in March 1943. (Imp. War Mus.)

Valentine, Infantry Tank Mk III By B. T. White

"The Brigade must have fired some of the last shots in the African campaign for it was on May 12 1943, that 23rd Armoured Brigade, led by 40th Royal Tank Regiment made physical contact with the leading troops of 6th Armoured Divison of British First Army. . . . The Brigade was the armoured spearhead of 30th Corps and 13th Corps and after El Alamein, from El Agheila onwards, they constantly led the way along the one and only road. One of the noteworthy features, which speaks volumes for itself is that many tanks in 40th R.T.R. covered more than 3,000 operational miles on their tracks and many in the 50th R.T.R. closely followed this record, which, to men who know and have fought in armour, is a tribute to the Brigade's work which needs no emphasising." *(Brief History of the 23rd Armoured Brigade, 1939–1945.)*

ALL the tanks of 23rd Armoured Brigade were Valentines. This well-proven British tank, available in good supply by 1942–1943, was able to play a prominent part in the later stages of the campaign in North Africa thanks to design work which had its origins some eight years earlier and to consistent development by the industrial concern most closely associated with British tanks—Vickers Armstrong Ltd.

DEVELOPMENT HISTORY

On St. Valentine's Day, 1938, the proposal by Vickers-Armstrong Ltd. for a new infantry tank had been deposited in the War Office.

The design was a private venture by Vickers—it had not been called for through the usual medium of a General Staff specification—and so had no "A. number" for a handy designation, and the name Valentine was chosen as a convenient and appropriate title. Valentine was also, incidentally, the second name

of Sir John V. Carden, whose genius was responsible for many tank designs including the immediate ancestors of the Valentine.

Two early Vickers cruiser tanks, the A.9 and A.10, must be mentioned here for the part they played in the evolution of the Valentine. A.9 was the General Staff specification for a simpler and cheaper medium tank than the famous Vickers "Sixteen tonner" (A.6) which was acknowledged as a very good tank but was frighteningly expensive at around £1,000 a ton.

The Army budgets of the 1930s gave little hope of the extensive re-equipment needed for the Royal Tank Corps at this cost (in fact, apart from the three experimental A.6s only three service vehicles—Tanks, Medium Mk. III—were built) and the A.9 specification drew up the essentials in armament, protection and performance for a more modest vehicle of around 12 tons using a commercial engine. The tank to meet these requirements was designed by Sir John Carden of

An A.9 (Tank, Cruiser Mark I) of 'C' Squadron, 1st Royal Tanks, 7th Armoured Division, 1940. (Imp. War Mus.)

An A.9 coming ashore from a landing craft during an exercise in the Middle East. (Imp. War Mus.)

Vickers—the Carden who had developed the highly successful Carden Loyd tankettes and carriers from their beginnings in V. G. Loyd's London garage that he once managed. It followed the same general layout as the A.6, although smaller, with a centrally-placed fighting compartment and turret, two smaller machine-gun turrets at the front, either side of the driver, and the engine at the rear. The suspension was not covered by armoured skirting plates, unlike the earlier mediums, and consisted of two units of three road wheels each side, with rear drive sprockets and front idler wheels.

The medium tanks in service with the Royal Tank Corps were used equally for infantry close support and for mobile operations, but War Office policy was then changing to the concept of two separate classes of

tank, for what were regarded as two distinct kinds of warfare each of which, it was felt, demanded special characteristics in tanks. Carden was accordingly asked in addition to design—to the A.10 specification—an infantry tank using the same chassis as the A.9 but with additional armour up to a 1 in. (25·4 mm.) standard, compared with A.9's 14 mm. basis; a speed of as low as 10 m.p.h. was considered acceptable as the price for the extra load of some 3 tons.

An A.9 in the Royal Armoured Corps Tank Museum at Bovington, Dorset. Next to it is a Cruiser Mk. IIA CS. (B. T. White.)

Front view of a Cruiser Mark I CS of 2nd Royal Tanks in 1940. This clearly shows the short barrel of the 3·7 in. howitzer used in early close support tanks. (Imp. War Mus.)

Tank, Experimental, A.10E1—prototype of the Cruiser Mark II. (Imp. War Mus.)

Cruiser Mark I CS (left) and two Cruiser Mark IIAs on patrol in the Western Desert in 1940. This picture brings out the chief external differences between the A.9 and the A.10, including the engine air louvres. (Imp. War Mus.)

THE A.9 AND A.10

Work on both tanks started within a few months of each other in 1934; the A.9 prototype A.9E1 was completed in April 1936 and the A.10E1 appeared shortly afterwards. The A.9 was originally fitted with a 15 pdr. mortar (with co-axial ·303 in. Vickers machine-gun) in the turret. This was, in fact, a low velocity close support weapon, but the alternative of a 3 pdr. was provided for in the design.

Unhappily Sir John Carden was killed in an air crash in December 1935 and so did not live to see the trials of his tanks. The A.9 performed well and could do a maximum speed of 25 m.p.h., but the suspension needed improvement, for the tank pitched badly on uneven ground, giving its crew an uncomfortable ride, and had a tendency to shed its tracks. Without Carden's guiding hand, development work took longer and it was not until the latter half of 1937 that the A.9

was considered satisfactory enough for the first production order—for 50 tanks—to be given. It was then officially designated Tank, Cruiser, Mk. I.

The infantry tank version, A.10, was by 1937 considered not heavily enough armoured for infantry support and was dropped. The following year it was, however, decided to produce it as a "heavy cruiser" and 75 were ordered initially.

The prototype built to the A.9 specification and known as Tank, Experimental Medium, A9.E1, was originally fitted with a Rolls-Royce Phantom II engine, but this was later replaced with an A.E.C. 6-cylinder 8·85 litre engine—a diesel converted for use with petrol. This in turn was replaced by a 9·64 litre engine, developing 150 b.h.p.

The production series, known as Tanks, Cruiser Mk. I (and later as Tanks, Cruiser A.9 Mk. I: finally reverting to the original title) also used the 150 b.h.p. A.E.C. petrol engine. One hundred and twenty-five of

An A.10 with 2 pdr. gun and coaxial Vickers machine-gun in the turret. On the right is an A.13, a Cruiser Mark III. (Imp. War Mus.)

Two Cruiser Mark IIAs followed by a Valentine. The similarities and the differences between the two types are apparent in this view. In the rear are two Matildas, Infantry Tank Mk. II. (Imp. War Mus.)

these tanks were built (50 by Vickers and 75 by Harland & Wolff, Belfast) of which a proportion were close support tanks (designated Mk. I CS) equipped with 3·7 in. howitzers in the turret instead of 2 pdr. guns. The turret, incidentally, was the first in a British tank to have powered traverse. All tanks were armed with three Vickers ·303 in. machine-guns, one co-axial with the main weapon in the turret and two in auxiliary turrets either side of the driver's cab. These auxiliary turrets were very small (even smaller in the prototype) and cramped and difficult to evacuate quickly in an emergency. They were omitted in the A.10 and in the Valentine.

A.9s were used in action by 1st Armoured Division in France in 1940 and later in Libya. They were also in service with the 7th Armoured Division in the early Desert battles up to 1941 and with the 2nd Armoured Division in Libya and in Greece.

The A.10E1, prototype of the intended infantry tank which was accepted into service as Tank, Cruiser, Heavy Mk. I, closely resembled A.9E1 except that the auxiliary machine-gun turrets were omitted, the driver's cab standing clear of the front sloping glacis plate. The front hull design in A.10E1 was later amended, however, to include a machine-gun position to the right of the driver. The A.E.C. engine was the same as that of A.9E1, although the cooling louvres were rearranged, and nearly all the mechanical features were similar. The extra weight brought about by the increased armour thickness reduced the maximum speed however.

The Heavy Cruiser designation was dropped in 1938 and replaced by Tank, Cruiser, A.10 Mk. I—eventually this confusing nomenclature was straightened out when the A.10 became simply Tank, Cruiser, Mk. II.

In the later production models, the co-axial machine-gun was a Besa—these tanks were designated Mk. IIA and were the first British tanks in which this weapon was introduced. There was also a Mk. IIA CS in which the turret 2 pdr. gun was replaced by a 3·7 in. howitzer which could fire smoke or high explosive ammunition.

Cruiser Mk IIs and IIAs were in action alongside A.9s in France in 1940 and in Libya in 1940–1941.

A.9s and A.10s could be used as pusher vehicles for the Anti-Mine Reconnaissance Caster Roller, a device originally designed in 1937 and intended to detonate by pressure contact anti-tank mines. It consisted of four rollers attached to a frame in front of the tanks so that two rollers, in tandem, were in front of each track. One version was designed by John Fowler & Co. (Leeds) Ltd., for the early cruiser tanks and another version, slightly modified, was intended for use with Valentine.

Cruiser Mark IIA CS (left) in the R.A.C. Tank Museum, Bovington, Dorset. The 3·7 in. howitzer of the close support tank can be compared with the 2 pdr. (40 mm.) gun of the A.9 alongside. (B. T. White.)

Left: *Valentine I of 23rd Hussars, 11th Armoured Division, on an exercise in the United Kingdom in August 1941. Note the headlamps reversed to avoid damage.* Right: *Valentine II with track sandshields and auxiliary petrol tank. Note the revolver port on the side of the turret: this was not present in all tanks of this Mark.* (Imp. War Mus.)

Left: *Valentine IV. This Mark was externally identical to the AEC-engined Valentines I and II.* (B. T. White.) Right: *Valentine V in Tunisia, January 1943. Note the Bren gun with drum magazine mounted on the turret for anti-aircraft use.* (Imp. War Mus.)

Valentine III of the New Zealand Tank Squadron on Nissan Island, Solomons group, during the Pacific campaign of 1945. This is one of the tanks in which the normal 2 pdr. gun had not been replaced by a 3 in. howitzer. (Sport & General.)

Left: *A Canadian-built Valentine in the Soviet Union. This is a Mark VII with the cast nose plate. Note the Bren anti-aircraft mounting and the Soviet unit signs on the turret.* (Sovfoto/R. J. Icks.) Right: *This view of the Valentine XI shows well the coaxial 75 mm. and Besa mounting and also the cast nose of the hull, introduced in this Mark from the Canadian design.* (Imp. War Mus.)

Valentine X—externally as Marks VIII and IX except for the modification to the turret face to accommodate the coaxial Besa machine-gun. The riveted front plates and 6 pdr. gun can be compared with the cast front plates and 75 mm. gun shown in the similar view of a Valentine XI. (Imp. War Mus.)

Valentine VIII—the Mark IX was externally identical and had the same turret armament of a 6 pdr. without a coaxial machine-gun. This tank is equipped with two 4 in. smoke dischargers mounted on the side of the turret. (Imp. War Mus.)

A carpet device for crossing barbed wire entanglements was tried out fitted to an A.9 in March 1939. The carpet—a roll of hessian—was attached to the tank by means of two arms and unrolled as the vehicle moved forwards. This experimental version was later developed for use by A.V.R.E.s for laying a path for vehicles over soft ground.

An A.9 was used in experiments at Christchurch, Hampshire, in connection with submerged running for water crossings. This was in 1940, shortly before the corresponding German experiments for Operation Sea-Lion—the hoped-for invasion of England. The system used on the Cruiser Mk. I was quite successful but War Office opinion was more in favour of floating devices. These culminated in the successful DD device, in the development of which the Valentines played an important part.

A.11—INFANTRY TANK MK. I

Before completion of A.9 and A.10 Carden had been asked to design another infantry tank, again on economical lines and using a commercial engine—this time a standard Ford V8 engine. This tank, the A.11, was intended to withstand any existing anti-tank

Valentine IIs of 48th Royal Tanks (21st Army Tank Brigade) on an exercise in Suffolk in June 1941. These tanks are fitted with the No. 11 wireless set, later superseded by the No. 19 set. The Brigade did not go into action with Valentines, but with Churchills (Infantry Tank Mk. IV), the first to do so—in Tunisia, 1943. (Imp. War Mus.)

A line up of Valentines (Marks I or II) of the Polish forces in Scotland in August 1941. These tanks all bear W.D. numbers in a special series allocated to the Polish forces serving with the British Army. This, the 1st Polish Armoured Division, fought in 1st Canadian Army, 21 Army Group, in North-West Europe. (Imp. War Mus.)

weapons but was required to mount only a ·303 in. Vickers machine-gun or alternatively the Vickers ·5 in. —a light anti-tank weapon.

Trials of the A.11 (known at the time as a "heavy infantry tank" in comparison with the A.10) went well and it put up the unspectacular performance required of it. Only a limited order for 60 was placed, though, as it was then thought desirable to concentrate on a larger infantry tank with at least the same protection but armed with a 2 pdr. gun and able to tackle enemy heavy tanks. The production order for A.11 was later extended to a total of 139 (excluding A.11E1, the prototype) and in action in 1940, despite the tactical limitations imposed by their two-man crews and low speed, their armour was found to come up to expecta-

tions and gave protection against most projectiles encountered.

VALENTINE PRODUCTION

Vickers-Armstrong's proposal for a new infantry tank in 1938 was based on elements of the three earlier Vickers types A.9, A.10 and A.11 from which a great deal of experience had already been gained. The main points were that it should have armour protection on a 60 mm. basis, as good as that of the A.11, but mount a 2 pdr. gun in a two-man turret and still have a relatively low silhouette and be as light as possible. It was intended to use as far as possible components—such as

Valentine II on a realistic battle exercise in the United Kingdom in August 1941. This tank is fitted with a No. 19 set. (Imp. War Mus.)

the engine, transmission and suspension—which had already been proved in the A.9 and A.10.

The scheme was at first turned down by the War Office, but in July 1939 the first contract for Valentine tanks was placed, with the delivery of the first completed vehicles to commence in May 1940. When World War II broke out in September 1939, Vickers-Armstrong were instructed to give absolute priority to production of the "Tank, Infantry, Mk. III", and concentrate their unrivalled experience in the design and manufacture of tanks on the Valentine.

The production of Valentine tanks was in the hands of three main contractors in the United Kingdom: Vickers-Armstrong Ltd. themselves, at their Elswick premises (near Newcastle—formerly the works of Sir W. G. Armstrong, Whitworth & Co. Ltd.); the Metropolitan-Cammell Carriage & Wagon Co. Ltd., an associated company of Vickers, at their Old Park Works, Wednesbury, Staffs., and later also at their Midland works; and the Birmingham Railway Carriage & Wagon Co. Ltd.

The other two firms, as well as Vickers, had experience in tank manufacture before the Valentine, both having been awarded small contracts for the production of A.10s which were nearing completion as the Valentine programme got under way.

The first Vickers-built Valentine to come off the production line was completed, on schedule, in May 1940, and ten tanks were runners by the following month. The first Valentine assembled by Metro-Cammell was delivered at the end of July 1940; and by the Birmingham Railway Carriage & Wagon Co. at about the same time.

Output of Valentines from Vickers, the parent firm, went up from the ten delivered by June 1940, to 45 per month a year later, rising through 1942 to 20 per week in 1943. At the end of that year production was eased off and closed in early 1945 when a grand total of 6,855 Valentines (including some special vehicles on the Valentine chassis) had been built in the United Kingdom. Of this output, 2,515 tanks were built by Vickers-Armstrong themselves and 2,135 by Metro-Cammell.

In addition, an order was placed in Canada in the spring of 1940 for Valentines to be produced by the Canadian Pacific Railway at their Angus Shops, Montreal, locomotive repair works. The production prototype was completed in June 1941, and full

Valentines of Headquarters 29th Armoured Brigade (11th Armoured Division) in Rottingdean, Sussex, in June 1942. (Imp. War Mus.)

Valentines in the Western Desert in July 1942. Note the Bren guns on anti-aircraft mountings. (Imp. War Mus.)

production was under way in the late autumn of the same year. Subsequent contracts brought the total order up to 1,420 tanks; delivery reached 80 tanks per month—comparing very well with that in the United Kingdom—and the last tank was completed in mid-1943.

The grand total of 8,275 Valentines manufactured in the United Kingdom and Canada was far greater than that of any other British tank, and the home output alone exceeded that of the Churchill, the runner-up.

THE VALENTINE DESCRIBED

The hull of the Valentine was of fairly straightforward construction. The vertical sides were made in two

Left: A Valentine carrying infantry of the Black Watch and towing a 6 pdr. anti-tank gun, Tunisia, April 1943. Right: Valentine of 23rd Armoured Brigade entering Tripoli on January 26, 1943 carrying infantry and a piper of the Gordon Highlanders. (Imp. War Mus.)

A gap in a Desert minefield marked by tapes, with a Valentine passing through, August 1942. (Imp. War Mus.)

halves, the plates riveted together at a lap joint about the middle. The top plates were screwed into the top edges of the side plates, and the hull bottom plates, forming a channel deeper in the middle, were screwed into the under edges of the side plates. In later production tanks riveting was used instead for attachment of the top and bottom plates. The vertical nose plate and the vertical rear plate were riveted to angle iron stiffeners. There were three cross members in the hull: the vertical plate in front of the driver and incorporating the driver's direct vision port; an internal bulkhead immediately behind the driver; and another bulkhead separating the engine compartment from the fighting compartment.

The driver's compartment housed only the driver, sitting centrally, and the driving controls. Steering, of the skid type operated by clutches and brakes, was controlled by means of two levers—one for each track. Each of these two levers was linked by two rods running the full length of the vehicle to the clutch and

brake assembly at the rear of the vehicle. With both levers right forward the steering clutches were engaged to transmit the drive through the tracks; if both levers were pulled right back the steering clutches were disengaged and the brakes applied. If only one lever was pulled back the tank would turn to that side. The clutch pedal was by the driver's left foot; the foot brake pedal and the accelerator pedal by the right. The gear change lever, with an open gate, was at the driver's right hand and a directional compass was mounted between his knees. The main driving instruments including the speedometer, oil pressure gauge, ammeter, starter switch and lighting switches were grouped on a panel at the driver's left.

Access for the driver was by means of either of two outward opening doors (hinged at the bottom) on either side of his compartment, level with his head when seated. There was also a downward opening emergency escape hatch in the hull floor beneath the driver's seat, which could be swung out of the way.

Left: Valentine XI, an anti-tank battery commander's vehicle, passing through Hopsten, Germany, in April 1945. Right: This view shows well the V-shaped under side of the Valentine's hull; also the arrangement of the inside of one of the front bogey units and the early type of twin-pin track. (Imp. War Mus.)

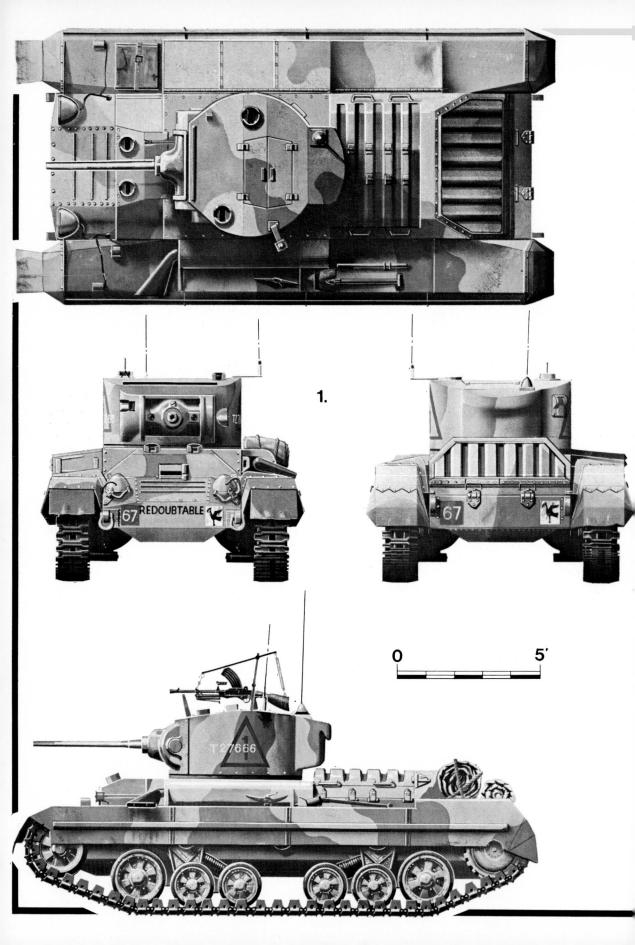

1.

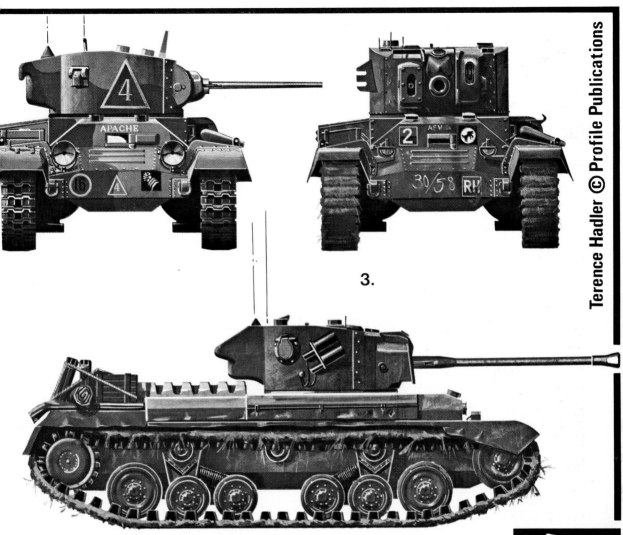

Terence Hadler © Profile Publications

3.

4.

5.

6.

1 Valentine II of No. 1 Troop "A" Squadron, 50th Royal Tank Regiment in 23rd Armoured Brigade. This was as the tank appeared at the time of the Mareth battle in Tunisia in March 1943, near the end of the North African campaign. The original 8th Army yellow desert camouflage has been modified for the Tunisian landscape

2 Valentine XI used as a command vehicle in a Corps Anti-Tank Regiment, Royal Artillery. North-West Europe 1944–45

3 Valentine I of "A" Squadron 17/21st Lancers, 6th Armoured Division, October 1941

4 6th Armoured Division sign

5 RA unit sign with serial number

6 Formation sign (30 Corps)

Looking down through the turret hatch on to the breech of the 2 pdr. gun. The elevating shoulder piece for the gunner can be seen on the left. The loader on the right is placing a 2 pdr. shell in the breech. (Imp. War Mus.)

The fighting compartment with the turret mounted on the roof carried the other two members of the crew —the gunner at the left and the commander/loader at the right (in the three-man turrets of Valentine III and V the commander sat in the rear of the turret). The turret, constructed of front and rear castings riveted to rolled side plates, was mounted on a ball race, the lower half of which incorporated a fixed traversing rack. Traverse was by means of a pinion operating on this rack through a reduction gear to a hand wheel for use in emergency and, for normal use, by electrical power. Control was through a spade grip and trigger in a control box: the further left or right the grip was twisted the further the turret rotated in that direction. Elevation of the turret guns was by a shoulder piece, without gearing except in the case of the 75 mm. gun of Valentine XI. The wireless was carried inside the rear of the turret—in early tanks a No. 11 set, with Tannoy equipment for crew intercommunication. Later the No. 19 wireless set which incorporated internal communications together with long range and short range networks was used.

In the rear of the hull, behind the rear bulkhead of the fighting compartment, was situated the engine, gearbox and transmission; the gearbox and bevel drive being assembled in one unit with the engine. The power was transmitted to the driving sprockets through multiplate steering clutches and a compound epicyclic reduction gear mounted on the hull side plates. The steering brakes were incorporated on the outside of the reduction gears in the drums which were a distinctive feature of the Valentine.

The suspension consisted of two groups of three road wheels each side. Each group contained two $19\frac{1}{2}$ in. diameter wheels and one of 24 in. diameter mounted on a primary and a secondary fork, sprung by means of a large spring incorporating a hydraulic shock absorber. The idler wheels were at the front and the drive sprockets at the rear; three rollers were mounted each side to carry the top run of the track. Early tanks had a twin pin type of track with 73 shoes, but later models had a shorter pitch single pin type which was standardised and consisted of 103 shoes. In a few early models a short pitch track with shoe profile like that of the Covenanter and Crusader

Carrier, Valentine, 25 pdr. Gun Mark I—a Bishop—in action in Sicily, 1943. (Imp. War Mus.)

cruiser tanks was also tried out. All types of Valentine track had twin horns, however, forming a path in which the road wheels ran.

THE VALENTINE MARKS

Eleven different marks of Valentine were built, together with sub-variants and versions for special tasks.

The original model, Tank, Infantry, Mk. III, known officially as Valentine I after June 1941, had an A.E.C. petrol engine like its predecessor A.10; and a two-man turret mounting a 2 pdr. gun and co-axial Besa

Rear view of a Bishop. Note towing hook, used for towing 25 pdr. field artillery limber. (Imp. War Mus.)

Self-propelled 6 pdr. mounting on Valentine I—experimental only. (RAC Tank Mus.)

Front view of S.P. 17 pdr., Valentine—an Archer. Note spare track plates, the front towing hook and the cable bracket on the right-hand side of the hull. (Imp. War Mus.)

machine-gun. Valentine II (Tank, Infantry, Mk. III*) was identical except that an A.E.C. diesel engine was used. The first 1,025 tanks to be built were of these two marks.

The A.E.C. diesel engine which powered Valentine II and also two later marks was developed from the A.E.C. Comet engine used in commercial road vehicles. It was a six-cylinder unit of 120 mm. bore and 142 mm. stroke with push-rod operated overhead poppet type valves. The pistons were of B.H.B. aluminium alloy. A gear type oil pump and dry sump lubrication system was used. The engine, clutch and gearbox were bolted together in one unit, the gearbox being a Meadows sliding pinion model with five speeds forward and one reverse, direct drive being on 4th gear.

A two-man turret had the disadvantage that the tank commander had to be also the gunner or the wireless operator-cum-loader with consequent difficulties in commanding the tank in action. This problem was intensified for troop commanders, who had to give orders to two other tanks besides their own. The Valentine III was given a modified turret with room for three men, therefore, which although larger was much the same in external appearance as that of Mk. II. The turret ring was the same size but more internal space in the turret was created by altering and extending the front plate so that the gun mounting was further forward and at the same time enlarging the rearward bulge of the turret. The weight of the three-

man turret increased to approximately $3\frac{1}{4}$ tons, compared with the $2\frac{3}{4}$ tons of the earlier two-man type.

The Valentine III formed the basis of the only close support version of the Valentine to be built. Matilda or later close support tanks were usually used in conjunction with Valentines but there was a special need for a Valentine close support tank for use with the 3rd New Zealand Division in the S.W. Pacific campaign. Only one squadron of tanks was to be sent in 1944 to support this Division and Valentines were chosen as the most suitable tanks available in New Zealand to form the equipment of this unit. However, they had the disadvantage that the 2 pdr. gun could not provide effective close support with high explosive considered essential for these operations. There was a 2 pdr. H.E. shell but this lacked the punch of the 18 pdr. shell of the 3 in. howitzer used in British close support tanks. Accordingly a conversion was designed in New Zealand to accommodate 3 in. howitzers, to be taken from Matilda IV CS tanks, in Valentine IIIs. The changes to the normal Valentine in the conversion to the 3 in. howitzer version included re-alignment of the telescopic sight bracket, provision of equipment to permit indirect fire, and resetting of the ammunition racks to take 3 in. ammunition, of which 21 of H.E. and 14 of smoke shells could be accommodated.

Nine Valentine close support tanks formed the strength of the New Zealand Tank Squadron, together with 16 normal Valentines (for which some 2 pdr. H.E. ammunition, made in New Zealand, was provided) and were used successfully in the S.W. Pacific opera-

Rear view of an Archer. Note how engine air louvres differ from those of the Valentine tanks. (Imp. War Mus.)

Tank, Infantry, Valiant (A.38). Side view, showing general similarity of layout to the Valentine. (Imp. War Mus.)

Valiant—front view. Note inverted-V top surface of cast nose plate. (Imp. War Mus.)

tions. Some of these tanks were still in use by the New Zealand Army up to 1955.

Valentine IV was similar in most respects to the earlier two-man turret models but introduced the General Motors diesel engine, used in all later Marks except one; and Valentine V was the three-man turret model using this engine.

The General Motors two-stroke diesel engine introduced in these two marks soon built up a good reputation for itself for its quiet running and high degree of reliability—two important qualities in any tank engine. The engine was bolted up in one unit with the clutch and Spicer synchromesh gearbox—this had five forward speeds and reverse. The six cylinders were 4·25 in. bore and 5 in. stroke, were fitted with overhead valves, and the pistons were a malleable iron, tin-plated. The lubrication system was of the dry sump pattern, forced feed with a gear type oil pump. Cooling was by means of two six-bladed 20 in. diameter fans which drew in air through the inlet louvres over the engine, blew it through the radiators (placed over the clutch and gearbox) and out through the outlet louvres. This engine, the General Motors Type 6–71, developed about 130 h.p. at 1,800 r.p.m.

The Canadian-built Valentines were designated Tanks, Infantry Mk. III*** at first and later as Valentines VI and VII. These were both two-man turret models, using the General Motors diesel engine.

The main armament was the 2 pdr. gun, but after the first 15 vehicles the co-axial Besa machine-gun was replaced by a ·30 in. Browning. In the Mk. VII a remote control grip and firing gear attachment was added to the Browning machine-gun, and the No. 19 wireless set replaced the No. 11 set. A sub-variant, Valentine VIIA, had a number of improvements, including an auxiliary fuel tank, an oil cooler, studded tracks, rear batteries, a convoy lamp and turret protection angles. To suit the Valentine to production in Canada, U.K. standards used in the drawings had to be converted to equivalents used in North America, but some more fundamental changes in the design, which made for simpler and better production, were introduced by the Canadians during the course of manufacture. These included a cast turret and cast engine armoured louvres to replace the fabricated types, and cast nose armour, replacing the built-up structure used in the original design. The cast nose was later adopted for British built Valentines.

The next British mark of Valentine, the Mk. VIII, had the A.E.C. diesel engine and a redesigned two-man turret mounting a 6 pdr. gun only, and the Valentine IX was the same vehicle but with the General Motors diesel engine. In some tanks of Mk. IX and subsequent marks an uprated 165 b.h.p. unit was used instead of the earlier 130 b.h.p. engine.

Although the 6 pdr. mounting used in the Valentine VIII and IX was designed at a time when it was urgently necessary to get a supply of 6 pdr.-armed tanks in the field without upsetting the existing production programme, the absence of a co-axial Besa machine-gun was a serious fault. This was rectified in Valentine X by a further redesign of the turret. The engine was again the General Motors diesel—the 165 b.h.p. model.

The final version, Valentine XI, was fitted with a 75 mm. gun and co-axial Besa machine-gun in a two-man turret, and was powered by the General Motors 165 b.h.p. diesel engine. It was during the course of production of this mark that the cast nose developed by the Canadians was introduced in the British-built tanks.

Throughout this progressive development over a period of 3½ years of quantity production the Valentine remained largely unchanged in external appearance

Left: *Valentine Bridgelayer—front three-quarter view with bridge folded. The rollers which take the weight of the bridge when it is being laid are at the front, above the driver's head.* Right: *Valentine Bridgelayer laying its bridge over a gap in a bridge in Burma.* (Imp. War Mus.)

Valentine with Anti-Mine Roller Attachment Mk. IB. The equipment has been damaged in exploding a mine. (Imp. War Mus.)

Valentine III or V with anti-mine "rake". (B. T. White.)

and retained its compact shape and low silhouette. Even when armed with the 75 mm. gun it was only about a ton heavier than the first tanks and its performance was virtually unaffected.

VALENTINE SPECIALS AND S.P.s

The Valentine chassis was also adapted for a number of special armoured vehicles and self-propelled mountings. Of the specialised armour the Valentine Bridgelayer was operationally the most important: these were issued on an establishment of six per armoured brigade equipped with cruiser or medium tanks and were used in action in Italy, North-West

Europe and in Burma. The "scissors" bridge was carried folded and was raised and placed in position, opened out, by means of a screw jack. The bridge could span 30 feet and take tanks up to 30 tons in weight.

A lightweight ramp tank known as Burmark using the Valentine chassis was designed for the Far East theatre. This was turretless and had decking built over the hull and hinged ramps at front and rear. It was not used in action or further developed because of the War's end.

The first production DD amphibious tanks were adaptations of the Valentine—Mks. V, IX and XI. The DD device, which was invented by Nicholas Straussler, was a means of increasing the freeboard of a tank to the point where it would float. Coupled with this was a means of transmitting power from the tank's main engine to a screw at the rear to propel the vehicle in water. The extra freeboard was achieved by the use of a collapsible canvas screen attached all round the hull, which was waterproofed, at the level of the track guards. The screens were raised by inflating rubber tubes by means of compressed air bottles. The screens could quickly be lowered by deflating the tubes as the tank came out of the water, allowing free use of the turret armament immediately.

Straussler's invention was first tried out on a 7-ton Tetrarch light tank and, when proved and accepted by the War Office, the design was adapted to the Valentine tank. Essentially the same pattern was used but a higher freeboard was needed to deal with the Valentine's weight, which was over twice that of the Tetrarch. The conversion of a total of 625 Valentine DD tanks was undertaken by the Metropolitan-Cammell Carriage & Wagon Co. Ltd., delivery first beginning in March 1943, and ending in 1944.

Valentine DD tanks were used widely for training in the United Kingdom and also in Italy and India, although their only operational use was in small numbers in Italy in 1945.

Tank flamethrower experiments in the United Kingdom were first conducted using Valentine tanks as the basis. Two different designs, one by A.E.C. Ltd. and the Petroleum Warfare Department and the other by the Ministry of Supply flamethrowing research section, both employed Valentine tanks with trailers containing the flame fuel. The Ministry of Supply vehicle had a cordite operated flame gun and the A.E.C. design used compressed hydrogen to project

Left: *Valentine Scorpion flail tank.* Right: *Valentine Scorpion towing a Centipede for dealing with anti-personnel mines.* (Imp. War Mus.)

the burning fuel. The latter design was chosen for further development in 1942 and formed the basis of the Churchill Crocodile flamethrower. A different form of flamethrower—a 9·75 in. mortar firing a combustible projectile—was also tried out experimentally on a turretless Valentine.

Various mineclearing devices were built on Valentines or designed as attachments, including the Anti-Mine Reconnaissance Caster Roller Mk. IB, a device with spiked rollers used in the Middle East, and Snake. The latter was a long tube of explosive pushed by the tank across a minefield and then exploded by remote control. A curious mineclearing "rake" with weighted tines, believed to have been designed by Nicholas Straussler, was also tried out experimentally on a Valentine. Probably the most important anti-mine device on the Valentine was the "U.K. Scorpion Mk. III". Although not used operationally, 150 of these flail tanks were built and in 1943-1944 used to train the flail regiments which later went into action with Sherman Crabs. Valentine II or III chassis were employed, with turrets removed and replaced by a fixed armoured box containing two Ford V-8 engines for the flail drive, which was transmitted via carden shafts to the rotors carrying the beating chains. This armoured structure also accommodated the tank commander and the flail equipment operator, the driver's position being unchanged. The Valentine Scorpion was quite effective but was replaced by the more powerful Sherman which also had the advantage of retaining its main armament.

Three self-propelled mountings were based on the Valentine. The first, a S.P. 6 pdr. mounted behind a shield in the fighting compartment of a turretless tank, was not developed because the Valentines VIII and later models had the same weapon in a turret.

Carrier, Valentine, 25 pdr. gun, Mk. I—known as Bishop—was produced urgently in 1942. The Valentine II chassis was used and 100 were built: they saw action in the Western Desert, Tunisia and in Sicily. The 25 pdr. was mounted in a simple armoured box structure with its ammunition carried in a towed limber.

S.P. 17 pdr., Valentine, usually called Archer, was developed from 1943, when the pilot vehicle was completed, and eventually succeeded the Valentine itself in production. Archer consisted of a 17 pdr. gun mounted facing rearwards in an open top armoured hull. The lower part of the hull was basically the same as the tank, however—the suspension was identical and so was the transmission, although the higher rated General Motors 6-71M, 192 b.h.p. diesel engine produced the higher speed of 20 m.p.h. Six hundred and sixty-five Archers were built and some were used in Italy in 1945 and others in the North-West Europe campaign. They remained in service with the British Army for some years after the War.

Miscellaneous vehicles based on the Valentine were the Valentine Dozer, an O.P. tank (carrying artillery observation and signals equipment and a dummy gun) and the Gap Jumping Tank. This last, designed at the end of World War II, could be propelled by rockets over minefields or other obstacles. The crewless Valentine performed in a highly spectacular way, but was eventually abandoned because it persisted in landing the wrong way up!

Valentine with a 9·75 in. mortar mounted in the fighting compartment. This mortar fired a combustible projectile. Experimental vehicle only. (Imp. War Mus.)

Valentine with cordite-operated flamethrower—experimental vehicle built by the Ministry of Supply. (Imp. War Mus.)

Valentine with gas pressure system flamethrower. This experimental vehicle, built by A.E.C. Ltd. in conjunction with the Petroleum Warfare Department, formed the basis of the later Crocodile flamethrower system. (Imp. War Mus.)

THE VALIANT

The final outgrowth of the Valentine was the 27-ton Valiant Infantry Tank which resembled its predecessor in several respects although it was, in fact, a new design. Design for the tank to specification A.38 was originally undertaken by Vickers-Armstrong, then was taken over by the Birmingham Railway Carriage

Valentine IX DD tank with the flotation screen folded. (Imp. War Mus.)

Valentine DD with flotation screen erected. (Imp. War Mus.)

Valentine V DD entering the sea from the bows of a tank landing craft. (Imp. War Mus.)

& Wagon Co. Ltd. (another firm in the Valentine production group). Finally, however, the design parentage was transferred to Ruston & Hornsby Ltd., of Lincoln, who built the pilot models in 1943–1944.

In the Valiant the cast nose plate of the Valentine was adopted although it had an inverted-V top surface and was much thicker, up to $4\frac{1}{2}$ in. The front plate of the turret was also a casting. The turret armament was either a 6 pdr. gun or a 75 mm., together with a co-axial Besa m-g. This was much like the later Valentines, although the turret held three men. The suspension consisted of six road wheels and three rollers each side—again like the Valentine. The Valiant's road wheels were all the same size and were similar in appearance to the Valentine's 24 in. diameter wheels. However, they were all independently sprung on wishbone arms, with coil springs.

The engine of the Valiant also followed precedent set by the later Valentines in that it was a General Motors diesel, although more powerful—210 b.h.p. A.E.C. engines were proposed as an alternative, and in a second version, Valiant II, either Ford V-8 or Rolls-Royce Meteorite engines were to be tried.

Rolls-Royce Ltd. joined Ruston & Hornsby as joint design parents for the Valiant II in order to further the development in this tank of the Meteorite engine which was derived from the Meteor, a de-rated Rolls-Royce Merlin aero-engine. The Meteorite 8-cylinder engine was designed for petrol or diesel fuel and foreshadowed the post-war multi-fuel tank engines.

The Valiant had several merits—it was compact and well armoured for its size and used some existing components, but the steering was found on trials to be unsatisfactory and the rear overhang caused problems with weight distribution. Also, the ground clearance of $9\frac{1}{2}$ in. was regarded as inadequate. These faults could no doubt have been corrected, but by 1944 it was felt that there was no longer a requirement for this particular type of tank.

VALENTINE IN SERVICE

The Valentine was intended as an infantry tank and was accepted into service as such, most of the first production vehicles being issued to Army tank brigades. However, production of cruiser tanks was insufficient to meet the needs of the new armoured divisions raised in 1940–1941 and so Valentines, which were coming off the production lines in good numbers by mid-1941, were issued in lieu of cruiser tanks to many armoured regiments in the United Kingdom. By October 1941, the 6th, 8th and 11th Armoured Divisions (each with two armoured brigades at that time) had some 900 Valentines between them, although the 11th was not fully up to strength and in the following year was re-equipped with cruiser tanks. Both the 6th and 8th Armoured Divisions took Valentines into action with them—the former in Tunisia at the end of 1942. The 23rd Armoured Brigade from the 8th Armoured Division joined the Eighth Army in July 1942 and was employed as an Army tank brigade in support of the New Zealand Division and the 9th Australian Division at the first battle of Alamein. The Brigade suffered heavy losses in this its first battle but helped to restore the faith of the infantry in tanks. The 8th Armoured Division, re-organised on the new establishment with only one armoured brigade, the 24th, arrived in Egypt in August 1942, equipped with Valentines, although these were not long afterwards replaced by Sherman tanks. Besides these formations some other units in the Middle East were also equipped with Valentines in part or completely, from around February 1942 onwards.

The organisation of tanks in both Army tank battalions and in armoured regiments was basically the same—three fighting squadrons, each squadron consisting of five troops of three tanks each. The armoured regiments of the 6th Armoured Division at the time of its arrival in Tunisia in most cases had two of the Valentine troops in each squadron replaced by 6 pdr. equipped Crusader cruiser tanks.

The specification of the Valentine made it acceptable as a cruiser tank and as such it had better protection than any British cruiser before the Cavalier–Centaur–Cromwell series, and also most contemporary German tanks, although the speed was lower than was considered desirable, even if it was better than that of the A.10, the Cruiser Mk. II. The lack of range of the 2 pdr. gun and also the absence of effective high explosive ammunition was a disadvantage shared by most British tanks up until 1942, when 6 pdr.-equipped tanks started coming on to the battlefields—some 6 pdr. Valentines were employed in North Africa towards the end of the campaign. The official concept of different specialised roles for "I" tank and cruiser sometimes inhibited the employment of the Valentine in "cavalry" roles which it could have undertaken quite effectively.

The main tactical drawback of the Valentine was that (with the exception of Mks. III and V) it was a three-man tank with the disadvantage that in battle the tank commander had to take on the role of gunner or wireless operator-cum-loader. The Valentine was also a fatiguing tank to drive, through the combination of a somewhat uncomfortable driving position and the effort required to operate the steering levers.

On the credit side, development of the Valentine had eliminated the less trustworthy features at an early stage. The amazing mileages put up by Valentines of the 23rd Armoured Brigade in 1942–1943 speak for

Valentine I with narrow tracks with a tread pattern like those of the Cruiser Mark III, IV, V and VI series. It was, however, of the twin guide horn type like other Valentines. The heavy armoured louvres on the rear deck show up well in this rear view. The formation sign on the left is of forces in Northern Ireland. (Imp. War Mus.)

The Rock of Gibraltar with a Valentine II of the Gibraltar Tank Squadron, November 1942. (Imp. War Mus.)

themselves and its mechanical reliability, particularly at a period when this was not a noteworthy feature of several British tanks, offset the Valentine's disadvantages from the point of view of its crews by whom it was generally well liked.

The most significant fact about the Valentine is, however, that it was a battleworthy tank coming off the production lines in quantity when it was most needed—firstly to help re-equip the British armoured units after Dunkirk in 1940 and then the new formations raised in 1940 and 1941. It is not surprising that the Valentine should have become the most widely distributed British tank of World War II. The North African theatre in 1942–1943 was its most important battle area, and Valentines were in their greatest numbers in the United Kingdom in units engaged in training and in Home Defence.

A large number of Valentines was sent to the U.S.S.R. in 1941–1943. These were tanks of nearly all marks except Mk. I, and included the whole Canadian production, except for the first 30 vehicles, which were retained in Canada for training purposes. Some 1,300 British-built Valentines were also despatched and getting on for 400 (British and Canadian production) were sunk by the enemy *en route*. The Russians made good use of their Valentines—some were sent into action only 40 minutes after arrival at the railhead for the battlefront.

The early Valentines' tracks gave some trouble in Soviet winter operations because at temperatures between zero and minus 20 degrees the snow packed in

them, although at temperatures colder than minus 20 degrees the snow powdered into a fine dust and blew away. Apart from the track troubles, which were eliminated later, and the 2 pdr. gun, which was felt to be too small, the Russians liked the Valentine very well. It was the sort of straightforward but effective design that was likely to appeal to Soviet tank crews. The Soviet Government Purchasing Commission in the U.S.A. wrote in August 1942, particularly asking for the number of Valentines shipped to the U.S.S.R. to be increased because "these tanks have given a fine performance in combat action."

The Valentine was used (in squadron strength) for the defence of the Rock of Gibraltar and also partly equipped some of the Special Service Tank Squadrons, one of which was engaged in an amphibious landing against heavy opposition in Madagascar in 1942. A New Zealand squadron of Valentine III's (some of which were converted to take 3-inch howitzers from Matilda close support tanks) was used in the Pacific campaign. Valentines were used for defence and training purposes in India, from where in 1943 was mounted a little known amphibious assault at Arakan in Burma, although the Valentine was not used in the full-scale campaign in 1944.

The Valentine, although by 1944 armed with the 75 mm. gun, had been rendered obsolescent by the Sherman, then available in large quantities from the United States, and by later-designed British tanks. However, it was found still possible to give them a useful role as battery commanders' vehicles—retaining full armament—in self-propelled 17 pdr. anti-tank regiments equipped with Archers, which were themselves developed from the Valentine, or M-10s. In this function the Valentine was in at the final stage of the War in Europe.

© *B. T. White*

A.F.V. Series Editor: DUNCAN CROW

SPECIFICATION:
TANK, INFANTRY, MARK III*—VALENTINE II

General
Crew: 3—driver, commander, gunner (the commander acted also as wireless operator-cum-loader or sometime took on the gunner's job, leaving another member of the crew as operator/loader).
Battle weight: 16 tons.
Power/weight ratio: 8·1 bhp/ton approx.
Bridge classification: 16.

Dimensions
Length overall and hull length: 17 ft. 9 in.
Height: 7 ft. 5½ in.
Width: 8 ft. 7½ in.
Track centres: 7 ft. 3 in.
Track width: 14 in.

Armament
Main: Ordnance Q.F. 2 pdr. Mk. IX or X and one Besa 7·92 mm. machine-gun mounted co-axially in turret.
Auxiliary: One Bren 0·303 in. machine-gun on collapsible mounting on turret roof. One 2 in. Smoke Discharger.

Fire control
Free elevation of main armament (by means of shoulder piece); traverse by electrical power with alternative manual operation. Guns fired by means of pistol grips.

Ammunition
2 pdr.: 60 rounds, stowed in fighting compartment.
Besa: 3,150 rounds.
Bren: 600 rounds.
2 in. smoke bombs: 18.

Sighting and Vision
Commander: Vickers tank periscope in turret roof.
Gunner: Vickers tank periscope in turret roof and Telescope, Sighting, No. 30, Mk. I or IA.
Driver: two Vickers tank periscopes on roof of compartment, and direct vision port.

Communications
Wireless Set No. 19 incorporating 'A' long range set and 'B' short range set, also intercomm. for all crew members. (Standard from February, 1943—earlier some tanks had the No. 11 Low Power set, with crew Tannoy equipment.)

Armour
Turret: castings, riveted and bolted, front 65 mm., sides 60 mm.
Hull: plates riveted and/or bolted. Nose plate 60 mm. at 21°. Glacis plate 30 mm. at 68°. Sides 60 mm. vertical.

Engine
A.E.C. Type A.190: diesel.
6 cylinders in line.
Capacity: 9·6 litres.
131 b.h.p. at 1,800 r.p.m.
Fuel: 36 gallons (31 gallons in main tank, 5 gallons in pressure tank—both in engine compartment on left side of engine).

Transmission
Meadows gearbox Type No. 22, sliding pinion, 5 speed and reverse.
Overall ratios: 1st 101·118:1, 2nd 48·528:1, 3rd 26·02:1, 4th 13·482:1, 5th 9·774:1, Reverse 142·914:1.
Drive to sprockets through multiplate steering clutches and compound epicyclic reduction gear mounted on hull side plates. Steering brakes incorporated on outside of reduction gears.

Suspension
Slow motion type: two groups of three rubber tyred wheels each side (each group one 24 in. wheel and two of 19½ in. diameter). Single spring in each group, damped by shock absorbers. Front idler wheels 24 in. diameter; drive sprockets at rear. Three track return rollers each side.
Tracks: single pin type, 103 shoes per set; pitch 4·36 in., width 14 in. (early twin pin track—73 shoes per set).

Electrical System
Service dynamo: C.A.V. Type G 5524B-3X.
Turret traverse dynamo: C.A.V. Type D.O. 7 L.X.-1.
Batteries: Four 6 volt.

Performance
Maximum road speed: 15 m.p.h.
Vertical obstacle: 3 ft. 0 in.
Trench: 7 ft. 9 in.
Wading: 3 ft. 0 in.
Range: 90 miles (road); 2½ miles per gallon.

Valentine V of 6th Armoured Division moving up near Bou Arada, Tunisia, in January 1943. It is towing a Rotatrailer containing spare fuel and ammunition. Note the spare track added to the nose plate for extra protection. (Imp. War Mus.)

TOG 1 with 75mm French howitzer in the hull front and A12 Matilda turret. Date on side is 4 October, 1940. TOG was the alternative to the A20 as a "shelled area" heavy I (infantry) tank. A picture of A20E1 appears in Volume Three. (Foster & Co. Ltd. Archives)

The Old Gang by Duncan Crow

SWINTON, Tritton, Stern, Wilson, Ricardo, Tennyson d'Eyncourt—these were the men who had pioneered Britain's tanks in the First World War. Swinton had visualized the tank and its employment; Tritton of Foster's at Lincoln had been the tractor expert and tank designer in co-operation with the brilliant automotive engineer Wilson; Stern had been the dynamic administrative genius who got the tanks produced, Ricardo had designed and built the engines for the Mark V onwards, and Tennyson d'Eyncourt as Director of Naval Construction had been chairman of the famous Landships Committee set up by Churchill to consider the practicability of "land battleships" and from which had stemmed the Mechanical Warfare Supply Department of the Ministry of Munitions. As far as tanks were concerned these men were The Old Gang indeed. Between 1915 and 1919 they had created the armoured fighting vehicles for a Tank Corps that grew to 25 battalions.

Twenty years after the tank supply department was disbanded these same men were grouped together again to design and build tanks—not, this time, as it turned out, a whole family of tanks, but a specific tank to deal with a specific problem. Their job was to design a super-heavy tank with a high trench-crossing capacity that would be capable of smashing through the new defences on the same Western Front as their Mark IVs and Vs had done in 1917 and 1918.

Despite the arguments of enthusiasts like Fuller, Liddell Hart, Lindsay, and Hobart, and the years of experiment with mobile forces in the shape of the Experimental Armoured Force and the Tank Brigade,

the idea of swiftly moving forces striking at the nerve- and brain-centres of the opposing army had not taken hold of the British military mind. Far from it. The concept that an army's rôle should be to bring about the strategic paralysis of the opposing force rather than destroy it physically was not acceptable. For one thing it was a most difficult concept to grasp and all the training and attitudes of military society were such as to exacerbate the difficulty. Whereas with traditional warfare the number of men and the number of guns and the rate of fire on each side could be calculated and the probable results assessed, this new idea was a bit like witchcraft—how did you know it would work? It was all so intangible. Furthermore, among those who did begin to grasp the idea there were some, perhaps many, who felt that, like witchcraft, this "strategic paralysis/mobile warfare" was not quite the thing. Attrition was an unpleasant word, but attrition was what warfare was all about. Thus, although mobile warfare was a useful subject for cocktail chat, the soldiers were really thinking about "Somme mud". When it became clear that there was going to be another war in Europe there came into most minds the vision of that line of trenches stretching from Nieuport to the Swiss frontier. And why not? This was what they knew and what they had told the next generation about. And wasn't it obvious that the brass-hats thought the same? There were the Maginot and Siegfried Lines to prove it.

Those who travelled across the Franco-Belgian frontier north of Sedan could see for themselves that there was no Maginot Line between there and

TOG 2 with mock-up turret and dummy 6-pdr. Date on plate is March 21st, 1941. (Foster & Co. Ltd. Archives)

the coast. There was a good political reason for this. But the fact that Germany had come through Belgium in 1914 and could come that way again was seldom mentioned, especially as the Ardennes, it was always confidently maintained, was quite unsuitable country for tanks.

So that although the door was open in the north for the new "mobile warfare"—the *Blitzkrieg* that had been so openly rehearsed in Spain and was so successfully demonstrated in Poland in September 1939 —the military mind was preoccupied with lines of trenches, and this, in the context of tanks, meant heavily armoured tanks able to cross shell-torn ground and assault fortifications.

A.20

One answer to the apparent need for this type of tank was a revision of the Infantry tank Mark I, the original Matilda. With the designation A.20 the specification

for this revision was proposed in September 1939 and the design was carried out by the Mechanisation Board and the engineering and shipbuilding firm of Harland and Wolff of Belfast. In December 1939 Harland and Wolff were given a contract to build four mild steel pilot models, of which the first two were produced by June 1940. A20E1 weighed 43 tons, $5\frac{1}{2}$ tons above the specified weight, and had an armour basis of 80-mm. Its main armament, even at this weight, was no larger than a 2-pdr. in a Matilda (Infantry Tank Mark II) turret, with a co-axial 7·92-mm. Besa. Trials of the A20E1 were disappointing and in June it was decided to abandon the project with only the two pilot models (A20E1 and E2) built. Nevertheless, the work was not wasted because the A.20 drawings and one of the pilot vehicles provided the basis for the A.22 which was embarked on immediately and became famous as the Churchill-Infantry Tank Mark IV.

TOG 2 with genuine turret mounting a 77-mm gun. (Imperial War Museum)

Side view of TOG 2* with 17-pdr. in Stothert and Pitt "Challenger" turret. Note covered-in aperture for sponson at side.

(Duncan Crow)

TOG

While the A.22 was under construction an alternative was also being built. On September 5, 1939, Sir Albert Stern had been asked by the Minister of Supply to form a committee to study tank requirements and design problems. He invited the members of The Old Gang to join him. In October they were officially named the Special Vehicle Development Committee of the Ministry of Supply. This title arose from their request to the General Staff for an outline specification for a heavy tank. The specification they were given was similar to that issued for the A.20, calling for a vehicle with all-round track able to cross shell-torn ground. Its armour was to be proof against 37-mm. and 47-mm. anti-tank guns and 105-mm. howitzers at 100 yards range. Its armament was to be a field gun in the hull front to demolish fortifications, sponsons mounting 2-pdrs., and Besa machine-guns covering all arcs. It was to be diesel-powered, have a speed of 5 m.p.h., and a range of at least 50 miles. The crew was to be eight. And it was to conform with the firmly understood rule that, like all British tanks, it had to be within standard loading gauge maxima on British railways. This meant in practice a maximum width of 9 ft.

The members of the Committee visited the BEF in France and studied the latest French tanks. In December 1939 the design for the new vehicle was drawn up at Foster's of Lincoln (where else?) and after a wooden mock-up had been built its construction was begun there in February 1940—at the same place as the first tanks of World War I had been built. Small wonder that the vehicle was named TOG, the initial letters of "The Old Gang".

The prototype appeared in October, several months after the reason for its design had been swept away by the German panzer divisions and especially by Guderian's advance through the Ardennes and breakthrough at Sedan. Despite this, TOG was not a waste of time and resources; it gave valuable experience and data, particularly in component design.

In appearance TOG 1 was very like a heavy World War I tank, with the same lozenge-like shape and all-round unsprung tracks. Especially was it like the Mark VI which had never gone beyond the wooden model stage. Like the Mark VI it had a main armament centrally placed in the hull front and a turret, but no sponsons. These had been dispensed with in design changes during construction, although the apertures for them had been left in the hull sides. The hull gun was a French 75-mm. howitzer, the same gun and mount as was fitted in the French Char B. The turret was taken from an A.12 Matilda and mounted a 2-pdr. Secondary armament, had it been fitted, would have been a co-axial 7·92-mm. Besa in the turret.

TOG 1 had a maximum speed of 8½ m.p.h. and weighed 63½ tons. It was powered by a Paxman-Ricardo 450 h.p. V-12 diesel engine developed to give 600 h.p. Because of the vehicle's weight it was decided to have electric transmission. Trials showed this to be unsatisfactory and the motors were burnt out on test. The engine drove two generators which in turn provided the power for a motor for each track. The steering wheel operated a potentiometer which increased voltage on the selected motor and thus increased track speed to turn the vehicle towards the other direction. The TOG method of converting braking energy into tractive power was very ingenious, but it needed a great deal of bulky equipment which made it less acceptable than the purely mechanical principles applied in the regenerative braking system designed by Dr. H. E. Merritt at Woolwich Arsenal in 1938. Merritt's double differential steering mechanism was used with a propulsion gearbox of Maybach design and Merritt-Maybach transmission was installed in the experimental heavy cruiser tank A16E1 in 1938. Merritt then developed a triple differential system, which, as the Merritt-Brown transmission, was generally adopted in British tanks.

In an endeavour to improve on the electric transmission which subjected the track and drive to great strain TOG was re-equipped with hydraulic transmission. This too proved unsatisfactory because the time lag involved in filling the fluid couplings made steering hazardous. In fact the poor steering ratio resulting from the very long ground contact in relation

Front view of TOG 2* showing name-plate of the builders, one of the most famous in the tank world: Wm. Foster & Co. Ltd. Engineers, Lincoln, England. (Duncan Crow)

TOG 1 with a 600 h.p. engine giving a maximum speed of just over 8 m.p.h. and a maximum cross-country speed of about 4 m.p.h. It could cross a 12 ft. trench and a 7 ft. vertical obstacle. It had a crew of six as against TOG 1's eight.

TOG 2 was to have a larger turret than TOG 1, as well as having the sponsons as originally designed. But the sponsons were never fitted and the turret on TOG 2 when it appeared in March 1941 was a mock-up with a dummy 6-pdr. Later this was replaced by a genuine turret with a 77-mm. gun. The working drawings for the vehicle show a low turret quite different from the one actually fitted, and it would appear that this had originally been intended for a development called TOG 2R (R for "revised") which was never built. TOG 2R was to have been 6 ft. shorter, without sponsons, and with torsion bar suspension.

By the time TOG 2 appeared the A.22 Churchill had been accepted as the new infantry tank, and although TOG 2 was used for trials, interest in the TOG concept had evaporated. Even so, early in 1942 TOG 2, with spring suspension, was given a new turret, mounting a 17-pdr. gun. The turret was intended for the Challenger, then being developed, and it was tested on TOG 2, now re-named TOG 2*. TOG 2* was thus the first British tank to mount a 17-pdr. It was fitting that this turret—which in modified form and with its associated Metadyne traverse system was used on the Challenger—was tested on TOG 2, because the turret was designed by Stothert and Pitt of Bath. Stothert and Pitt was the firm which had built the Pedrail "landship" machine, one of the experimental precursors of the tank. TOG indeed!

to width was TOG's greatest weakness. With its hydraulic transmission the vehicle was called TOG 1A.

Before TOG 1 was complete a second prototype was begun. In order to reduce the height of the hull TOG 2's tracks were recessed. This gave the vehicle a more modern appearance. It was 33 ft. 3 in. long, 10 ft. 3 in. wide, and 10 ft. high. It weighed 80 tons, with armour of 63 plus 13-mm. maximum and 25-mm. minimum. Mechanically it was the same as

Three-quarter view of TOG 2* now on display at the RAC Tank Museum, Bovington Camp, Dorset. (Duncan Crow)

The Carden-Loyd Mark VI Light Armoured Vehicle with sprung suspension, Vickers machine-gun and sponson stowage boxes over the tracks.
(Col. R. J. Icks)

Tankettes and Tracked Carriers

GENERAL Estienne's concept of light tanks for use as armoured skirmishers to give armoured mobility to infantry in the *battue* conditions of the Western Front trench warfare resulted in the Renault FT. Estienne's idea was revived in Britain in the early 1920s by Colonel (later Major-General) J. F. C. Fuller and put into practical effect by Major (later Lieutenant-General Sir Gifford) le Q. Martel and Carden-Loyd.

The firm of Carden-Loyd Tractors Ltd. was run by two former officers—Captain Loyd and Captain (later Sir John) Valentine Carden. Loyd owned a London garage which Carden managed. Carden had served in the Army Service Corps in the war and was familiar with that great stimulator of armoured fighting vehicle development, the Holt tractor. He too believed that the infantryman must be given mobility. To this end he built a very low track-laying vehicle powered by a Ford Model T engine in the front, with Ford transmission, and final drive in the rear. It weighed 700 lb. and carried one man, who lay prone and controlled the machine by means of handle-bars. The *ventre à terre* design was the sole protection for there was no armour. The vehicle gave a rough ride, its suspension system having neither springs nor rollers, and although it ran fairly well on smooth ground it had a tendency to gallop on hard going. The first demonstration, in an empty field in Kensington, London, was widely reported in the press.

Meanwhile Martel's home-built one-man tank (see page 25) was also receiving considerable publicity. Carden called on Martel who suggested he approach Colonel (later Major-General) S. C. Peck, Director of Mechanization at the War Office from 1924 to 1928. At a period when money and official enthusiasm were in short supply Peck did much to encourage armoured mobility during the four years he held this appointment. He was impressed by Carden's idea and recommended an order for an experimental machine.

D.C.

The Carden-Loyds by Colonel Robert Icks

IN THE first finished machine the driver sat astride the engine. Steering and braking were accomplished by foot pedals actuating brake drums mounted on the axle, the final drive having been moved to the front. Gears were shifted by means of a lever similar to the airplane "joystick" of the period. The radiator at the rear of the hull was unprotected. The muffler was below the hull on the left side. The suspension comprised a track frame with 14 rollers but no springs. Instead of upper track rollers, double metal strips acted as track support and track guide. The conveyor chain tracks of the experimental machine, which had a life of about 20 miles, were modified, increasing track life to about 80 miles.

By the time of a meeting of the Dominion Premiers in 1926, Captains Carden and Loyd had formed the small company of Carden-Loyd Tractors Ltd. and had applied for patents. A demonstration arranged by the War Office for the Premiers at Camberley on November 8, 1926, was able to show, among other vehicles, not only the one-man Mark I vehicle but several other Carden-Loyd models, as well as other vehicles then in use. The Mark I had been fitted with a small turret-like shield carrying a machine rifle

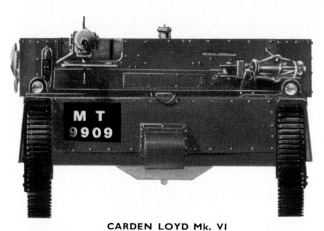

CARDEN LOYD Mk. VI

This only known survivor in Britain of one of the most famous fighting vehicle series of the inter-war period is preserved in the Royal Armoured Corps Tank Museum at Bovington. Its War Department No. 612 confirms that it was a standard Machine Gun Carrier, built in 1929 and issued to 2nd Batt. Lincolnshire Regt.

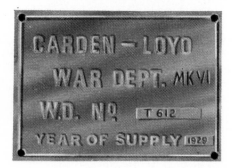

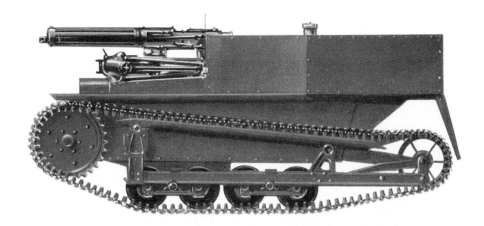

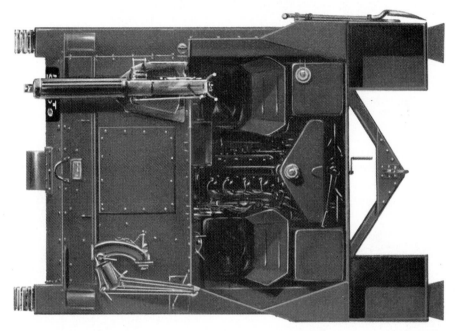

The second one-man Carden-Loyd machine, showing the general construction of the unarmoured vehicle and the position of the operator, features which were carried into the third machine, the Mark I. (N. Payne-Johnson)

as well as a wedge-shaped air scoop open at the top which protected the radiator.

One of the newer models was the Mark I*. It was the same as the Mark I but a three-wheeled tricycle arrangement enabled it to run on either tracks or wheels. During World War I heavy tanks had been brought as close as possible to the front by rail because track life seldom exceeded 50 miles. Light tanks as employed by the French were moved in rear areas by truck, trailer or tracklaying tractor, again because of short track life. The track life of the little Carden-Loyd also was limited so this device—parallel with the thinking of J. Walter Christie in the U.S.—was

expected to enhance mobility and increase track life because it provided a built-in carrier. A large automotive type pneumatic tyred wheel on either side near the drive sprocket supported the front of the vehicle and a small solid tyred steering wheel supported the rear. The wheels could be dropped on crank arms by means of a front and rear screw arrangement operated by hand in the rear and through dog clutches on the axle in front. A chain drive from the sprockets to the large wheels and operated by an outside lever disconnected the sprockets from the tracks and connected the chain drive to the wheels. Because of the small amount of track clearance the wheels were not sprung so the vehicle rode roughly on either tracks or wheels.

The third model built in 1926 and also shown at the Camberley demonstration was the first two-man vehicle. It was very low and considerably wider but the suspension remained substantially unchanged. No Mark was assigned to it.

MARKS II—V

Early in 1927 extensive tests were conducted at Bovington. By then the Mark II had appeared. This was the same as the Mark I but had the suspension changed to comprise four large soft rubber tyred bogie wheels on a solid frame without springs and with a new drop-forged track. This track lasted longer but by 300 miles it had stretched so badly that replacement was necessary. The bogie wheel tyres wore out rapidly and the vehicle rode roughly. Nevertheless, the rubber tyred bogie wheel principle

Carden-Loyd Mark I Tankette without the turret-mounted machine-rifle showing the muffler mounted below the left side of the hull. (Col. R. J. Icks)

Three-quarter left front view of the Carden-Loyd Mk. V showing the unsprung soft rubber-tyred bogie wheels, the sprocket throw-out and engagement device and the changeover housing in the centre glacis covered over in this vehicle. (Col. R. J. Icks)

Three-quarter right rear view of the wheel-cum-track Carden-Loyd Mk. V illustrating the change to a large rear steering wheel and the crank device for raising and lowering the rear wheel. (Col. R. J. Icks)

Carden-Loyd Mk. I Tankette from the right rear as operated on wheels, showing the small rear solid rubber-tyred steering wheel.* (Col. R. J. Icks)

Right: *Original Carden-Loyd two-man vehicle with shield open at the rear and armed with light machine-rifle, showing the metal upper track support guide.*
(Royal Tank Corps Journal)

Below: *King George V inspecting one of the eight Carden-Loyd Mk. IV Tankettes issued to 3rd Battalion, Royal Tank Corps in 1928.* (Central News)

was to be permanent and eventually was adopted by practically every tank designer in the world.

The Mark III was the same as the Mark II but with the wheeled tricycle device used on the Mark I*. By now, however, it had become apparent that one man could not drive and handle a weapon at the same time so the one-man concept was abandoned. The Mark IV was a two-man vehicle with the soft rubber tyred bogie wheels of the Marks II and III. The hull was wider and lower. On the right of the hull the armour was higher in front of the gunner and an additional slotted shield could be raised to make it even higher. This model was armed with an automatic rifle. The vehicle also was of the wheel-cum-track variety with a device similar to that on the Marks I* and III.

The Mark IV vehicles, of which eight were made, were considered tankettes and were to act as scout or reconnaissance vehicles together with eight Morris-Martel tankettes in the Mechanised Force.

At about this time the firm of Vickers-Armstrong Ltd. became involved. They had been supplying tanks to the British army and were interested in developing an export market. This would have advantages in many ways. By producing more vehicles more experience would be gained and development speeded. Early in 1928 Vickers absorbed the small Carden-Loyd Company, acquiring their patent rights as well as the services of Captains Carden and Loyd.

The last vehicle to be produced by the original firm was the Mark V. Again it was a wheel-cum-track vehicle and with the springless soft rubber tyred bogie wheels. However, in this model, the rear steering wheel was a full-sized wheel but still with a solid rubber tyre. The track was a malleable cast iron track with double guides. The pitch remained at $1\frac{3}{4}$ in. but the track width was increased to $5\frac{1}{4}$ in. This track remained virtually unchanged thereafter and its design was to influence track design in many countries. As Micklethwait said in 1944: " . . . the development of tracks for the Carden-Loyd tankette founded a dynasty in which a very large number of modern tracks can trace ancestry."*

The numbers produced by the Carden-Loyd company between 1925 and 1928 were approximately as follows: One-Man Original 1; One-Man 1; Mark I 3; Mark I* 1; Mark II 1; Two-Man Original 1;, Mark III 1; Mark IV 8, plus one believed to have been sold to Hungary; Mark V 1. Total 18 or 19.

MARK V*

The first vehicle to be produced by Vickers-Armstrong Ltd. was the Mark V*. There was very little change in the hull but a big improvement was made in the suspension. It now paired the rubber-tyred bogie wheels by means of connecting flat leaf springs pivoted so that the bogie could move with the movement of the track over undulating ground surface. The differential housing continued to be unprotected. One

* *Tracks for Fighting Vehicles, E.W.E. Micklethwait, School of Tank Technology, Chobham, 1944.*

Carden-Loyd Mk. VI with armoured head covers as supplied commercially to various countries in Europe, South America and Asia. (Col. R. J. Icks)

Carden-Loyd Mk. VI variant with bevelled armour and split transverse roof hinged fore and aft. This was the type used in the Gran Chaco. (Col. R. J. Icks)

of these vehicles was modified by providing a guide rail having six small rollers for track return in place of the double metal rails previously used. This seems not to have been considered a worth-while change since it was not continued in later Marks. Nine Mark V*s were produced.

MARK VI

The Mark VI appeared before the end of 1928. It was very similar in appearance to the Mark V* but the front of the hull now was armour instead of sheet metal and the differential housing was protected by a removable armour cover. In addition, sponson boxes useful for stowage were added over the tracks at the rear on either side.

The Mark VI became one of the best known and most discussed armoured vehicles ever produced. In addition, it marked the point where the design concept it represented pointed the way to two lines of development, the machine-gun carrier and the light tank. Although there was then as well as later a great deal of criticism of the original concept as well as of the two resulting design paths, the matter must be considered in the context of the period.

The limitations imposed by the need for economy may be difficult to realize today, when military expenditures throughout the world reach such staggering proportions. There also existed the struggles between military branches seeking to get as much of the available fiscal appropriation as possible, partially based on the age-old desire on the part of some to get back to the comforts of conventional peace-time soldiering. All in all, the size of the British army, the reduced appropriations, an incomplete acceptance of mechanization by the army, and last but not least a belief that the main task of the future would be colonial warfare rather than a Continental war, were the factors which bore on the direction that design and development had taken and would take.

The publicity which the Carden-Loyd received was out of all proportion to the numbers produced in its early stages. Not all of it was due to the vehicle alone although the novelty of its diminutive size as contrasted with the British tanks of World War I certainly accounted for some of it. But the hope that future war, should it come, might avoid the slaughter of World War I by the promise of armoured mobility probably played an even greater part in making the whole subject of mechanization good newspaper and magazine copy.

CARDEN-LOYD MARK VI DESCRIBED

The Carden-Loyd Mark VI Light Armoured Vehicle was a very satisfactory, simple, cheap and inconspicuous vehicle with a low centre of gravity which inhibited tipping. It was powered by a Ford Model T engine of 22·5 b.h.p. which drove the vehicle through a standard Ford planetary (or epicyclic) transmission and special reduction gear through a Ford differential, with final drive in front. Standard Ford foot pedals were used. That is, the left foot pedal engaged low and high gear, the centre pedal engaged reverse and the right pedal was the brake.

A lever for engaging the reduction gear was provided and another right hand lever steered the vehicle. Pushing it forward produced a right turn by actuating a brake on the right axle. Pulling on the lever produced a left turn by actuating a brake on the left axle. The differential effect made this possible. Turning radius was 13 ft.

The driver was on the left, the gunner on the right, sitting in curved-back seats which helped to brace them against vehicle motion. Peep slots were provided for the driver on the front and the bevelled side and for the gunner on the right side. The crew's heads projected but they could crouch down below the top level of the hull.

The machine-gun mount was pivoted at three points so that the weapon could be elevated and also quickly dismounted. Since the vehicle was an unstable gun platform and firing on the move was not very accurate, it was usually done from a halt. In its rôle as a machine-gun carrier, the gun could be dismounted and remounted on a tripod normally carried on the left glacis.

The engine was insulated with asbestos and located between the driver and the gunner. The fuel tank was behind the crew. Fuel capacity originally was 6½ Imperial gallons, sufficient for about 52 miles but in the Mark VI it was increased to 10 gallons, enough for about 100 miles. The radiator was behind the engine and could be protected by double doors which could be opened or closed from the inside. Below the radiator the frame ended in a truss on which there was a pintle for towing. The muffler was on the left rear. The front plate was armour and the differential was protected by a removable armour cover.

The Mark VI was capable of speeds up to 30 m.p.h. It could climb a vertical wall a little over 1 ft. and could ford up to a depth of 2 ft. It weighed about

Carden-Loyd Mk. VI variant "Infighter" with slightly curved gun shield and raised forward hull armour for better crew protection. (Col. R. J. Icks)

The Czech MV4/T 11 Tankette of 1931 which was an outgrowth of the Carden-Loyd Mk. VI with armoured head covers built under licence in Czechoslovakia. (Globe)

2,600 lb., was 8 ft. 1 in. long, 6 ft. 6½ in. wide and 4 ft. high. The suspension comprised two pairs of rubber tyred bogie wheels, each pair on a pivoted flat leaf spring.

VARIANTS AND DERIVATIVES

Various experimental models of the Mark VI were built in a search for greater fighting efficiency. Other models were developed for a variety of uses. The Mark VI was used in service as a tankette, a machine-gun carrier, a ·50 cal. machine-gun carrier, a 47-mm. self-propelled gun, a 3·7-in. howitzer tractor, an A/T gun tractor, a mortar carrier, a smoke producer, and it had yet other uses. Some, for example, were used with bench seats as an observer's or umpire's vehicle for manoeuvres in the U.K. A total of some 389 Mark VIs of all sorts, including experimental models, were produced, a few of them by the Royal Ordnance Factory.

Over 100 Mark VIs and variants were exported to other countries where, in some cases, they were also built under licence, often emerging with a different design from the original.* The Czechs produced one such variation of their own, the MV4/T11 of 1931 which was a blend of the Mark VI and the Polish TK. The Polish TK variations were of several kinds. The Italians produced 25 under the designation CV29 (Carro Veloce '29) and then produced a re-design which became the CV3/33 and, a later design, the CV3/35. These became almost as well known as their progenitor, also being available commercially. The Russians produced a variation called the T-27.

There were other far-reaching influences of the little Carden-Loyd Mark VI on vehicle design. The Cunningham Scout built experimentally in the United States owed its existence to the influence of the Carden-Loyd although the only one built was never completed. It had a tiny cylindrical turret on the left

with the gunner having a headcover on the right. The Marmon-Herrington series of light tanks beginning with the CTL-1 also resulted from Carden-Loyd influence. Although originally equipped with endless rubber band tracks similar to those on U.S. half-tracks, later models had tracks almost identical to Carden-Loyd tracks and included the M.22 Locust airborne tank of World War II which was built by Marmon-Herrington.

The French purchased one of the tractor type vehicles with the single upper track roller. Some of these were produced as the Latil Tracteur N. The Carden-Loyd influence is plain in the French Tracteur d'Infanterie UE. This vehicle not only became a maid of all work in the French Army but many were taken over by the Germans after the fall of France in 1940. Some were used without change but many also were modified into machine-gun carriers and into light tanks.

The Belgians built some of the tractor type vehicles, modifying some of them with additional armour shields and mounting a 47-mm. anti-tank gun. And, without doubt, the Straussler light tanks in Hungary, the designer of which later came to England, also were influenced by the Carden-Loyd.

The Carden-Loyd Mark VI, as has been said earlier, was the point at which development divided between the machine-gun carrier and the light tank. So far as the British army was concerned, the Imperial General Staff in 1929 laid down specifications based on experience with the Carden-Loyd to begin the development of a long series of light tanks, both conventional and amphibious. At this time armoured track-laying vehicles were being designed by the War

* Vehicles were furnished at least to the following countries (quantities approximate): Arabia—not recorded; Belgium —1 Tractor and licensing of Fabrique Nationale; Bolivia— 5; Canada—4; Czechoslovakia—5 with head-covers and licensing of Skoda; Chile—5; Finland—2; France—1 Tractor and licensing of Latil; Italy—1 with licensing of Fiat-Ansaldo; Japan—5; Netherlands—4 with headcovers; Poland—1 and licensing of Pantswowe Zaklady Inzyniernij; Portugal—6; Sweden 1; Thailand—60; U.S.S.R.—6 with headcovers and licensing of Soviet government. Total—107+.

Carden-Loyd Mark VI Mortar Carrier with removable base plate and mortar tube carried at rear of hull. (Col. R. J. Icks)

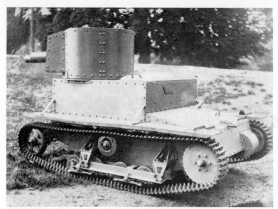

Carden-Loyd Patrol Tank in its original form with 40 h.p. Meadows engine and selective transmission showing final drive offset to the left. (Col. R. J. Icks)

Polish Tanketka on manoeuvres in Poland in 1938, a year before the German and Russian invasion of Poland during which they were used in combat. (R. M. Ogorkiewicz)

Office as well as by Vickers, both sometimes being submitted to a single specification. The more promising of the two would then be given a Mark and the other would be dropped. Since the commercial firm thus was in the design business, a third direction of development began in the area of producing light tanks for export.

One of these was the Vickers-Carden-Loyd Patrol Tank of 1932. It was a glorified Mark VI with a small rotating turret mounting a Vickers machine-gun in an armoured jacket. The weight rise made the suspension unequal to the task and a new suspension with double rubber tyred bogie wheels and coil springs and a wider centre guide track was adopted. One each of these was sold to Denmark, Finland, Portugal and Sweden. Swedish light tanks later produced by the Landsverk firm undoubtedly also were influenced. However, this was a makeshift vehicle which lost many of the advantages of predecessor vehicles without acquiring enough attributes to offset these losses. The firm had by then embarked on a programme of marketing a series of light tanks designed as such, one of which was the Vickers-Armstrong 6 Ton tank.

From the Mark VI there also stemmed a long series of light tractors or dragons. These included the Carden-Loyd 3-ton Tractor, the Cavalry Carrier, Light Dragons Marks I through III and some others. In 1935 Vickers-Armstrong Ltd. also returned to the original machine-gun carrier concept. They proposed to the War Office a carrier somewhat larger than the Mark VI. This culminated in the famous Universal Carrier of the World War II period. However, it is curious that after all the developmental work which preceded it Vickers-Armstrong during World War II did not manufacture a single one of the over 40,000 carriers produced in England, Canada, Australia, New Zealand and the United States.

The original thought of General Estienne embodying the use of armoured skirmishers never really materialized. In the first place, not enough of the early Carden-Loyd vehicles were purchased to make such a use even experimentally possible. The chequered history of the British Mechanized Force itself indicates the indecision as to tactics which existed. The few vehicles of this type which were available were used as light tanks, as reconnaissance vehicles, as machine gun carriers and as tractors.

The final abandonment of the Mechanized Force was partly political and partly financial. When the period of re-armament began prior to World War II a decision had already been reached to use heavily armoured tanks to accompany infantry, fast lightly armoured cruiser tanks for long-range operation and light tanks for reconnaissance. The Universal Carrier became an all-purpose vehicle, being used in many capacities, not the least of which was the original Carden-Loyd concept of a machine-gun carrier.

The British Carden-Loyd Mk. VI Light Armoured Vehicle appeared on the military scene at a time when no major war was in progress. Nevertheless it did see combat service, even though on a minor scale only, in the Bolivian Army during the Gran Chaco War with Paraguay in 1932-35. (See also page 61.) Derivatives or copies in the service of other nations saw widespread service during the Italian-Abyssinian War, the Spanish Civil War, and, not least, during World War II. Above all, the little Carden-Loyd Mk. VI was a progenitor which spread its design influence throughout the world; its long and distinguished lineage in the light tank and carrier class is equalled only by that of the Christie M.1928/31/32 in the medium class.

SPECIFICATION

LIGHT ARMOURED VEHICLE, CARDEN-LOYD MK. VI.

Crew: Two—driver and gunner. Battle weight: 1·5 tons. Dry weight: 1·3 tons.

Dimensions
Length overall: 8 ft. 1 in. Height: 4 ft. Width: 5 ft. 7 in. Width over tracks/overall: 6 ft. 6½ in. Track width: 5¼ in.

Armament
Main armament: One Vickers ·303 R.C. Class "C" Land Service water cooled machine-gun, mounted right front.

Ammunition
1,000 rounds ·303 R.C. minimum.

Armour
Face hardened, riveted, 9-mm. front and back plates. 6-mm. sides, all vertical.

Engine
Ford Model T Petrol with Zenith type F.D. carburettor and Watford F.M. 4 magneto, 4 cylinders, in line, 22·5 b.h.p. Fuel capacity 10 gal.

Transmission
Ford Model T two speed, epicyclic, with supplementary low gear.

Suspension
Four rubber tyred bogie wheels each side in two pairs, each pair connected by flat leaf spring pivoted to girder track frame. Track of malleable iron 5¼ in. wide, 1¾ in. pitch; weight per track link 1¾ lb. 108 shoes.

Electrical System
Magneto.

Performance
Maximum road speed: 28–30 m.p.h. Maximum gradient: 25°. Vertical obstacle: 1 ft. 4 in. Trench: 4 ft. Wading depth: 2 ft. Ground clearance: 9 in. Fuel consumption: 100 miles road range. Miles per gallon: 10.

Universal Carrier Mark II with Canadian crew south of Caen in the battle for Falaise, August 9, 1944. Note mudguard shape and Stacey towing attachment. Vehicle has been modified as a medium machine-gun carrier.

Carriers

By Peter Chamberlain and Duncan Crow

"IS a Bren gun carrier an AFV?"

That was a question in the military quiz which appeared regularly in the Army Bureau of Current Affairs' fortnightly publication *War*. This one was in issue No. 19 of May 30, 1942. The date is interesting because by mid-1942 carriers were preponderantly of the Universal type; but the name Bren stuck and for most of World War II was eponymous for carrier.

It is almost impossible that anyone who saw *War* did not know what a Bren carrier was. The carrier was the most ubiquitous vehicle in the British army and in any general action photograph there is almost invariably a carrier somewhere in shot. But only, it must be added, if the photograph is of British or Commonwealth troops. The tracked carrier was peculiar to the British and Commonwealth armies—although when carriers fell into enemy hands they were soon put to use.

But while most *War* readers must have known what a Bren gun carrier was, it is probable that many could not answer the question correctly. The answer was:

"No. It is a fire power transport. Its crew fight dismounted."

In practice, however, this was not always true. The carrier was often an AFV in deed, if not in name.

EARLY DEVELOPMENT

The carrier stemmed from the idea of giving armoured mobility to infantry—"armoured skirmishers" the French General Estienne envisaged them as. Development in Britain began simultaneously at two points in 1925. Major (later Lieutenant-General Sir Gifford) le Q. Martel, who had been G.S.O.2 at Tank Corps H.Q. in France during the war, built a "one-man tank" at his home near Camberley; and Captain (later Sir John) Carden, who was to become one of Britain's most brilliant and ingenious tank designers, built a one-man track-laying vehicle at the garage in London which he managed for Captain V. Loyd.

Martel's vehicle was a "one-man tank" in two senses. Not only was it designed to carry one man, but it was built by Martel himself alone. In the evenings when he got home from his job at the War Office, and at week-ends, he constructed his "tankette"—as this type of vehicle came to be called —using the engine from an old Maxwell car and the back-axle from a Ford lorry. The tracks, which were the most costly item, were specially made for him by the Roadless Traction Company, the firm founded by another famous tank designer, Lieut.-Colonel Philip Johnson of Medium D fame. In all, Martel's out-ofpocket expenses were about £400. In August 1925 the home-made tankette was tested on the heathland outside his garden gate. Its performance, according to Liddell Hart in his history of *The Tanks,* was 20 m.p.h. on the level, 6-8 m.p.h. on rough ground, and up hill it climbed four-foot banks and slopes of 1 in 1. It was eight feet long, five feet high, and four-and-a-half-feet wide. The track was shorter than the length of the vehicle and a pair of wheels was added at the back "to steady the machine, increase its gap-crossing span, and check the risk of over-turning when climbing a steep bank."

After the demonstration the War Office ordered four Martel machines, which were built by Morris Motors using ordinary commercial parts except for the tracks and the armour. There was a 16 h.p. engine and the weight of the machine was just over two tons. The first two were delivered in March 1926, one of which was a two-man version as it was decided that one man would not be able to carry out all the duties effectively. In subsequent models the tankette's length was increased to twelve feet, the tracks being seven feet long. Eight of the two-man improved models were built for the Experimental Mechanized Force and during the two years of the Force's existence they proved more reliable than eight Carden-Loyd machines which were also built for and issued to the Force. But Morris Motors were too busy with building cars and Martel was too busy at the War Office to develop the Morris-Martel tankettes any further, and it was through the Carden-Loyds that the main stream of carrier development continued.

Carden's first machine had emerged from a cycle-car that he built soon after the war as a way of making motoring inexpensive. While his cycle-car was popular with the public his experimental machine for giving the individual infantryman mobility aroused no interest in military quarters until Martel's machine was described by Liddell Hart in the *Daily Telegraph* of which he had just become military correspondent. Carden sought Martel's advice. Martel suggested he contact Colonel (later Major-General) S. C. Peck, Director of Mechanization at the War Office. Peck backed the idea, and a machine was ordered.

From this beginning the Carden-Loyd Tractors company improved on the design, producing seven successive types, mostly with a wheel and track device and mostly of one vehicle only, until the Mark IV arrived. It was eight of this type that were built for the Experimental Mechanized Force. Thereafter came a Mark V, and then a Mark V* which was the first vehicle to be produced by the newly-merged Vickers-Carden-Loyd company. In 1928 the Mark VI appeared.

The Carden-Loyd Mk. VI Light Armoured Vehicle soon became one of the most talked about military vehicles ever produced. Basically it was a low two-man machine weighing 1·5 tons and capable of a speed of 25 m.p.h. It proved to be the progenitor of a long line of tracked carriers. Nearly 400 Mark VIs were built, some of them experimental models in a search for a more battle-worthy machine, others for use in a variety of ways. Mark VIs were used as tankettes, carriers of light and medium machine-guns, mortar carriers, smoke projector carriers, and light gun tractors. In the machine-gun carrier rôle the Vickers machine-gun could be dismounted from the front of the vehicle and re-mounted on a tripod that was normally carried on the front left side.

Morris-Martel two-man Tankette. Eight of these machines were built, with eight Carden-Loyd Mark IVs as experimental scout machines or the Experimental Mechanized Force of 1927.

Tractor with 40 mm. Equipment. The VA.D50 tractor with re-worked suspension and converted as a self-propelled mount for a Vickers 40-mm. gun.

MACHINE-GUN CARRIERS

The next stage in carrier development occurred in late 1934 when, as a commercial project, Vickers-Armstrong built a vehicle that could be adapted to the rôles either of a machine-gun carrier or of a towing tractor for a light field gun. The vehicle, VA.D50, was fitted with Horstmann-type suspension with solid idler wheel and two return rollers on each side. The driver and front machine-gunner were enclosed in an armoured compartment, and there was a bench with a folding back on each side of the vehicle behind this compartment for seating the independent machine-gun unit or the field gun crew.

This vehicle was later tested as a self-propelled mount for a 40-mm. Vickers gun and was designated Tractor with 40 mm. Equipment. The conversion consisted of mounting the gun and trail on the engine behind the driver's compartment to achieve a 360 degrees traverse; other changes included the removal of the folding seats and the reversal of the front suspension unit with a reduction to one return roller each side.

On February 1, 1935, a meeting was held at the War Office to discuss this new type of vehicle as a replacement for the expensive and complicated light dragons then in use as gun towers. The War Office decided to purchase two modified versions of this machine for test purposes, one as a machine-gun carrier, the other as a light dragon. Designated Light Dragon Mark III, 69 of the vehicles in the latter rôle were eventually built. "Dragon", incidentally, was a generic name given to certain tracked vehicles used for gun-towing or troop-carrying.

In the machine-gun carrier rôle the vehicle was to have a driver, gunner, and machine-gun in an armoured front section so that enemy fire could be returned as the carrier advanced. There was also to be room to carry a machine-gun team of four men, with a machine-gun, tripod and ammunition, who could leave the carrier and operate independently. It was in fact to be a "fire power transport" as defined in the answer to *War's* quiz question.

One machine, designated Carrier, Machine-Gun Experimental (Armoured) (WD No. T1583, Regd.

No. BMM939) was built to this specification. The basic chassis was similar to that of the 40-mm. SP equipment Tractor with improved suspension, but the top superstructure was considerably altered. The independent unit was seated on benches behind the compartment for the driver and the front gunner on either side of the Ford V-8 engine which was positioned centrally. The compartment for the driver and the front gunner was an armoured box with stowage bins fitted on each side, the engine was protected by steel hinged plates mounted on a frame, and the machine-gun unit was protected by two folding armoured back-rests fitted to the vehicle's rear sides which could be folded down inwards when not in

VA.D50. This was a projected design by Vickers-Armstrong Ltd. as a light tractor to replace the Light Dragons in service as gun towers. Fitted with a modified coil spring Horstmann suspension. The driver and crew member sat protected in an armoured compartment with folding bench seats provided for the auxiliary crew. Note the mount for the fitting of a front Vickers machine-gun.

Three-quarter front view of VA.D50 with the Vickers machine-gun in position.

One of the two experimental machines ordered by the War Office, this version was to become the Dragon, Light Mark III. The suspension had again undergone modification, being strengthened and fitted with a new type of idler wheel.

The second experimental machine, designated Carrier, Machine-Gun, with same type of chassis as that of Light Dragon Mk. III but with superstructure adapted for its rôle of machine-gun carrier. Note stowage bin and folding armoured side, and one of the methods of mounting the machine-gun.

use. In 1937 the vehicle was given a converted super-structure and called a General Service Vehicle. Around the top of the front gunner's compartment was fitted a grooved rail in which was enclosed a four-wheeled pinion mount carrying a Boys anti-tank rifle. The gunner was able to use this travelling mount to traverse the gun from the front to the side of the vehicle. A Bren LMG was carried in the normal machine-gun housing. This was an experimental prototype for the Scout Carrier.

In the next version of the machine-gun carrier the fundamental decision was taken to abandon the idea of carrying an independent machine-gun crew. The crew was reduced to three with just the front machine-gun, fitted with a small armoured shield, as armament. The folding sides were dispensed with and the left side of the superstructure was made a fixture forming a compartment for the third member of the crew. The right side of the vehicle was left open and was used for stowage. Designated Carrier, Machine-Gun No. 1, Mark I, a small batch of these machines was built in mild steel (WD Nos. T1828-T1840, T1921)

and introduced into service in 1936. Weight was 3·15 tons, armour was 10 mm. basis, engine was a Ford V-8 30 b.h.p. (liquid cooled). Six of these machines were later converted as pilot models for Carrier, Machine-Gun No. 2, Mark I, Cavalry Mark I, and Scout Mark I, while the remainder were used as instructional machines. Carrier, Machine-Gun No. 1, Mark I, was the prototype of the Machine-Gun and Bren carrier series.

Carrier, Machine-Gun No. 2, Mark I, appeared early in 1937. It was basically similar to No. 1, Mark I, but with a number of improvements. The Vickers machine-gun was mounted in an armoured housing on the left front, the engine air ducts which had been introduced on the No. 1, Mark I were modified, the steel boxes on the headlamps which the No. 1, Mark I had were removed, and a stowage box was put on the right side of the vehicle. The super-structure on the left side was improved and an armoured folding back-rest was fitted for the third man's protection and comfort. These vehicles were later equipped with the Bren LMG and/or with the

Carrier, Machine-Gun, No. 1, Mark I. Developed from the Experimental Machine-Gun Carrier, this was the prototype of the carriers of the Machine-Gun and Bren series. The view shows the armoured box front headlamps and the small armoured shield for the machine-gun.

Bren Carriers of 4th Indian Division resting on a desert road march in Egypt, May 1940.

Above: *Carrier, Cavalry Mark I. Picture shows the prototype vehicle of this series. As the personnel sat facing outwards, safety guards were provided to protect their legs; a hinged hand rail was also fitted.*

Top right: *Carrier, Machine-Gun No. 2, Mark I. View shows the redesigned front superstructure that was typical of the Bren and Universal Carriers.*

Bottom right: *Bren Carrier showing right side. Bren is on AA mounting, Boys anti-tank rifle in left front.*

Below: *Carrier, Scout Mark I, showing the pedestal-mounted Bren gun, with an alternative anti-aircraft mount. On this class of vehicle the built-up superstructure was reversed from that on the Bren Carrier.*

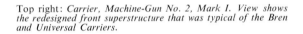
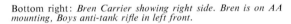

Boys anti-tank rifle which replaced the Vickers ·303 machine-gun and were re-worked to Bren carrier standards.

During 1938 one of these No. 2, Mark Is was fitted with a 2-pdr. mounted above the engine and arranged to fire to the front through a fixed shield. The ammunition was carried in racks on the off-side of the gun. The crew numbered four and the vehicle (T2335/FME890) weighed 3·9 tons.

After Vickers had built 43 No. 2 Mark I carriers (T2294-T2336) their work on this type of vehicle came to an end. The development work which went back to Carden's first experimental machine and the production of thousands of carriers which was to follow now passed to other firms. These included Thornycroft (which built No. 2 Mark Is numbered T2531-T2621), Morris (T2832-T2982), Aveling Barford (T3231-T3291), and Sentinel Wagon (T3716-T3915).

Carrier, Bren, No. 2, Mark I. Basically the Carrier, Machine-Gun, No. 2, Mark I, but adapted to carry the Bren light machine-gun.

THE BREN CARRIER

Built primarily to carry a medium machine-gun, the No. 2 Mark I carrier was modified late in 1938 to mount the Bren Light Machine-Gun, which was a Czech weapon modified by the small arms section of the Director of Artillery's Design Department. In their new guise, with improved armour protection and modified machine-gun housing, some of them mounting a Boys anti-tank rifle as well as or instead of a Bren, the carriers were designated Carriers, Bren, No. 2, Marks I and II.

Carrier, Bren, No. 2, Mark I. Three-quarter rear view showing the built-up left side.

Carrier, Armoured, 2-pdr. Conversion of the Carrier, Machine-Gun, as a self-propelled mount for a 2-pdr. gun. The view shows the ammunition racks on the right-hand side of the fixed armoured shield.

Scout Carriers of the British Expeditionary Force in France, September or October, 1939. Note left side open for stowage. Rear vehicle has base for wireless aerial fitted.

The weight of the carrier laden was 3·75 tons, the engine was a Ford V-8 85 b.h.p. (liquid cooled), speed was 30 m.p.h., and there was a crew of three. Bren carriers were issued to British infantry on the scale of ten per battalion and first saw action in France and the Low Countries in 1940. It was the beginning of a long battle experience for carriers.

The pilot model of the Bren carrier, a re-worked Carrier, Machine-Gun No. 2, Mark I, was converted by Thornycroft. Production was carried out by Thornycroft and other firms. WD numbers of the Bren carriers built were T2622-T2831, T2983-T3230, T3292-T3425, T4349-T4384, T4515-T4664, T4716-T5084, T5883-T5908—a total of 1,173. Production was also begun in Australia and New Zealand by 1941 and ended in 1943 after a total of 5,501 machines had been built in the Antipodes. The Australian version was welded, whereas the Bren carriers produced in Britain were of riveted construction.

SCOUT AND CAVALRY CARRIERS

Also introduced into service before the outbreak of World War II in 1939 were two variants of the Bren carrier. The first of these was the Carrier, Scout, Mark I. This was very similar to the machine-gun and Bren carriers but provision was made for carrying either an extra man or a No. 11 wireless set, the batteries for which were stored in a bullet-proof box housed on the rear axle cover plate. Wire screens were put over the openings in the rear of the engine cover to suppress interference. In the Scout Carriers the built-up superstructure was reversed (except in the pilot model T1834/CMM992). A Boys anti-tank rifle was mounted in the front and there were sockets in the rear compartment for the Bren gun. The

vehicle weighed 3·25 tons unladen. 647 were built, their WD numbers being T3966-T4165, T4485-T4514, T5255-T5550, T5616-T5756.

Scout carriers were designed for the Mechanized Divisional Cavalry regiments of which there were seven in the BEF in 1939-40. Each regiment had 28 light tanks and 44 scout carriers.

Major P. E. C. Hayman, Technical Adjutant of the 15th/19th King's Royal Hussars, which was one of the Mechanized Divisional Cavalry regiments with the BEF in 1939-40, described the scout carrier in the following somewhat uncomplimentary terms in an appendix to the regimental history (by Major G. Courage, Gale and Polden, 1949, p. 267):

"The scout carrier was a low-sided open box on tracks divided into three compartments. Across the full width of the front was a compartment for the driver and gunner or Commander; behind this, down the centre of the carrier, lay the engine, a 90-b.h.p. Ford V-8, and transmission on either side of which (and close against them) were narrow compartments for the rest of the crew which totalled four and, in the Troop Commander's carrier only, a wireless set which replaced one man. The carrier was thus cramped and uncomfortable, open to the elements, yet made desperately hot in summer, especially for the crew in the side compartments, by the engine. It was also even more vulnerable than the light tank: its armour, 10-mm. in front and 7-mm. elsewhere, was proof only against small arms fire and splinters and except at the front was too low to provide complete cover to the crew. It must, however, be remembered that the carrier was not intended to be used tactically as an AFV in armoured battles [although, perforce, it was often used as a close contact fighting vehicle in May-June 1940], nor indeed, apart from its lack of armour, could it do so successfully with the armament provided. This consisted of a ·303-

inch Bren LMG which could be fired either from a limited traverse mounting in the front compartment or from rests fitted in the sides and back of the carrier, and a Boys ·55-inch single shot anti-tank rifle which could be fired from the front compartment or the ground.

"Mechanically, perhaps the most interesting feature of the carrier was its steering system: for sharp turns one track could be slowed down and the other speeded up—a process that could be continued until one track was locked and a skid turn resulted—but for gradual turns both tracks could be disaligned by forcing the centre bogie wheels away from the hull to left or right."

While the scout carrier had the rôle of reconnaissance the second variant, the Carrier, Cavalry, Mark I, was designed to carry the dismounted personnel of the cavalry light tank regiments in the Mobile Division. With the evolution of the Mobile Division into the Armoured Division and the change in its organization the rôle for the Cavalry Carrier disappeared and only 50 were built (all by Nuffield, WD numbers T3916-T3965). The vehicle had seating accommodation for six men in addition to the driver and gunner, benches being fitted on either side behind the driver's compartment which was the only part that was armoured. A metal frame was fitted to carry a canvas hood for protection against the weather. The engine cover had sliding access doors and a louvre at the rear.

A third variant, which was virtually a variant of the scout carrier itself, appeared soon after September 1939. Known as Carrier, Armoured OP, Marks I and II, it was designed for use in the Royal Artillery as an armoured observation post. The principal modification from the scout carrier was an adjustable shutter in the machine-gun housing instead of the gun aperture. This was to allow protected vision for binoculars. The armoured OP carriers

had a No. 11 wireless set, a cable drum fitted at the rear, and a Bren LMG. Ninety-five were built (T5984-T6078).

THE UNIVERSAL CARRIER

The proliferation of versions of a basic machine to carry out a variety of rôles was clearly uneconomic. Consequently in 1940 a Universal type of carrier was produced for all purposes, any special requirements being met by minor modifications. Designated Carrier, Universal, Marks I, II and III, this remained the standard combat carrier throughout the remainder of the war.

The general construction of the hull of the Universal was a combination of both the Bren and Scout carriers, but with protection plates on both sides, the earlier machines only having armour plate on one side—right on the Scout, left on the Bren. The engine cover had bullet-proof plates on top only, the side plates being of mild steel and easily detachable. Angular mud deflectors were fitted on the front track guards, and there was a rear step on each side of the vehicle.

The carrier had a front compartment for the driver and gunner and two rear compartments, the right-hand one for the third member of the crew, the left-hand one for passengers or gear. The main weapon fitted in the gun-housing varied; it was either a ·303-inch Bren LMG or a ·55-inch Boys anti-tank rifle, or—common practice on Australian carriers—a Vickers ·303-inch medium machine-gun. When the Bren was fitted the vehicle was almost invariably, and erroneously, called a Bren carrier, retaining the old generic name.

In the front compartment the driver sat on the right with a car-type steering wheel mounted ver-

Carrier, Universal, Mark I.

Universal Carriers, Mark I, of 49th Division (the "Polar Bear" div.) in Iceland.

Universal Carriers with sand shields, Bren gun, and Boys anti-tank rifle, manned by Free Greek troops in the Western Desert.

Carrier, Universal, Mark II, showing stowage for a vehicle of the carrier platoon of an infantry battalion.

Universal Carrier No. 1, Mk I of Training Battalion, Grenadier Guards, Catterick, September, 1940.

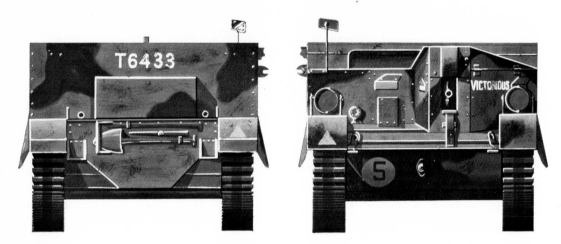

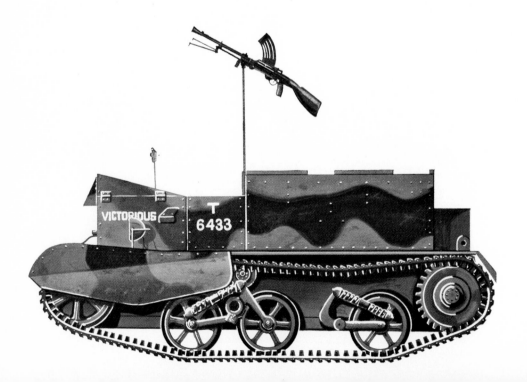

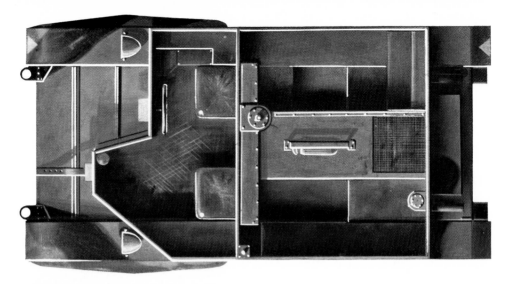

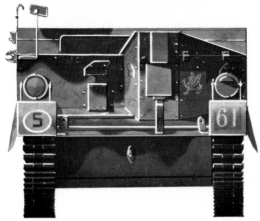

Universal Carrier No. 1, Mk I Battalion Commander's vehicle of 4th Battalion, Dorsetshire Regiment, 43rd (Wessex) Division, October, 1942.

rtin Lee
Limited.

Universal Mark IIs towing 6-pdr. anti-tank guns in Holland, October 1944.

Carrier, Armoured OP No. 1, Mark II. Three-quarter rear view showing standard rear fittings including cable reel.

Three-inch mortar Carrier, Mark II, with ·50 Browning machine-gun mounted in front.

tically in front of him. The gunner's compartment projected forward and provided alternative gun ports: the one in the centre of the face plate was for the Bren, while the hinged flap at the top could be dropped to allow the Boys to be mounted. When not in use the Boys anti-tank rifle was stowed longitudinally in the left rear compartment and the Bren in a rack in the gunner's compartment. Clips for rifles were also provided as well as a rack for a rifle or a spare Bren. There was an AA mounting at the front and rear of the right-hand rear compartment and in the centre of the left-hand rear compartment on the inside wall. Ammunition was carried in the front two compartments as well as in the right rear compartment and there was a box for two grenades in each of the compartments except the gunner's. Three fire extinguishers were carried: one on top of the engine cover, one on the inside of the front protection plate to the left of the gunner, and one on the division plate to the right of the driver. Various storage containers were fitted to the back of the carrier. The detailed stowage arrangement of equipment depended on the rôle the vehicle was to undertake, whether as a scout, a Bren, or an infantry carrier.

Universal carriers were often re-armed in the field to suit users' requirements. The weapons mounted included ·30-inch Browning MG, ·50-inch Browning MG, and German 20-mm. Solothurn anti-tank gun. These were usually mounted on the AA pintle sockets in the rear compartments. Light weapons like the PIAT were sometimes fitted in the front compartment. Some carrier units with Mark I Universals unofficially mounted a 2-inch mortar on the engine cover. This additional fire-power proved so useful

that a more satisfactory mounting was designed to be fitted in the gunner's compartment. The new mounting became a standard fitting in 1943 and was included in all Universals of Mark II standard.

The Mark II, as well as having a 2-inch mortar on the left side of the gunner's compartment, or a 4-inch smoke discharger, differed from the Mark I in various other particulars. It had a welded water-proofed hull, a new type of stowage arrangement, and a valance that enclosed the front quarter of the track run. Four foot steps, two on each side of the vehicle, were fitted. A spare wheel and tow rope were carried on the front and a large kit box across the rear.

As compared with the Mark I the Carrier, Universal, No. 1, Mark II, had a crew of four instead of three, weighed $4\frac{1}{4}$ against $3\frac{3}{4}$ tons, but its Ford V-8 engine still developed only the 85 b.h.p. of the Mark Is. Both had a speed of 30 m.p.h. and an armour basis of 7-10 mm. The Mark III (Carrier, Universal, No. 1, Mark III) had a welded hull like the Mark II, but with modified air inlet and engine cover. Crew, weight, b.h.p., speed, and armour basis were the same.

Universal carriers were modified for use as artillery armoured OP and command vehicles, as 3-inch mortar carriers (in 1942), and as Vickers medium machine-gun carriers (in 1943). Various marks and models of each were produced. Although occasionally the 3-inch mortar was assembled and fired from the front gunner's compartment, normal practice was for the mortar, bipod and base-plate to be secured at the rear of the vehicle with the ammunition stowed in racks inside and to be carried to the firing position where the crew dismounted and assembled the weapon

Carrier, 3-inch Mortar, No. 1, Mark I. Rear view showing the complete stowage of mortar and ammunition.

Canadian 3-inch mortar in action. Note Canadian Army prefix "CT" on carrier.

Universal Mark I (in foreground) mounting Bren gun and Boys anti-tank rifle. Compare with Bren Carriers at rear mounting medium machine-guns. Australians in the Western Desert.

Universal Carriers with track ways carried on sides advancing east of the Chindwin, December 1944.

for action. In the case of the vehicle's use as a medium machine-gun carrier the gun was sited behind the driver's compartment on a pedestal mount which was fitted on a strengthened engine cover. This position allowed an all-round field of fire. The gun could also be dismounted and fired from a tripod that was stowed on the vehicle. A crew of four was carried.

RONSON AND WASP

There was also a modified Universal for use as a Wasp flame-thrower. The first carrier flame-throwing equipment was the Ronson device. This was pressure-operated, with two 60-gallon flame-fuel tanks attached to the outside rear of a Universal. The flame-gun was mounted on top of the front gunner's superstructure and the flame fuel came through a flow pipe that ran along the left side of the vehicle. Because the fuel tanks were outside the carrier had room for its normal crew. The Ronson, however, was not accepted for service by the British War Office. The Canadian army on the other hand was interested and Ronsons

were produced in Canada. Twenty were sent from Canada to the Pacific theatre at the request of the U.S. Marine Corps who fitted them in M3A1 Light Tanks and renamed the equipment "Satan".

During 1941 and 1942 work by the Petroleum Warfare Department in Britain resulted in a new type of flame-thrower called the Wasp. There were three marks of Wasp Universal carrier:

Wasp Mk. I (FT, Transportable, No. 2, Mk. I). This had the two flame-fuel tanks (40 and 60 gallons), pressure bottles, and connected equipment stowed inside the carrier. The flame-projector, of new design, had a range of 80 to 100 yards and was mounted over the left front of the carrier. Normal armament was discarded and there was a crew of two. An order for 1,000 was placed by the War Office in September 1942; production was completed by November 1943. Mark Is were then relegated to training purposes while production was switched to the Mark II. Several Mark Is were used in flotation trials.

Wasp Mk. II (FT, Transportable, No. 2, Mk. II). The first prototype was tested in August 1943. It was markedly superior to the Mark I, the main

Ronson flame-throwing equipment under test.

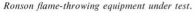

difference lying in the flame-projector which was of a completely new design and was mounted in the machine-gun housing of the carrier, making the vehicle less easily recognizable as a flame-thrower.

Wasp Mk. IIC (FT, Transportable, No. 2, Mk. IIC). "C" stood for "Canada" because the IIC was developed by the Canadian army and was first used by Canadian units in August 1944 during the battle of Falaise. The IIC differed from the II in that only one flame fuel container of 75 gallons was carried, mounted outside at the rear of the vehicle. This left room for a third crew member with a Bren LMG or a 2-inch mortar. The flame-gun was as in the Mk. II and mounted in the same place.

The Canadians had designed their Mk. IIC so that it could fulfil the rôle of a normal carrier as well as being a flame-thrower, and they accepted the disadvantage of the exterior-mounted fuel tank to attain this. Experience showed they were right. After the production programme of the Mk. II was completed in June 1944 all production was switched to the Mk. IIC. Some local conversions were also made in 21 Army Group by mounting the Mk. II's 60-gallon tank at the rear. Plastic armour was also fitted to the fronts of Mk. IIC Wasp Carriers in 21 Army Group for additional protection against German 7·92 mm. AP shells and 20 mm. fire.

By the beginning of 1945 the Wasp Mk. IIC had replaced the Mk. II in 21 Army Group. Most infantry battalions were issued with six. By the end of the war it had been accepted as the standard British carrier-borne flame-thrower. Three Wasps were sent to Russia for evaluation in February 1945.

As well as being modified as armoured OPs and to carry Wasps, mortars, or medium machine-guns, Universals were used in a number of specialized rôles, such as mine-clearing, demolition, and as ambulances in armoured units. There were a variety of miscellaneous types, some of which are illustrated. Many of these were experimental.

Close-up of the Wasp Mk. II flame projector.

Universal Carrier in Italy fitted with ·50 Browning machine-gun in rear compartment.

NORTH AMERICAN AND AUSTRALASIAN PRODUCTION

Used initially in the Western Desert and subsequently in all campaigns in all theatres of war, Universal carriers were supplied to all Allied armies (Russia receiving 200) except the U.S.A. Carriers formed the greater part of the vehicle strength of the Reconnaissance Corps regiments which were raised after the 1940 campaign to relieve the mechanized cavalry of the reconnaissance rôle in British infantry divisions. These regiments each had 63 carriers and 28 Humber scout cars. Carriers also equipped the support companies in British infantry rifle battalions, and there were 109 carriers in the 1940-41 type British armoured division of which each of the two motor battalions had 44.

The demand for the Universal carrier far exceeded the numbers that could be produced in the United Kingdom. Production was therefore also undertaken by Australia, which supplied its own army and sent 1,500 to China; by Canada, which built 33,987, supplying more than one fifth of British carrier needs; by New Zealand where a few were built for home use; and by the United States where many of the carrier engines were built. Both Canada and the United States also carried out experimental work aimed at designing a more satisfactory vehicle, for it was generally accepted that the Universal, useful as it was, was overloaded and under-powered.

The different models of engines and Universals built in Canada and the United States were:

Carrier, Universal, No. 2, Mk. I—similar to No. 1, Mk. I, but with Ford V-8, 85 b.h.p. GAEA engine built in U.S.A. for Allied use.

Carrier, Universal, No. 2A, Mk. I—as for No. 1, Mk. I, but with Ford V-8, 85 b.h.p. GAE engine. built in U.S.A. for Allied use.

Carrier, Universal, No. 3, Mk. I*—as for No. 1, Mk. I, but with Ford V-8, 85 b.h.p. engine. Built in Canada.

Carrier, Universal, No. 2, Mk. II—as for No. 1, Mk. II, but with a Ford V-8, 85 b.h.p. GAE engine built in U.S.A. for Allied use.

Carrier, Universal, No. 2A, Mk. II—as for No. 1, Mk. II, but with Ford V-8, 85 b.h.p. GAEA engine built in U.S.A. for Allied use.

Carrier, Universal, No. 3, Mk. II*—as for No. 1, Mk. II, but with Ford V-8, 85 b.h.p. engine. Built in Canada.

Carrier, Universal, No. 2, Mk. III—as for No. 1, Mk. III, but with Ford V-8, 85 b.h.p. GAE engine built in U.S.A. for Allied use.

Carrier, Universal, No. 2A, Mk. III—as for No. 1, Mk. III, but with Ford V-8, 85 b.h.p. GAEA engine built in U.S.A. for Allied use.

Carrier, Universal, No. 3, Mk. III*—as for No. 1, Mk. III, but with Ford V-8, 85 b.h.p. engine. Built in Canada.

These vehicles were also adapted to the rôles of armoured OPs, medium machine-gun carriers, flame-throwing and mortar carriers.

The Canadians also built 213 Carriers, 2 Pdr Equipped. These were Universals Mk. I* and Mk. II* modified to allow the mounting of a 2-pdr. with necessary ammunition and stowage. The ammunition was stowed along the sides and the front of the division plate. The engine cover was re-designed to provide adequate clearance for recoil. These carriers were used for training in Canada.

The Universals built in Australia for the Australian army were modified in detail to suit local conditions. The various components of the carriers, except the power units which were imported from North America, were made by engineering sub-contractors and the carriers were then assembled in Australian state-owned workshops.

There were three Australian local pattern carriers:

Carrier, Machine-Gun, Local Pattern, No. 1, was basically similar to the British Bren gun carrier in appearance but it had welded armour and other minor differences.

Universal Carrier, MG, Local Pattern, No. 2, had the Universal superstructure, and was fitted with 1938-39 Ford heavy duty commercial truck-type rear axles. Instead of having large stowage lockers on the right side as in Local Pattern No. 1, No. 2 had them at the rear.

Universal Carrier, MG, Local Pattern, No. 2A, was No. 2 with 1940 Ford heavy duty truck-type rear axles.

The Australians also built a Carrier, 2 Pdr, Tank Attack, and a Carrier, 3-inch Mortar. In both the weapon was fired from a turntable which allowed a 360 degree traverse and was in the rear of the vehicle, the engine being moved to the left of the driver. The Universal carrier, Local Pattern, was also used as a mortar carrier, the weapon being mounted on and fired from the top of the engine compartment. It could also, of course, be dismounted and fired from the ground, as could the mortar in the Carrier, 3-inch Mortar.

The carriers built in New Zealand were also modified to suit local conditions and the two models (Carrier, MG, Local Pattern, No. 1 and No. 2) were identical in virtually all respects to those built in Australia, which supplied the working drawings and machine-tools. Canada provided the Ford engines and the New Zealand State Railways workshops were the carriers' builders. Only 40 of No. 1 were built and both these and the more numerous No. 2 model were used almost exclusively in New Zealand, the New Zealand forces overseas using Australian-built carriers.

Universal Carrier, MG, Local Pattern, No. 2, Australian-built, all welded and Australian manned.

Praying Mantis in travelling position.

Carrier, Medium Machine-Gun No. 3, Mark I. Canadian built
Universal Carrier adapted to the MMG rôle.

Universal Carrier fitted for wading with heightened hull dis-
embarking on Ramree Island, Arakan, January 1945.

Universal Carrier fitted with PIAT in front.

Praying Mantis elevated for firing and revealing the reason for
its name from its resemblance to the insect. Constructed from
Universal Carrier parts, the idea was to use natural cover to
best advantage by raising the armoured driving and fighting
compartment to maximum of 12 ft. above the ground. Design
work and testing extended intermittently from 1937 to 1944 but
the machine was never used operationally.

Universal Carrier with Kid explosive device for demolition of
small concrete walls. The name "Kid" was a diminutive from
the similar "Goat" device used with the Churchill tank.

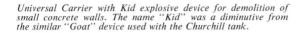

Carrier, Tracked, Personnel Carrying. The Loyd Carrier as a personnel carrier.

THE T16

The experimental work carried out in the United States to improve on the Universal resulted in the T16. This was basically the Universal with a larger chassis, four bogie wheels and a larger engine. The original vehicle was designated Cargo Carrier T16 but was re-designated Universal Carrier T16 in order to be uniform with British nomenclature. It was designed in 1942 partly for British requirements and partly for United States army operations against the Japanese. The British were supplied with 2,625 T16s in 1944 and 604 the following year. The T16 was not considered entirely satisfactory by the British General Staff in spite of its improvements over the Universal in certain particulars because, at least until a late stage in the war, it was mechanically unreliable and furthermore had a payload even smaller than that of the Universal. A few T16s were used operationally in S.E.A.C. at the end of the war.

A modified version, the T16E2, was built late in 1945. This had altered bogie spacing to reduce track wear.

THE WINDSOR

Canada's experimental work on carriers resulted in a much more promising design. This was the Windsor, produced in 1943 by the Ford Motor Co. with considerable backing from the Canadian Department of Munitions and Supply. Despite the fact that 90 per

Universal Mark I during the advance into Syria, 1941. Manned by Australians, it mounts a Vickers machine-gun, a Boys anti-tank rifle, and a Bren LMG.

cent of its components were from the Loyd carrier (see below), the Windsor's design was also based on that of the Universal, though it was larger and more powerful. It was specifically intended to replace the Loyd as a towing vehicle but it proved so satisfactory in its early trials that serious consideration was given to using it in the rôles of the Universal.

After the design had been approved and production begun at the rate of 500 a month mechanical troubles disclosed themselves. As a result the Windsor was only in operational use in small numbers by the end of the war in 1945. It was used in 21 Army Group as a towing vehicle for the 6-pdr. anti-tank gun. It is reported that "the project was not pursued by the General Staff with very great energy because, when it was first considered, the demand for carriers in general was too great to allow use of production capacity on an unproven design."

THE LOYD CARRIER

In 1940, the year in which the Universal was introduced, a second new carrier was also produced. It was built by the firm of Vivian Loyd & Co. Captain Loyd, of Carden-Loyd fame, left Vickers, where he had been engaged in the foreign marketing side of the business, after the death of his close colleague, Sir John Carden, in an airplane accident in 1935. The new carrier which he designed and which bore his name was intended by him to be suitable for a variety of rôles, including the carriage of weapons ranging from machine-guns to anti-tank guns, the transport of troops and stores, and even as a one-man fighting machine—the "armoured skirmisher" idea revived yet again! The chassis was composed largely of Ford commercial vehicle parts to assure cheap and rapid production, but this had the disadvantage that it lacked mechanical reliability and was inferior to that of the Universal.

Unfortunately for Loyd, the demand for light tracked vehicles was limited when his new carrier made its appearance and initially it was used by the British army only as a troop carrier. In this rôle it had the great advantage over the Cavalry carrier of being able to carry eight men. It was tested as a 2-pdr. anti-tank SP, but was considered less suitable than the portee vehicle in which the anti-tank gun was mounted, facing the rear, on the open back of a four-wheeled lorry. Nevertheless, its importance grew. It was later adopted as a towing vehicle, thus taking the place of the pre-war dragon that had been discarded in favour of the four-wheel drive tractor. When the portee vehicle too proved unsuccessful, as well as the four-wheel drive tractor, for giving close support to AFVs, the Loyd came into its own. Its major importance arose from the urgent requirement for large numbers of mobile anti-tank guns, especially in the Western Desert fighting. As well as this the Loyd was the only general utility carrier available and was employed in many ancillary rôles, especially cable-laying and for carrying slave batteries which were of supreme importance for AFVs which ran their own batteries flat on constant wireless watch.

As a result of the demand for the Loyd as a towing vehicle for the 2-pdr. and later the 6-pdr., a need arose

Carrier, Universal, T.16. Designed and built in the United States, this was an attempt to develop a more satisfactory vehicle than the Universal Carrier. The principal changes in design were the use of the controlled differential steering system, Ford Mercury engine, two two-wheeled bogies on each side, refinement of the track and suspension, and a lengthened welded hull structure.

Right: Carrier, Windsor. Built in Canada and based on the design of the Universal Carrier, this machine incorporated 90 per cent of Loyd components. Like the T.16, the Windsor was a much bigger vehicle than the Universal, incorporating a four-wheeled bogie suspension very similar to that used on the Loyd Carrier. This rear view of the vehicle shows the towing attachment.

Carrier, Tracked, Cable Layer, Mechanical—one of the variants of the Loyd Carrier. This three-quarter front view shows the three cable drums mounted on the front and the cable laying unit mounted in the centre of the rear compartment. Mounted on the side are the linesmen's poles and ladders.

for its load capacity and tractive ability to be improved, for both were considered inadequate for a gun tower. Work was therefore undertaken to develop several improved models of the Loyd during 1943, but due to the continued demand for the vehicle as a 6-pdr. gun tractor in quantity its mechanical weakness was perforce accepted and no modifications were allowed that would delay production of some 10,000 vehicles.

While the Universal could have undertaken the Loyd's rôle as a gun tower, it was decided that it should stick to its own rôles except in emergency. To provide for these emergencies the Stacey towing attachment was fitted to all Universal carriers (except the OP version) built in 1943, thus enabling them to tow the 6-pdr. over short distances. The troops themselves preferred the Loyd to the Universal as a tower because its steering and handling were simpler. The training of drivers was consequently simpler too.

The limitation of carriers to the two basic types, the Universal and the Loyd, considerably reduced production problems, especially as there were components common to both vehicles. Production of the Loyd was also undertaken by the Ford Motor Co. of Canada. Some designs for airborne tanks grew out of the Loyd carrier but were not adopted.

THE OXFORD (CT20)

The Windsor carrier at a later stage in its development was regarded merely as a stop-gap until a long-term replacement for the Universal matured. This intended replacement was the Oxford—officially designated Carrier, Track, CT20 (Carrier, Oxford, Mark I). The Oxford was the last of the series of carriers developed from the early machine-gun carrier of 1934, and of which the "family characteristic" was the Horstmann suspension.

The Oxford was to replace the Loyd and the Universal as an all-purpose carrier. In the event only a few were made and they were tested at the very end of the war for towing 6-pdr. and 17-pdr. anti-tank guns and as a 3-inch mortar carrier. The Oxford was an open armoured box with a double floor as a protection against mines. It had improved Horstmann suspension, weighed just over 7 tons, was 14 ft. 9 in. long, 7 ft. 6 in. wide, and 5 ft. 7 in. high. It was powered by a Cadillac V-8, 110 b.h.p., liquid cooled engine, had a top speed of 38 m.p.h., and a range of 126 miles. Its armour basis was 20 mm.

With the demise of the Oxford, the future of carriers, after some hesitancy with the FV.401 Cambridge, turned at last in the late 1950s to the essential armoured personnel carriers of today.

A.F.V. Series Editor: DUNCAN CROW

CARRIER DETAILS

	M.G., No. 1 Mark I	Bren, No. 2 Marks I & II	Scout Mark I	Universal Mark I
Weight (tons and cwt.)				
Fully laden	3 3	3 16	3 16	3 16
Unladen	2 17	3 5	3 5	3 5
Dimensions (feet and inches)				
Height	4 8	4 9	5 2½	5 2½
Length	11 6	12 0	12 0	12 0
Width	6 9	6 9	6 9	6 9
Width, track centres	5 2¼	5 2¼	5 2¼	5 2¼
Width, outer edge of tracks	5 11¾	5 11¾	5 11¾	5 11¾
Performance				
Ground clearance	0 8	0 8	0 8	0 8
Trench	4 6	4 6	4 6	4 6
Speed	30 m.p.h.	30 m.p.h.	30 m.p.h.	30 m.p.h.
Fuel capacity (gallons)	20	20	20	20

Carrier, Tracked. C.T.20 (Carrier, Oxford, Mark I). The last of the series that was descended from the Experimental Machine-Gun Carrier. The view is of the Oxford in the rôle of Mortar Carrier. Note the mortar in the front compartment and the base plate carried on the front of the machine.   (Imperial War Museum—as are all the photographs in this Profile)

1921 Rolls-Royce. These cars were 1920 Rolls-Royce chassis with Indian pattern body as shown here. Instead of an open box at back the armour was brought down to the rear of chassis. Two Vickers machine-guns are mounted for maximum fire-power. The alternative was to have one facing forward and the other to the rear on opposite sides.
(R.A.C. Tank Museum)

Armoured Car Development in the Inter-War Years

by
Major-General N. W. Duncan

THE armoured car story between the wars is that of slow and reluctant realization that commercial and military requirements rarely march hand-in-hand. Only a car designed to meet the peculiar circumstances in which it is required to operate can carry out its task properly; this is unfortunately a costly business owing to the limited market. One of the main attractions of the armoured car on a commercial chassis is its low cost. Country after country fell into the trap and tried to make do before resorting to specially built cars to obtain the necessary performance with the weight of armour and equipment that had to be carried if the armoured car was to carry out its diverse rôles with success.

The evolution from the 4×2 cars with which Great Britain ended the First World War and the 4×4 vehicles that came into service from 1939 onwards can be divided into three phases:
  (a) The adaptation of ordinary commercial vehicles.
  (b) The use of specialized 6-wheeled chassis adapted from commercial practice.
  (c) The provision of special vehicles for the armoured car rôle.

THE EMPLOYMENT AND ROLES OF THE ARMOURED CAR

Armoured cars had carried out some spectacular operations and done much hard slogging work during the First World War and they had won for themselves a place in the post-war army. They were however a

little like a Hollywood starlet, spotted and engaged by a talent scout but uncertain either of the parts to be played or even of the clothes to be worn on stage.

Some ideas about their employment emerged in the early '20s culled and consolidated from the various tasks allotted to them in Ireland, India, the Middle East, with the Experimental Mechanized Force in 1927/28 and seasoned with experiences during the late war. From all this experience it appeared that they might profitably be used,

in peace, (a) For the control of large sparsely inhabited areas.
          (b) For the control of civil disturbances.
in war,   (c) For reconnaissance.
          (d) For exploitation of enemy rear areas after his defences had been penetrated.
          (e) For independent raids.
          (f) To hold a line of observation or to guard a threatened flank.

Armoured cars were used in Iraq from 1920 onwards to control the country. This was accomplished by a series of patrols—virtually flag-showing. The columns were often supported by air and eventually the Tank Corps armoured car companies which had inaugurated the patrols were replaced by R.A.F. units to make the co-ordination of air and ground operations easier to accomplish.

The Egyptian frontier was continually patrolled by armoured cars operating across the Western Desert as far as the limitations of equipment would allow. They

Front view of Peerless armoured car in the R.A.C. Tank Museum.
(Duncan Crow)

Rear view of Peerless. Ex-Austin armoured car twin-turretted bodies were fitted on Peerless chassis. These were too long for them and the side members protruded beyond the armour plate. Despite its appearance the Peerless was staunch and long-lived.
(Duncan Crow)

were also used by the Sudan Defence Force to keep areas of country which were suitable for their use under observation. In Ireland in 1920 armoured cars were in constant demand as escorts to convoys; clashes were frequent, with operations greatly hampered by the lack of cross country ability in the Rolls-Royce and Peerless cars which were used there.

In Shanghai, Palestine, Egypt and India armoured cars were continually used in civil disturbances. They were suitable for patrolling restless areas but they were seriously handicapped in crowds since the use of their only defensive weapon, the machine-gun, inevitably involved heavy casualties among demonstrators if they were to be kept at a distance from the cars. When they were not, as happened in Peshawar, cars could be rushed suddenly, pushed over by sheer weight of numbers and subsequently burnt at the mob's leisure. Following this incident the cars were electrified so that anyone touching the armour plate would receive a severe shock; but this was only a palliative and disregarded the fundamental unsuitability of a wheeled vehicle coming into close contact with a hostile populace.

Armoured cars were used as the spearhead of the British Force sent into the Saar in 1935. Even though

Rear end of Peerless showing protruding chassis.
(Duncan Crow)

mechanical faults and bad design features hampered their performance they demonstrated their suitability for long-range far-reaching operations ahead of, or to the flank of, an advancing force. At this time their performance in either of these rôles was apt to be unpredictable owing to lack of communications: many a promising exercise was ruined by the sudden arrival of armoured cars before operations had really begun, for in addition to the secrecy imposed by lack of wireless facilities the speed of the cars was liable to be considerably underestimated.

So far so good: the possible rôles which the armoured car starlet might be called on to undertake began to become clear. Her clothes, in the shape of the actual vehicles, were quite a different story. The performance of an armoured car in any of the tasks enumerated above depended on its mechanical capability and ability. Capability was fairly easily solved and depended on the elimination of the weak design points which showed up as mechanical failures in use. Faulty parts were redesigned and replaced and mechanical breakdowns became rarer and rarer. Ability was quite a different story and depended on the design of the car. Any 4×2 car carrying the extra weight of an armoured body was bound to be hampered on any but very good cross country going. Equally a car might often expect to find its military task difficult of accomplishment while its only armament was a machine-gun. The advent of the anti-tank machine-gun—the ·5-in. Vickers—lessened the problem so far as hostile armoured cars were concerned but offered no solution to an enemy post which had been dug in, nor to the problem of holding a defensive flank. Finally the problem of communications was a very real one: without wireless, information could only be transmitted by detaching cars with the consequent delay in getting messages through and the depletion of the available force. Signalling lamps and heliographs used to be issued in early days but the chances of using visual communications satisfactorily were slim at the best.

The history of the inter-war years armoured cars is therefore intimately bound up with three problems:

(a) The increase of cross country capacity.

(b) The evolution of armament.

(c) The development and application of wireless.

It is a salutary thought that in 1914 the R.N.A.S. armoured cars were supported by their own lorries carrying 6-pdr. guns. It was not until 1963, when the Saladin armoured car came into the service, that regiments carrying out this rôle had an armoured car with HE capacity in its main armament.

ADAPTING COMMERCIAL CHASSIS FOR ARMOURED CAR WORK

At the end of the First World War there were three types of armoured car in extensive use together with a miscellaneous collection of other machines. The three principals were Peerless cars in Ireland, Rolls-Royce in Ireland, Iraq, Palestine, Egypt and India, and a number of Model T Fords in Light Car patrols in the Middle East.

India played a prominent part in the development of armoured cars in the early part of the period under discussion. The Government were firm believers in the value of armoured cars which they had used extensively during the war, both for the control of civil disturbances in the interior of the country and on the North-West Frontier. Provision had been made for the inclusion of armoured cars in India's post-war army. However, after prolonged discussion with the British Government India agreed to accept nine armoured car companies of the Royal Tank Corps on their establishment and these arrived in the country from 1920 onwards. A heterogeneous collection of cars had survived from the war and to reinforce them some Rolls-Royce 1920 pattern cars were ordered and fitted with an Indian designed body which differed materially from the old Admiralty pattern body that had been used on all Rolls-Royce cars up to that date.

The Indian pattern body had no open box at the back; instead the armour was brought down to the rear of the chassis. Side doors were provided as well as double doors at the back and a dome-shaped turret with ball mountings for four unarmoured Vickers guns replaced the old cylindrical pattern. A cupola with all-round independent traverse which could be completely opened when required was provided for the commander. The engine compartment and front radiator doors were amply provided with louvred openings for ventilation and the whole of the interior of the body

A famous Rolls-Royce armoured car—No. 2641 as originally armoured and armed in India in 1915. It was a Silver Ghost standard 40/50 h.p. built in 1911 and belonged to the Rajah of Ticca who presented it to the Government at the beginning of the First World War. (R.A.C. Tank Museum)

was lined with asbestos to render life tolerable for the crews; even so the temperature inside a car standing in the sun on riot duty would rise to 140–150 degrees, not perhaps the ideal conditions for cool calculated thinking!

For one reason or another, probably capital cost, the Rolls-Royces were abandoned by the Indian Government who replaced them with Crossley armoured cars adapted from a truck chassis mounting the Indian pattern armoured body. These cars, 4×2, had a 50 h.p. Crossley engine, 4-cylinder, with a four-speed truck gearbox with straight cut pinions. NAP (normal air pressures) tyres, which had been used in India since the days of the Jeffrey Quad, were fitted and gave an uncomfortable ride, despite their description as semi-solid. The Crossley was not popular with armoured car crews, who found it underpowered and underbraked with the weight of the armoured body. For some reason the foot brake acted on the transmission while the hand brake operated the rear wheel shoes; there were no front wheel brakes and handling these cars especially in the wet on the roads of the N.W. Frontier could be a hair-raising business.

In 1939/40 the Crossleys were scrapped after continuous service since 1923. Their armoured bodies were transferred to Chevrolet 4×2 truck chassis. These vehicles, with ample power and large size pneumatic tyres, had a much better cross country performance than the Crossley. They proved extremely useful, not only in civil disturbances during the war years but also in the campaigns fought on the frontiers of India from 1939 to 1945.

1920 Rolls-Royce in the R.A.C. Tank Museum. Sides of bonnet have been removed to display engine to visitors. The towering turret and "Bishop's Mitre" of a Mk. II Lanchester can be seen beyond the Rolls. (Duncan Crow)

Disc wheels and turret shape were identifying features of the 1920 Rolls-Royce. (Duncan Crow)

Car No. 2641 fitted with a new armoured body—the Indian pattern type—designed by the 1st (HQ) Armoured Motor Brigade and built by the Gun Carriage Factory at Jubbulpore 1919-20. Soon afterwards the car was used as a bridal coach at the wedding of the 1st Brigade's adjutant and was consequently named Wedding Bells. It remained in service until 1940.
(The Tanks)

Chevrolet armoured cars of the 13th (D.C.O.) Lancers, Indian army, formed up for the entry into Teheran, September 17, 1941, when British and Russian contingents entered the city simultaneously. (R.A.C. Tank Museum)

Chevrolet 4×2 on patrol. These cars had the Crossley armoured bodies on Chevrolet truck chassis. (R.A.C. Tank Museum)

1924 pattern Rolls-Royce. Differences from 1920 pattern were new turret shape with cupola, vision slits in hull, side doors, different wheels—all seen in this photograph of a Rolls of A Squadron, 11th Hussars, in Palestine 1936.
(The Eleventh at War)

Crossley 4×2 showing bonnet raised, front radiator doors, vizors, side and rear doors open, and searchlight on cupola. These cars were adapted from a truck chassis with the Indian pattern armoured body.
(R.A.C. Tank Museum)

Vickers-Guy 6 × 4 on test at the Royal Tank Corps Centre, Ahmednagar, India. (R.A.C. Tank Museum)

At home Morris entered the armoured car field in 1935 and produced an experimental armoured car based on their 25 h.p. truck chassis. It had a square rotatable turret mounting a ·5 and ·303 VMG side by side in a Mark V light tank mantlet. The body was an adaptation of the Indian pattern armoured car body, squarer in outline, which gave the driver a poor view of the road owing to the length of the bonnet in front of him.

Morris also produced a reconnaissance car. This had an open topped turret which mounted a Bren LMG and a Boys A/Tk rifle side by side. Great play was made because these weapons could be dismounted from the turret at need and handled from the ground, but crews hankered for the fire-power of the Vickers and in any case were trained to fight with their weapons from the car and not from the ground. The smaller size of the Morris was an advantage by comparison with the bulk of the 6-wheeled armoured cars which had become the standard equipment of armoured car regiments at that time. Apart from that it was disappointing that the Morris should show no new features and should follow such a conventional pattern of design. These cars were used by the 12th Lancers in France in 1939/40 and were also used in the Western Desert.

INTRODUCTION OF THE 6-WHEELED ARMOURED CAR

In the post-war years considerable developments were taking place in the civilian world designed to improve the cross country performance of the ordinary 4×2 car or lorry. M. André Citroen had made an impressive start to this new phase when he crossed the Sahara

desert with a convoy of Citroen Kegresse cars. These were the ordinary Citroen 4×2 cars with the rear wheels replaced by a self-contained tracked assembly incorporating a rubber track with a driving sprocket, an idler wheel for adjusting tension, and small bogies to distribute pressure. His success led to a spate of semi-tracked and 6-wheeled cars and lorries. Every variation of fixed and floating axle was developed for lorries. By 1927 a 6-wheeled lorry with two semi-rigid back axles was being marketed as a commercial proposition and in 1928 the Indian Government ordered enough Vickers-Guy 6-wheeled armoured cars to equip the 10th Armoured Car Company RTC then stationed at Lahore.

The Vickers-Guy armoured cars were very big; they weighed approximately 9 tons; they were over 20 feet long and were powered by a 120 h.p. engine. They had a standard 4-speed gearbox with an auxiliary 2-speed box to give low ratios and had the same turret as the Crossley armoured car on a body that was longer to suit the extended chassis. The cross country performance was quite good but the cars were so big that they were entirely unsuitable for the narrow tracks and acute turns that were encountered around Quetta where the company moved on to. The local bridges could not stand up to the weight and the cars proved so cumbersome that they were withdrawn from service in 1934.

Two cavalry regiments in the British army were converted to an armoured car rôle in 1929. The 11th Hussars, who were then stationed in Tidworth, were issued with Lanchester armoured cars, while the 12th Lancers, who were then in Cairo, took over the 1920 pattern Rolls-Royce cars of the 3rd and 5th Armoured Car Companies of the Royal Tank Corps.

Austin 7, Vickers-Guy 6×4, and Crossley 4×2 with its cupola open—all three types of car were in use by R.T.C. Armoured Car Companies in India about 1929.
(R.A.C. Tank Museum)

The Lanchesters were 6-wheeled cars with two driven semi-rigid axles. They were armed with three machine-guns, a ·303 and a ·5 in the turret and another ·303 alongside the driver, so that they could operate effectively against other armoured cars of the time. Two versions of the Lanchester were produced with only minor variations between them. They suffered from the same disadvantages as the Guy; they weighed $7\frac{1}{2}$ tons, were 21 feet long like the Guy and stood 10 feet high. They were hard to manoeuvre in confined spaces and the long bonnet gave the driver a very inadequate view of the road. They had quite a good cross country performance but they were very hard to hide on account of their bulk, a serious failing in time of war and in view of the tasks they were likely to have to undertake.

The 12th Lancers who had exchanged station with the 11th Hussars took the Lanchester cars to the Saar in 1935 as part of the joint Anglo-French force sent there to supervise the elections to determine the future nationality of the region. Trouble was experienced with the cooling on this occasion but the trouble was later rectified. These cars were phased out of the service before the start of the Second World War but they were used in the Malayan peninsula before this was overrun by the Japanese.

Crossleys entered the 6-wheeled field with two experimental prototypes, D2E1 and D2E2 in 1930. Domed turrets of the pattern fitted to the Indian armoured car body were used on these machines and they were followed by three more experimental cars which had cylindrical turrets similar to those which were being tried out on the first light tanks. They only mounted one machine-gun and turret room was very cramped. The final version of the Crossley used a Light Tank Mark IIA turret but still had only one MG

Prototype Lanchester 6×4 D1E1 (ML8688) designed in 1929 with single machine-gun in turret and no cupola. There is a second machine-gun alongside the driver.
(R.A.C. Tank Museum)

in the turret; a second one was mounted alongside the driver. The earlier twin rear wheels were replaced by large diameter single tyres which were used all round. The Crossley was a little smaller than the other 6-wheeled armoured cars with a length of 17 feet and a height of 7 feet; but even then it was big to conceal and cumbersome to handle. Crossleys were tried out by the R.A.F. in Iraq and by the Royal Tank Corps companies in India. They were not very successful in either theatre. Under-gunned and under-powered—50 b.h.p. for a weight of 6 tons—they compared unfavourably on all grounds except that of silence in movement with the light tanks which were being developed concurrently with them.

EVOLUTION OF THE SPECIALIST ARMOURED CAR

This phase is concerned with the appearance of the armoured car specially built to fulfil that rôle and, except for use of suitable components, not an adaptation of some vehicle already on the civilian market. By 1934 armoured car designers were beginning to exhaust most of the tricks in the adaptation of commercial chassis for armoured car work. They had reinforced springs, fitted extra petrol tanks and twin wheels, reinforced chassis members, and provided lower gear ratios to compensate for the extra load. None of these devices had radically improved the cross country performance of the 4×2 chassis and resource was then had to the 6-wheeled chassis which basically conformed to current civilian practice. General mobility was improved at the cost of unacceptable bulk and it became evident that no adaptation of a standard vehicle was likely to provide an acceptable solution to the armoured car problem.

The first specialist armoured cars in Britain were two Hungarian vehicles: they were Straussler 4×4 cars designed by Mr. N. Straussler, who later was responsible for the design of the DD tank, the first really practicable solution to the problem of making a tank float. The Straussler cars were fast and had a good cross country performance, but they were not considered entirely satisfactory from the gunnery angle. A number of trials were carried out with these two machines but no action was taken as a result.

Another specialist vehicle now enters the scene, the scout car. When cavalry regiments were first mechanized they were given the Austin Buckboard. This was an Austin 7 with no wind-screen, two bucket seats and a wooden platform over the rest of the chassis. The contraption was so light that it could be manhandled out of trouble and it proved very useful as a fast speedy scout. Based on its successful use the Mechanization Board issued a specification for a small armoured vehicle with a crew of two, armed with a machine-gun and having 4-wheel drive to give it a high degree of mobility.

Alvis produced the Dingo in answer to this specification, a car with a tubular backbone, a rear-mounted engine on one side of the car, and 4-wheel drive with the propeller shafts inside the tubular backbone. It had 14-mm. of armour and all round traverse for the machine-gun. The name caught the popular fancy and for a long time Dingo was used generically, both in the Army and in the outside world, to denote a scout car—which sometimes caused considerable confusion.

Vickers-Guy armoured cars on patrol in India.
(R.A.C. Tank Museum)

The Dingo was followed by another version built by BSA. This had 4-wheel drive and 4-wheel steering as well. A 6-cylinder engine with a fluid flywheel and an epicyclic gearbox took the drive through a transfer box, which incorporated a reverse available on all gears, and thence through separate shafts to each wheel. The short wheel base and all wheel steering made it tricky to drive and the steerable rear wheels were later discontinued. The BSA version, which was cheaper than the Alvis, was selected for production and was built by the Daimler company.

Concurrently with the Dingo, other tests were being carried out on two Straussler armoured cars. These differed considerably from the earlier versions and from each other. One had two Ford 3·6 litre engines, disposed on either side of the car between the wheel arches, and each driving a front and back wheel. Any variation in power output must have produced some striking directional variations or deviations but no detailed record of their performance exists. The other car was powered by a 4-litre Alvis engine with optional 4-wheel drive and an alternative steering position for use when in reverse gear. Brakes were operated by air pressure, the tubular backbone being used as an air reservoir. One VMG was mounted in each version and both carried 8-mm. of armour.

These Straussler cars were tested against a 4×4 armoured car built by Alvis and also against a Steyr Daimler-Puch which was an Austrian production also built round a tubular backbone but fitted with air-cooled engines. These trials were very detailed and thorough and aroused a great deal of interest. The performance of all competitors was considerably better than that displayed in the 1934 trials and as a result 4-wheel drive was not only recognized as a

Crossley 6×4 D2E1 with twin rear wheels.

Lanchester 6×4 Mark I 1929 with cylindrical cupola, two VMGs (·5 and ·303) mounted coaxially in the geared traverse turret, a third VMG alongside the driver, and radiator louvres modified from prototype design. There were also Marks IA, II and IIA which differed in cooling, carburation, armament and cupola design: for details see table on p. 140. (R.A.C. Tank Museum)

necessity but there seemed some probability of getting a satisfactory version into production in place of the earlier very unreliable types.

All this activity in specially designed armoured wheeled vehicles bore fruit in 1939 when the Guy Armoured car, or as it was originally announced, the Guy Wheeled tank, appeared. This was a compact 4-wheeled armoured car mounting a ·303 and a ·5 machine-gun in a turret with all round traverse. It had 4-wheel drive, taken from a centrally placed gear-box to front and rear driven axles, the engine being placed at the rear. The Guy is notable on two counts; it was the first of the modern armoured cars, compact, light, reasonable in size and with a good cross country performance; and secondly the plate used in its construction was welded in many places instead of being located with straps and rivets. This was a major breakthrough and Guy's had solved a problem which had defeated many other builders. Before this satisfactory welds had only been achieved at the risk of damaged armour plate; either the plate in the vicinity of the weld became brittle and liable to crack under impact, or it was softened by the heat and liable to penetration.

Quite apart from ease of construction the ability to weld armour plate simplified repairs and gave new life to the word "modification". Improvements and alterations for increased efficiency and greater comfort

Vickers-Guy and Lanchester armoured cars. The Guy carries the wireless aerial supports fitted to these cars. The Lanchester D1E2 (ML8689) has two machine-guns in the turret as well as one alongside the driver. (R.A.C. Tank Museum)

Experimental Scammel 6×4 armoured car with wooden mock-up body showing rear MG turret. Experiment was abandoned because car was considered too big, heavy, and slow.
(R.A.C. Tank Museum)

were easily effected, a wonderful change though one which brought some difficulties in its train. Two pieces of armour plate butt jointed and secured by a welded fillet had not the strength of the old-fashioned joint with a strap and securing rivets. It took some time before the need to mortice plates of armour where they were to be joined was realized. The Germans appreciated the necessity for this technique in the Panther and the Tiger series, but as late as Churchill VII the glacis plate was only held in position relative to the nose and side plates by a welded joint. A mortar bomb on the nose plate broke the joint and allowed the plate to fall, trapping the driver's feet. The failure was easily cured by welding a shaped strut to the side plate which took

the weight of the glacis plate and relieved the weld of the task of holding up this heavy piece of metal in its proper place.

In 1940 the Guy was followed by the Daimler based on the design of the Daimler scout car. These cars were armed with a 2-pdr. gun and an MG which assured them of superiority over any other current types of armoured car but which did not solve the problem of overcoming a dug-in enemy post. An alternative steering position was provided and the transmission was the same pattern as that of the scout car, a pre-selector gearbox, a transfer box which allowed all gears to be used in reverse, and independent driving shafts to each hub where there was a special

Crossley 6×4 with a light tank turret. A machine-gun is mounted alongside the driver but the turret still carries only one. Single wheel all round.
(R.A.C. Tank Museum)

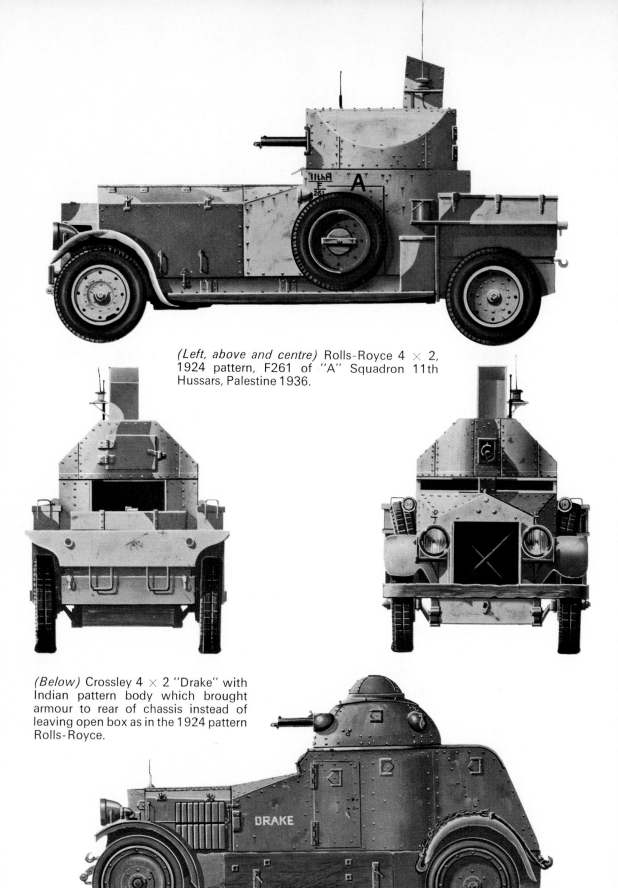

(Left, above and centre) Rolls-Royce 4 × 2, 1924 pattern, F261 of "A" Squadron 11th Hussars, Palestine 1936.

(Below) Crossley 4 × 2 "Drake" with Indian pattern body which brought armour to rear of chassis instead of leaving open box as in the 1924 pattern Rolls-Royce.

DRAKE

(Above) Lanchester 6 × 4 Mark I, one of the armoured cars the 12th Lancers took to the Saar during the Plebiscite, January 1935.
(Centre and below) Vickers-Guy 6 × 4, side view showing aerial supports in place.

Martin Lee © Profile Publications Ltd

Early days in the desert for the 11th Hussars. Maintenance on 1924 pattern Rolls-Royces in 1935 soon after the 11th had exchanged station with the 12th Lancers.
(The Eleventh at War)

Straussler armoured car 1938. This vehicle was one of a type ordered by the Dutch East Indies Government. Those tested in England had no hull gun. (Alvis Ltd.)

A 1924 pattern Rolls-Royce of the 11th Hussars stuck in Western Desert sand. Note rear doors open.
(The Eleventh at War)

Morris armoured car of the 11th Hussars at a desert well, 1940.
(The Eleventh at War)

Straussler armoured car in the Sinai Desert 1935. This vehicle was driven from Port Said to Baghdad when trials were carried out on guarding the oil pipe-line. (Alvis Ltd.)

Morris 4×2 experimental armoured car 1935. The sighting vane shows clearly in front of the cupola on the square rotatable turret. Note 4-in. smoke dischargers on far side of machine-guns. (Morris Motors Ltd.)

reduction gear to compensate for the weight of the car. The Daimlers had a good performance and although some mechanical trouble was experienced for the first two years, it was rectified and they proved very reliable cars.

The third of this trio, the Humber armoured car, appeared in 1941. It is included here because it was like the Daimler and Guy in size and general compactness. It was armed with a 15-mm. and a 7·92 Besa MG and its transmission was the same pattern as the Guy with driven transverse axles. Front wheel drive could be engaged at will. The cross country performance was not as good as that of the Daimler and the 15-mm. Besa was not a very satisfactory weapon. By the time of the invasion of Europe these cars were obsolescent and some of them were converted to AA armoured cars with four Besa 7·92-mm. MGs mounted in an open topped turret.

ARMAMENT AND MOUNTINGS

In 1919 two types of machine-gun were used in armoured cars: the water-cooled Vickers in Rolls-Royces and the air-cooled Hotchkiss in the Peerless. Both were ·303-in. calibre and both fired rimmed cartridges. The Vickers on its crosshead dropped into a socket on the turret and fired through a rectangular hole in the front, the gunner being virtually unprotected. The Hotchkiss fitted into a ball mounting with a small sighting aperture. The ball was closely shrouded and the likelihood of splash was much reduced. Both mountings provided for elevation and a limited traverse. The turret was retained in position by clips which incorporated rollers running on the turret ring; the turret was moved by man power for major changes in direction, fine laying being accomplished on the mounting.

The Indian pattern armoured car body provided for four machine-gun mountings for VMGs, two usually being mounted, one facing forward, the other on the opposite diagonal facing aft. Improved rollers made the turret easier to move and in some models optional geared elevating gear was incorporated. The other innovation was a cupola for the commander which could be rotated independently of the turret and opened at will to provide an opportunity of observing and controlling fire power.

The Guy 6-wheeler turret was traversed by gearing, but otherwise the gun arrangement was the same as for the standard Indian pattern body. The VMG water jackets were unarmoured and were liable to be penetrated with a consequent loss of water; plasticine to effect a temporary repair was a standard issue in the gun kit. The Crossley 6-wheelers used light tank turrets with geared traverse and shoulder control for the single VMG they carried in the turret, which by this time was of Tank Corps pattern with a pistol grip and an ejector tube to take spent cartridge cases outside the tank.

When the Lanchester was introduced the ·5 VMG appeared for the first time, mounted coaxially with a ·303 in the Mark V Light tank mantlet. The guns were held in armoured jackets which had appeared for the first time in armoured car history on the Crossleys. The bow gun was held in a gimbal mounting with a curious square armoured box to guard the aperture. Telescopic sights with apertures in the armour plate

Crossleys of the 1st Armoured Car Company, Royal Tank Corps, on the North-West Frontier, India, 1936. (*The Tanks*)

were provided for both turret and bow guns. Geared traverse was provided for the turret, this could be disengaged at will for quick movement. A seat for the commander moved with the turret and he also had a cylindrical cupola capable of independent rotation. Mark IIs had the "Bishop's Mitre" pattern cupola like those fitted to the Vickers Medium tanks. The guns were shoulder controlled for elevation.

The curious square turret of the Morris armoured car, mounting a ·5 and a ·303 VMG, saw the first introduction of the 4-in. smoke discharger, two being fitted. These also featured on the Morris Light Reconnaissance car which mounted a Bren LMG and a Boys anti-tank rifle, both of which could be dismounted for ground use.

The Straussler armoured cars had geared elevation for their MGs in addition to geared traverse. Possibly owing to the unsatisfactory elevating arrangements on the Vickers Medium tanks, geared elevation never found favour with British armoured units before the war. Shoulder control was feasible with the light mountings in use and was considered far better for shooting on the move which was common practice in those days.

The 1924 pattern Rolls-Royce had a body like the 1920 pattern but with side doors in addition to the back opening and a deeper open-topped turret; there were no side bevels. Their armament was increased by the addition of a Boys A/Tk rifle which was fitted on the right-hand side of the front plate of the turret and a Bren LMG for AA work which was mounted on the rear rim.

VMGs, ·5 and ·303 in a Mark VIB Light tank turret appeared on the Guy armoured car Mark I and these

Morris 4 × 2 Light Reconnaissance Car 1939. The aerial has been lowered along the side of the open topped turret. The Boys anti-tank rifle, smoke discharger, and Bren light machine-gun can be seen at front of turret. (Morris Motors Ltd.)

guns had geared traverse and shoulder control for elevation; the Mark IA shows the first real armament change with the introduction of the 7·92 and 15-mm. Besa machine-guns air-cooled, adapted from a Czech gun, firing rimless cartridges and destined to become the standard machine-guns of the Royal Armoured Corps. Telescopic sights were used and periscopes were provided for both the commander and the gunner. The Guy was replaced in 1941 by the Humber which was very similar in design. Humbers Marks I, II and III which all came out the same year used the two Besa machine-guns, Mark IV which appeared in 1943 had a 37-mm. gun. Geared traverse was fitted to all Humbers, the guns being shoulder controlled. A locking device was incorporated in the traverse operating handle, a very necessary precaution in view of the weight of the turret. The reduction gear was 69 to 1 so that traverse was not particularly speedy: no provision was made for disengaging the traverse gear for rapid movement in an emergency which anyhow would easily have been impossible if the car was on any slope.

A marked change takes place with the introduction of the Daimler armoured car in 1940. The 2-pdr. with a coaxial Besa is used for the first time to give the car some chance against a hostile armoured car or a light tank. No provision was made for any HE capacity and armoured car regiments were only able to solve the problem of the dug-in enemy by the introduction of assault troops who could take dismounted action in case of need. The Daimler had a platform suspended from the turret which rotated with it taking the commander and gunner. Hand traverse was used and turret movement was slow on account of the low gear

that had to be used. Twin 4-in. smoke dischargers were mounted.

The change in armament is very small over the twenty years; from free elevation and traverse of a single gun to geared traverse of a co-axial ·303 in. and a ·5 in., and then to their air-cooled equivalents in millimetres. Finally "à la fin de siécle" the introduction of a shot-firing gun inadequate to deal with a medium tank and incapable of turning an enemy out from any dug-in position.

WIRELESS IN ARMOURED CARS

Communications were always a difficulty with the early armoured cars. The only control available to a commander was by hand or flag signal between cars and the only method of passing information was by heliograph or Lucas lamp provided that it was possible to establish a visual link between the man who had the information and the headquarters who needed it to formulate their plans.

Wireless was an obvious solution but the sets available in 1919 were not suitable for armoured cars, they were too bulky and required too much skilled handling to make them operate efficiently. Various attempts were made to solve the problem without much success until 2 Armoured Car Company in India built their own wireless sets as a private venture and were able to control sub-units while on the move. They were aided by a code which enabled the necessary signals to be condensed into letter groups which could also be sent by flag or lamp signal.

This wireless was also fitted to the Vickers-Guy cars when these came out to India in 1928: rectangular

Guy 4×4 Armoured Car Mark I, 1939—the Guy Wheeled tank. Prototype with riveted, not welded, nose. (Guy Motors Ltd)

Above: *Daimler Scout Car. Designed by B.S.A. in 1937, it was preferred to the Alvis "Dingo", appropriated its name, and was produced by the Daimler Company from the end of 1939 onwards.* (Daimler Co. Ltd.)

Top right: *Humber 4 × 4 Armoured Car Mark I, 1941, mounting 7·92 and 15-mm. Besas.* (Rootes Motors)

Bottom right: *Guy 4 × 4 Armoured Car Mark IA (T10388) mounting a 7·92 and a 15-mm. Besa in place of the ·5 and ·303-in. Vickers in the Mark I.* (Guy Motors Ltd.)

external aerials were used and sufficient room was allowed for the turret to be traversed within the rectangle of aerial wire. This type of aerial was not used on British armoured cars after 1934 although a similar pattern was used by the Germans on their vehicles.

No major progress was made until the introduction of the No. 1 set about 1930. This was a compact battery-operated set with a nominal range of 2–5 miles. It was erratic and temperamental but, with an external wire aerial, voice communication was established between Cairo and Tidworth—to the dislocation of many European broadcasting stations. These sets were fitted in Rolls-Royce cars in Egypt and in the Lanchester Mark IA and IIA which had the bow gun removed to make room for the set. As sets became more powerful they were also fitted to these cars using an outside rod aerial. After the Lanchesters the wireless set was always fitted in the turret, although this necessarily involved the complication of a rotary junction to allow for turret traverse. In contrast to this

the German tanks and armoured cars mounted the wireless set in the hull and usually made the bow gunner responsible for operating it.

Closely connected with the wireless set was the question of inter-communication between members of the crew. A loud voice was really the only practical solution until wireless sets with a built-in inter-communication system such as the 19 and 22 sets became available after 1939. 19 sets, which incorporated a short range VHF set for local work, were fitted in Humbers and Daimlers in the turret and introduced their own problems in connection with the drain on batteries experienced by armoured cars on observation. Under these circumstances batteries ran down because there was no opportunity to run the engine. To overcome this the Daimler Mark 2 which appeared in 1941 had a special two-speed dynamo which provided a high rate of charge when the engine was only idling and thus enabled battery charges to be maintained.

Daimler 4 × 4 Armoured Car Mark 2 with 2-pdr. coaxial 7·92-mm. Besa, and smoke dischargers. Vehicle is closed down and no wireless aerial is fitted though 19 set base can be seen behind smoke dischargers. (Daimler Co. Ltd.)

Daimler 4 × 4 Armoured Car Mark 1, 1940. No Besa is mounted in this picture, which illustrates way in which rear half of roof folded back. Differences from Mark 2 included type of gun mounting and modifications to driver's escape hatch and engine covers. (Daimler Co. Ltd.)

Type	Wt/tons	Length	Width	Height	Engine b.h.p./r.p.m.	Transmission	Speed m.p.h.	Radius of action	Armament/Amn	Crew	Remarks
Crossley 4 × 2	5	16'6"	6'0"	7'1"	Crossley 4 cyl. 50/	Sliding pinion gearbox 4F IR	40	125	2 × VMG/ 3500	4	Armour 5·5 mm. Autovac petrol feed and auxiliary gravity tank. N.A.P. tyres.
Vickers Guy 6 × 4	9	20'4"	7'7"	9'4"	Guy 6 cyl. 120/	Sliding pinion 4F IR + 2 speed low ratio box	40	150	2 × VMG/ 6000	4	Armour 6 mm.
Lanchester Mk I and II	7·5	20'2"	6'4"	9'10"	Lanchester 6 cyl. 88/2200	Epicyclic gear box 3F IR + auxiliary 2 speed box for low ratios	45	200	1 × ·5VMG/ 1000 2 × ·303 VMG/5000	4	Engine fitted with dual ignition. Autovac feed. Mark I has cylindrical cupola, and twin rear wheels. Mark II has "Bishop's Mitre" cupola and single wheels. Mk. IA and Mk. IIA have no bow VMG but have provision to mount a wireless set in lieu. Dual steering. Armour 8–6 mm.
Guy 4 × 4 (Guy Wheeled tank)	4·5	13'3"	6'6"	8'1"	Guy 4 cyl. 61/2600 Rear mounted	Sliding pinion 4F IR and transfer box incorporating optional f.w.d.	35	100	1 × ·5VMG/ 600 1 × ·303 VMG/2500	3	Single steering position. Mk. IA had 1 × 15 mm. and 1 × 7·92 Besa guns. Welded armour 15–5 mm.
Daimler Mark 1	7·5	13'0"	8'0"	7'4"	Daimler 6 cyl. 95/3000	Pre-selector epicyclic 5 speed + transfer box with reverse gear. Wheel hub reduction gear. Separate drive shafts to each wheel	50	150	1 × 2 pdr./ 52 1 × 7·92 Besa/2700 1 × Bren /500	3	Fluid flywheel. Mk. 2 had 2 speed dynamo. No separate chassis, power train located in hull. Mk. I CS mounted 3·7" mortar in place of 2-pdr. Armour 15–5 mm.
Humber Mark I	5	15'0"	7'2"	7'8"	Humber 6 cyl. 90/3430	Sliding pinion 4F IR + 2 speed transfer box for low ratios. Optional f.w.d.	45	180	1 × 15 mm. Besa 1 × 7·92 Besa	3	Marks II and III similar but Mark III had 4 man crew. Armour 15–5 mm.

Humber Mark II, 1941.   (Rootes Motors)

The first armoured formation in the world—the Experimental Armoured Force drawn up in review order on Salisbury Plain, 1928. Medium Mark IIs in the centre of the picture. (Imperial War Museum)

British Armoured Units and Armoured Formations (1919-1940)

by
Duncan Crow
(Late 5th Royal Inniskilling Dragoon Guards)

DESPITE the immobilization of cavalry by the machine-gun during the Great War, as it was called in those days, the horse survived on the military scene. The traditions of a thousand years of cavalry dominance on the battlefield were too strong to be rejected simply because of experience in Flanders during the years of trench warfare from September 1914 to November 1918. Indeed those die-hards who refuted the predictions of the enlightened minority of cavalry officers that there was no future for the horse in warfare could point to Allenby's brilliant cavalry success in Palestine in 1918 as proof that cavalry was still the dominant arm.

Thus in the post-war reduction of the army the cavalry was not disbanded—an unthinkable suggestion!—nor was it mechanized to take the place of the youthful Tank Corps which was thereby allowed to survive. Even so the cavalry did not escape untouched. Its 30 regular regiments were reduced to 22 by amalgamating a number of them in 1922.

The 22 regiments were:

The Life Guards

Royal Horse Guards (The Blues)

1st King's Dragoon Guards

The Queen's Bays (2nd Dragoon Guards)

3rd Carabiniers (Prince of Wales's Dragoon Guards)
  Formed by the amalgamation of
    3rd Dragoon Guards (Prince of Wales's) and
    The Carabiniers (6th Dragoon Guards)

4th/7th Royal Dragoon Guards
  Formed by the amalgamation of
    4th Royal Irish Dragoon Guards and
    7th Dragoon Guards (Princess Royal's)

5th Royal Inniskilling Dragoon Guards
  Formed by the amalgamation of
    5th Dragoon Guards (Princess Charlotte of Wales's) and
    The Inniskillings (6th Dragoons)

1st The Royal Dragoons

The Royal Scots Greys (2nd Dragoons)

3rd The King's Own Hussars

4th Queen's Own Hussars

7th Queen's Own Hussars

8th King's Royal Irish Hussars

9th Queen's Royal Lancers

10th Royal Hussars (Prince of Wales's Own)

11th Hussars (Prince Albert's Own)

12th Royal Lancers (Prince of Wales's)

13th/18th Royal Hussars (Queen Mary's Own)
  Formed by the amalgamation of
    13th Hussars and
    18th Royal Hussars (Queen Mary's Own)

14th/20th Hussars
  Formed by the amalgamation of
    14th King's Hussars and
    20th Hussars

15th/19th The King's Royal Hussars
  Formed by the amalgamation of
    15th The King's Hussars and
    19th Royal Hussars (Queen Alexandra's Own)

The first Mediums, Mark A "Whippets"—seen here moving up to the front in 1918—were still in service in 1919-1920 with the 17th Bn. R.T.C. in Ireland. Other Whippets were sold to Japan and were in service there at least until 1930.
(Imperial War Museum)

Johnson's Light Infantry Tank, 1921. Though smaller than the Medium D it had a similar configuration.
(Imperial War Museum)

16th/5th Lancers
  Formed by the amalgamation of
    5th Royal Irish Lancers and
    16th The Queen's Lancers
17th/21st Lancers
  Formed by the amalgamation of
    17th Lancers (Duke of Cambridge's Own) and
    21st Lancers (Empress of India's)

The Tank Corps (which received the "Royal" prefix on October 18, 1923) suffered equally draconian reduction. Most of its battalions were disbanded in 1919 and on September 1, 1923 it was constituted in permanent form, having only five battalions and eleven armoured car companies. The battalions were the 1st (Depot), (which had its name changed to the "Royal Tank Corps Depot" on June 18, 1925), the 2nd, 3rd, 4th, and 5th. The armoured car companies were the 1st, 2nd, 3rd, 5th, 6th, 7th, 8th, 9th, 10th, 11th and 12th. All these armoured car companies, together with the 4th which was disbanded in 1922 after service in Palestine, were formed between March 1920 and July 1921. They were raised in response to the demand for armoured cars to control large sparsely inhabited areas and for the control of civil disturbance.

ARMOURED CAR UNITS

Within months of their formation all the Tank Corps armoured car companies except the 5th and the 12th were serving abroad in the Middle East and India, and these two exceptions were in Ireland where The Troubles were at their height.

Medium Mark C, the "Hornet", was the main equipment of the post-war Tank Corps until the arrival of the Vickers Medium Mark I from 1923 on.
(Imperial War Museum)

The emphasis on armoured cars had a direct effect on horsed cavalry; in 1920 eight out of the 55 yeomanry regiments in the army were converted to Territorial armoured car companies and were subsequently entitled the 19th to 26th Armoured Car Companies, Royal Tank Corps. The eight regiments were:

Derbyshire Yeomanry (Dragoons)—24th Armoured Car Company.
Royal Gloucestershire Hussars—21st Armoured Car Company.
Lothians and Border Horse (Dragoons)—19th Armoured Car Company.
Fife and Forfar Yeomanry (Dragoons)—20th Armoured Car Company.
2nd County of London Yeomanry (Westminster Dragoons)—22nd Armoured Car Company.
3rd County of London Yeomanry (Sharpshooters) (Hussars)—23rd Armoured Car Company.
Northamptonshire Yeomanry (Dragoons)—25th Armoured Car Company.
East Riding of Yorkshire Yeomanry (Lancers)—26th Armoured Car Company.

These eight regiments were the first cavalry units in the army to be mechanized.

The first regular cavalry regiments to be mechanized were the 11th Hussars and the 12th Lancers. In 1928-29 they were converted to what were then called "cavalry armoured car regiments". The 11th Hussars, stationed in England, took over the armoured cars of the 12th Armoured Car Company, R.T.C., on March 31, 1929. The 12th A.C. Company was then disbanded much to the chagrin of the R.T.C.

Medium Mark B showing the revolver ports in the protruding doors which allowed close-in covering fire along the sides of the tank. Medium Bs served in Russia in 1919 and equipped a company of the 17th Bn. R.T.C. in Ireland.
(Imperial War Museum)

Vickers Medium Mark IA (T33/ME9939) with box bogies. The first thirty Mediums were Mark Is. Main external distinguishing feature was the driver's hood. In the Mark I it folded back as a complete unit; in the Mark IA, as seen here, it divided in three, the top plate alone folding back on to the superstructure. (Imperial War Museum)

The 12th Lancers, in Egypt, took over the armoured cars of two RTC armoured car companies—the 3rd which was in Egypt, and the 5th which had been in Shanghai from March 1927 to January 1929 and was to leave its cars in Egypt on the way home for disbandment. In the event both the 3rd and the 5th were reprieved; the 3rd to be equipped with tanks so that it might examine the technical problems of using tanks in a desert campaign, the 5th to train the 12th Lancers in handling armoured cars. Skilful administrative moves by the RTC kept averting War Office instructions to carry out the disbandment of the 5th, and in 1932 the 3rd and the 5th were officially fused and formed into the 6th Battalion Royal Tank Corps stationed in Egypt.

At the end of 1934 the 11th Hussars and the 12th Lancers exchanged stations and equipment, the 11th Hussars leaving behind at Tidworth the Lanchester armoured cars with which they had been equipped since 1931. The AFV establishment of an armoured car regiment on service in Egypt at that time was 34 "1920–24" pattern Rolls-Royces and 5 Crossleys. The regiment was divided into Regimental Headquarters and A, B, and C Squadrons, each sub-divided into a headquarters and three (later, four) Troops, each of three Rolls-Royces. The Crossleys, which were equipped with wireless, were allotted to RHQ and the squadron headquarters. In 1938 the Crossleys were replaced by Morrises. The regiment consisted of 23 officers and 408 other ranks.

An armoured car company of the Royal Tank Corps in India had an establishment of 12 officers and 141 other ranks, and was divided into a Company HQ and 3 sections of five cars each. Its full vehicle equipment was 16 armoured cars, 6 motor-cycles, 1 motor-car, 4 three-tonners, 7 thirty-cwts., and 1 Trailer, Water Tank, of 110 gallons. After the demise of the

12th A.C. Company and the conversion of the 3rd and 5th Companies to other rôles in 1929, all the remaining RTC armoured car companies—that is, the 1st, 2nd, 6th, 7th, 8th, 9th, 10th, and 11th—were located in India.

In 1932 a start was made on converting all these armoured car companies to light tank companies, the first two being the 2nd and 7th. Each of the Light Tank Companies, RTC, had an establishment of 12 officers and 130 other ranks and was divided into a Company HQ and 3 sections. Its full vehicle equipment was 25 light tanks, 8 motor-cycles, 1 motor-car, 4 three-tonners (including a breakdown lorry), 7 thirty-cwts., and 1 Trailer, Water Tank, of 110 gallons.

THE EXPERIMENTAL MECHANIZED FORCE, 1927

Before continuing with the development of armoured units between 1919 and 1940 it is convenient to bring the story of armoured formations up to the same point in time. The idea of an independent force consisting entirely or largely of tanks and operating on its own initiative instead of simply in support of infantry had been mooted since November 1916 when Captain G. le Q. Martel, Brigade Major of the Heavy Branch, Machine Gun Corps, wrote a paper on "A Tank Army". And Colonel Fuller's "Plan 1919" had postulated an armoured force consisting of heavy and medium tanks for a massive breakthrough on a 90-mile front, with a "pursuing force" of fast Mediums to attack German headquarters and lines of communication, the whole attack being supported by aircraft and lorried infantry.

Another factor in developing the idea of the armoured formation was General Estienne's concept of light tanks for use as armoured skirmishers, which

Mark IA with side Vickers machine-guns in place. (The Tanks)

One of the many variations of the Carden-Loyd Mk. VI Light Armoured Vehicle, this one mounting a 47-mm. gun to form a light self-propelled mount.

(Taschenbuch der Tanks—Heigl)

Front view of the one-man Morris-Martel tankette, 1926. In action the driver/rifleman could lower himself to observe through the horizontal loop-hole and fire his rifle through the vertical one.
(R.A.C. Tank Museum)

B11E4 Carrier (Carden-Loyd Mk. VI Machine-gun Carrier, India Pattern) with sunshade provided for crew comfort in that country. (Imperial War Museum)

Major Martel demonstrating his home-made "one-man" tankette on the heathland outside his garden gate at Camberley in August 1925. (The Tanks)

Carden-Loyd Mk. VI Tractor drawing a personnel-carrying tracked trailer and a track-mounted anti-tank gun.
(Royal Tank Corps Journal)

resulted in the Renault FT 17 in France, and which was revived in Britain in the early 1920s by Fuller, and put into practical effect by Martel and Carden-Loyd with their tankettes.

In 1927 the missionary work and pressures of the enthusiasts on a reluctant War Office were successful. The first armoured formation in the British army—indeed the first armoured formation in the world—was formed. It was called the Experimental Mechanized Force and comprised the following units:

3rd Bn. Royal Tank Corps.
5th Bn. Royal Tank Corps.
2nd Bn. The Somerset Light Infantry.
9th Field Brigade, Royal Artillery.
9th Light Battery, Royal Artillery.
17th Field Company, Royal Engineers.

The 3rd Bn. RTC, which formed the Force's reconnaissance group, consisted of HQ, 2 companies of armoured cars (one of 2 sections of four cars each, the other of 3 sections of four cars each), and 1 company of tankettes (eight Morris-Martels and eight Carden-Loyds) organized in 4 sections—a total of 20 armoured cars and 16 tankettes plus HQ.

The striking force of the main group was the 5th Bn. RTC, consisting of HQ and 3 companies, each of 3 sections, of five Vickers Medium Mark II tanks each. There was also a radio telephone section of four wireless tanks.

The 2nd Somerset Light Infantry was a machine-gun battalion consisting of HQ and 3 companies, each of 3 sections, each of four Vickers machine-guns. The battalion was carried in Crossley-Kegresse half-tracks and 6-wheeled Morrises.

The field artillery consisted of HQ and 4 batteries, 2 of them Dragon-towed, 1 in Crossley-Kegresse half-tracks, and the fourth with self-propelled mountings. The Dragon was a full-track vehicle with a Vickers tank chassis. The light battery of artillery, equipped with 3·7-in. howitzers, was carried in half-track lorries.

The engineers, commanded by Major Martel, were carried in 6-wheeled vehicles.

Air support in most of the Force's exercises was provided by No. 16 (Army Co-operation) Squadron, R.A.F., in many by No. 3 (Fighter) Squadron, and in a few by No. 11 (Bombing) Squadron.

It will be noticed that the Force had no infantry apart from the specialized machine-gun battalion. This was in accordance with the school of thought that believed the infantry element would be needed only in a defensive rôle: to hold ground won by the armour and to protect the armour when it was harboured. But there was another school of thought, which included the Force's commander, Colonel R. J. Collins, who also commanded the 7th Infantry Brigade, which maintained that ordinary infantry should be a component part of the Force provided that it was lorry-borne. Consequently the 2nd Bn. Cheshire Regiment was attached to the Force for a number of its exercises.

It should be noted that there was also a third school of thought which believed that infantry would also be needed in helping the armour to clear obstacles but that to do this it must be "armoured infantry".

In 1928 the name of the formation was changed to Experimental Armoured Force—a change of title which, says Liddell Hart in his history of the RTC,

"expressed an aspiration rather than any change in reality. The only difference of composition from the improvised force of 1927 was the provision of some more 6-wheeled lorries and a few half-track carriers —all *unarmoured* vehicles."* The Force's 280 vehicles were of some 15 different types, a variety which complicated handling and limited the tactical value of the exercises.

Despite its limitations the Armoured Force had shown that it carried within it the key to machine age warfare. The lessons it demonstrated were not ignored abroad, especially by the German light infantry officer, Heinz Guderian. But the British General Staff turned its back on the Armoured Force. In November 1928 it was announced that the Force was to be dispersed and in January 1929 a Staff Conference on the two-year experiment concluded with a statement by the Director of Staff Duties, Major-General Charles Bonham-Carter, on "Future Policy Regarding Mechanization." The Armoured Force had been given three rôles for trial: first, strategical reconnaissance; second, "a wide movement on the battlefield culminating in an attack on the flank of an enemy engaged with our main force"; and third, "a special operation involving a long movement up to the full capacity of the force, which will have to maintain itself for 48 hours at a distance from the main army." Bonham-Carter announced that for the first rôle the General Staff proposed a light armoured brigade, consisting of a regiment of armoured cars, two battalions of light tanks, with a close support unit and an anti-aircraft unit. For the second rôle a medium armoured brigade was proposed, consisting of one battalion of medium tanks, two battalions of light tanks, two close support units and an anti-aircraft unit. For the third rôle field artillery, engineers, and infantry should be added to it.

Two points should be noticed about these proposals. First, the high proportion of light tanks; and second, that while motorized infantry might be necessary for a particular operation they should not be a permanent part of an armoured brigade. Both these points had stemmed from the trials of the Experimental Force. The preponderance of light tanks was the result of the conclusion that "medium tanks cannot effectively operate unless accompanied by a high proportion of light tanks." They were, it was argued in what was later to prove a dangerous tactical analogy, like destroyers protecting the main battle fleet. The absence of permanent motorized infantry arose from the conclusion that no fixed proportions of different arms would make the armoured force suitable for all its rôles. The difficulties of movement and deployment inherent in a force that had armoured and unarmoured elements also favoured the tank brigade as the basic unit with other arms attached for specific tasks.

In the 1929 training season the main tank experiment ordered by the War Office was a test of "the employment of light and medium tanks, combined in one formation." In fact the test was carried out with light and medium tanks combined in one unit; the 2nd Bn. RTC was re-organized with two companies of medium tanks (16 in each) and one company of 32 light tanks.

*The Tanks, Cassell, London, 1959. Vol. I, p. 259.

Rolls-Royce armoured car at a Palestine road-block.
(The Eleventh at War)

Rolls-Royce armoured cars of "A" Squadron, 11th Hussars, at "Windy Corner" on the road between Tulkarm and Nablus, Palestine, 1936—the only road between Tel Aviv and Haifa at that time.
(The Eleventh at War)

"1st BRIGADE, ROYAL TANK CORPS", 1931

The next stage in the development of British armoured formations was the "Mixed Tank Brigade" which came into existence on April 1, 1931 and lasted for six months until September 30. Its official title was "1st Brigade, Royal Tank Corps". Although it was actually assembled for barely a fortnight—at Tilshead Camp on Salisbury Plain—this temporary formation, says Liddell Hart in *The Tanks,* "proved the most significant experiment carried out by the British Army since the end of the war. Indeed, when viewed as the foundation upon which the more advanced training of the brigade was developed after its permanent establishment in 1934, it may justly be considered as the most important step in tactical experiment since the training of the Light Brigade at Shorncliffe Camp, prior to the fight with Napoleon's armies in the Peninsular War." (p. 287).

The "1st Brigade, Royal Tank Corps", commanded by Brigadier (later Lieut-General Sir Charles) Broad, consisted of the 2nd, 3rd, and 5th Bns. RTC, together with a skeleton Light Battalion which was attached for administration to the 2nd Bn. This Light Battalion was formed by taking the light companies from each of the permanent battalions. It was organized in three companies, each of three sections of five "nominal" light tanks apiece.

The 2nd, 3rd and 5th battalions were organized on a development of the "mixed" pattern that had been tried out by the 2nd Bn. in 1929. Each battalion (less its light company) comprised three mixed companies and a section of five close support tanks. Each mixed company had two sections—one of five medium tanks, the other of seven light tanks. In point of fact the light tanks still had to be represented by Carden-Loyd machine-gun carriers as only about a dozen of the new Mark II Light Tanks were available and these were used mainly by commanders and liaison officers.

The success of the brigade exercises raised hopes in the RTC that the Tank brigade would be made permanent in 1932. But the General Staff turned down the idea. Nor would it allow the formation of a permanent Light Battalion at this stage. The furthest it would go was to agree that the brigade should again be temporarily formed for summer training.

The 1932 brigade, commanded by Brigadier K. M. Laird, had an "action" strength of 230 machines, 50 more than the 1931 brigade. These extra 50 were new Mark II Light Tanks that had been built in the interim. They enabled a complete Light Battalion to be formed, and this was extensively tested for five weeks before being broken up and distributed so that the 2nd and 5th had proper light tank sections in each of their mixed companies. The 3rd had to continue with Carden-Loyds, of which there were 80 in the brigade. In the final week of the exercises the Light Battalion was re-formed.

THE 1st TANK BRIGADE, 1934

The tank brigade was not re-assembled in 1933, but following a decision taken in November four battalions of the Royal Tank Corps were permanently brigaded under Brigadier (later Major-General Sir Percy) Hobart, on April 1, 1934. The 1st Tank Brigade consisted of the 2nd, 3rd, and 5th Bns. RTC, together with the new 1st (Light) Bn. which was created by transferring the light company from each of the older battalions. Various types of organization were tried out in the three companies of the Light Battalion. One company had three sections each of five light tanks; the second had four sections of three light tanks; and the third had four sections of four light tanks.

The 2nd, 3rd, and 5th Bns. were now called "medium" instead of "mixed" battalions, although they were still on the "mixed" pattern. Each battalion had a headquarters and three mixed companies. Each company had a medium tank as headquarters, and three sections—one of seven light tanks, one of five medium tanks, and one of two close support tanks. 15 tanks in each company, 49 in the battalion.

This organization was more impressive on paper than in actual fact. The Medium tanks were the old Marks I and II, almost ten years old on average; and while the first of the three-man light tanks (Mark V)

146

had arrived that year there were still a larger number of Cardens-Loyds in service.

Two Territorial Armoured Car Companies, RTC, took part in the 1934 exercises of the 1st Tank Brigade —the 22nd (Westminster Dragoons) and the 23rd (Sharpshooters).

THE MOBILE FORCE EXERCISE, 1934

Over the years since 1927 the champions of armoured warfare had seen their vision slowly materialize despite the delaying tactics of their numerous opponents; they had achieved a permanent tank brigade; they were on the crest of a wave. But in the process they had become hubristic—or at least their critics in the older arms thought so. And those critics were now to ensure that, as in a Greek tragedy, hubris was to lead to nemesis.

At the time the decision was taken to form the 1st Tank Brigade in November 1933 Hobart immediately began to discuss the possibilities of using armour in an independent rôle, as Martel's "Tank Army" and Fuller's "Plan 1919" had first proposed. Brigadier G. M. Lindsay, a former Chief Instructor of the RTC Central Schools and former Inspector of the RTC, who had just returned from a tour as Brigadier, General Staff, in Egypt, suggested that the time had come to "organize and experiment with a Mobile Division", a type of organization tentatively proposed in the official War Office manual *Modern Formations* issued in 1931. Such a division, Lindsay considered, should have a motorized cavalry brigade, a tank brigade, and a motorized infantry brigade heavily armed with light automatics, machine-guns, and anti-tank weapons.

In February, 1934 after a Southern Command war game which featured a Mobile Force consisting of a horsed cavalry brigade, a tank brigade, and a motorized infantry brigade, Lindsay wrote a long paper on an "Experimental Mobile Division", in conjunction with his brigade-major, and sent it to the CIGS. While hoping that a Mobile Force could be tried out later in the year he warned the CIGS that unless the commander, staff, and signals were given the opportunity of working together before the exercise the formation was "not likely to function with success, and that in such circumstances there is a grave risk that the experiment will be stultified, or, in other words, put back for at least 12 months."

Thus was nemesis unconsciously invited. At the very end of the 1934 manoeuvres the GOC-in-C Southern Command, General Sir John Burnett-Stuart, ordered a "Mobile Force Exercise". The Force consisted of the 1st Tank Brigade, the 7th Infantry Brigade (which was carried in civilian motor buses), the mechanised 9th Field Brigade, R.A. (which had been part of the Experimental Mechanized Force in 1927 and 1928), and various auxiliary units. There was no motorized cavalry brigade in existence, so that particular part of Lindsay's proposed organization could not be adopted, and the horsed cavalry brigade that had been "imagined" as part of the war game was omitted as unsuitable in practice. Mechanized reconnaissance, instead of being at brigade strength as envisaged in Lindsay's Mobile Division, was in fact limited to part of one armoured car regiment, the 11th Hussars. In his paper Lindsay had urged that three cavalry regiments should be mechanized in 1935 in order to provide mechanized reconnaissance for a Mobile Division.

Burnett-Stuart was a convert to armoured warfare but he thought that the Tank Brigade was having too easy a run and that the older arms needed a boost to their drooping morale. He made sure they got it.

Typical Indian frontier scenery. A light Tank Mark IIB being guided round an acute hairpin bend. (RAC Tank Museum)

147

Vickers Mediums and Carden-Loyds of the "1st Brigade, Royal Tank Corps" during an exercise on Salisbury Plain, 1931 . . . "the most important step in tactical experiment since the training of the Light Brigade." Note the wireless aerials on the Mediums.

(The Times)

Lindsay's force was given no opportunity for training together, his staff had never worked together before, the signals were improvised, and the exercise was so arranged that the Mobile Force had to advance on "an independent raid" under limitations of timing and movement that severely handicapped it and against "defenders" who were informed of the objectives. "The obviousness of the objective, the canalization of the advance, and the timing handicap made frustration almost a certainty before the operation started. It foreshadowed the similar result from similar causes of the British armoured push for Arnhem exactly ten years later, in September 1944."*

Burnett-Stuart, who had, says Liddell Hart, "a rather impish sense of humour," may have had some justification in demonstrating that a mobile force

*The Tanks, Vol. I, p. 333.
†Lt.-Col. L. B. Oatts, I Serve, 1966, p. 247.

cannot always expect to have everything its own way. In doing so he was supporting those who held that the cult of armour was exaggerated. They decried the idea that the slaughter of the Western Front could be avoided in future by having a small professional army that made up for its lack of numbers by mechanical mobility. They felt that those who assumed that God was no longer on the side of the big battalions were wrong and believed that "the idea that the pace of an army in the field could be speeded up from the three miles an hour of the infantryman to the 40 miles an hour of the motor car was completely false." †

Burnett-Stuart may also have been justified, from a tactical point of view, in boosting the morale of the older arms by artificial restrictions on the younger. Major-General Norman, who commanded the 9th Lancers when the regiment was mechanized in 1936, has recorded that the advice on armoured tactics given

Medium Mark IIs and light tanks advancing in close order on a Salisbury Plain exercise. The manoeuvre is being controlled by wireless from the tank in the top left. Learning to communicate by wireless between tanks on the move was a key step in the efficient handling of armoured units and formations. Three Mark II*s, a Mark II**, and a Light Tank Mark II can be identified.   (RAC Tank Museum)

by the cadre of RTC officers attached as instructors was often critically received. "We found it difficult entirely to accept the theories about the employment of armoured troops which held sway at this period, since they seemed to us to put too high a value on armour in comparison with the other arms. Our instincts in these matters proved to be sound, for the experience of the war soon showed that the tank alone cannot perform all the tactical rôles and that the co-operation of all arms in the right proportions is as necessary as ever for success in battle. We also believed that all ranks should continue to be trained in the use of ground weapons and in dismounted action, since there would certainly be periods when, for one reason or another, tank crews would find themselves 'unhorsed' and obliged to defend themselves like any other troops. This belief too was borne out by experience."**

The immediate outcome of the Mobile Force Exercise, however, was that the sceptics of armoured warfare triumphed and the waverers, who could see both sides of the question, sided with the victors. Not only was there a strong reaction against the use of a mobile armoured force in the third of the rôles specified by Major-General Bonham-Carter at the 1929 Staff Conference, namely a long-range strategic stroke, but the rejection of this rôle seem to imply the rejection of such a force altogether. If it was no good for that rôle, what use could it be at all? Thus, as Liddell Hart says, "although the project survived, there was a diminished sense of urgency in War Office discussion of the measures needed to carry it out, and more emphasis was now given to the programme for renovating the infantry divisions—although even this was a slow process." (*op. cit.* p. 336).

While it would be going too far to say that the longer range outcome of the exercise in September

**Ed. Joan Bright, *The Ninth Queen's Royal Lancers 1936-1945,* Gale and Polden, 1951, pp. xx-xxi.

1934 was that the success of the German blitzkrieg in 1940 was militarily assured, there can be no doubt that there is an element of truth in the assertion. Other factors, political and financial, played a part as well as military controversy, and even if the soldiers had agreed on what was wanted they would not have got it. Nevertheless, their sharply divided counsels assisted the other factors which were delaying the creation of a modernized army. The delay was almost fatal, for in Germany Guderian, despite some opposition, it is true, was rapidly building an armoured force. In 1934 when the British had a tank brigade the Germans were forming their first tank battalion. A year later the British still had only a single tank brigade; the Germans had three armoured divisions. By the end of 1937 when the British were forming their first ill-balanced Mobile Division, the Germans had four panzer divisions and were still expanding.

ARMY TANK BATTALIONS

Apart from the two-company strong 6th Bn. in Egypt the only battalion of the RTC not included in the 1st Tank Brigade was the 4th, which was stationed at Catterick. In 1934 the General Staff issued a directive on army re-organization. There would, it said, be two types of division. The first of these was a Mechanized Infantry Division. Its transport, apart from the divisional artillery, would be motorized, and its brigades would each have three rifle battalions and one machine-gun battalion, equipped with armoured machine-gun carriers. Furthermore—and this was the important point for the RTC—each infantry division would have one battalion of "infantry tanks" which were to be slow, heavily armoured vehicles whose rôle was to be "the intimate support of infantry." They were to be known as "army tank battalions." The 4th Bn. was designated as the first of these. A second was to be raised in three years time (1937–38), and

The "medium" battalion of the 1st Tank Brigade, 1934, carrying out close order drill. Right hand tank is a Mark II, in front of it is a Mark II**. In the left foreground are Carden-Loyds which deputised for light tanks.* (The Times)

Brigadier P. C. S. Hobart, commander of the 1st Tank Brigade, giving his orders over the air during the Salisbury Plain exercises in 1934. With him in the turret is General Sir John Burnett-Stuart who ordered the "Mobile Force Exercise" which had such far-reaching results. The tank is one of the only three Medium Mark IIIs to be built and was modified for use as a command tank. Note extra aerial round turret.
(Imperial War Museum)

two more in 1938–39. The 4th Bn's experimental organization was three companies each of three sections of five "I" (infantry) tanks. These tanks were, of course, symbolical for it was not until October 1935 that the project was started for building an "I" tank under the code name "Matilda".

MOBILE DIVISION PROPOSED

The second type of division was to be the Mobile Division. It was to replace the horsed Cavalry Division. It would have a reconnaissance echelon of two cavalry armoured car regiments; a fighting echelon consisting of a tank brigade of RTC units and a mechanized cavalry brigade; and a support echelon of two RHA brigades, a field squadron of engineers, and possibly a cavalry machine-gun regiment. The mechanized cavalry brigade would consist of three regiments mounted in light trucks and one regiment mounted in light tanks. The truck-borne regiments would fight dismounted, fulfilling the rôle of infantry in the division.

Side-view of Medium III with Hobart in the turret.
(Imperial War Museum)

Thus the inevitability of mechanizing the cavalry was at last recognized, even though the decisive step was glossed over by the pretence that it was merely a tentative "toe in the water". Moreover, and most satisfactorily for the champions of the older arms, the hubristic Tank Corps had been thwarted in its ambition to expand. If the horsed Cavalry Division had to go—and the cavalry itself was far from unanimously persuaded of the necessity—then it would be insufferable if the upstart Tank Corps took over its rôle. The Tank Corps had been created as a supporting arm for the infantry and that is exactly what it should remain. The cavalry rôle, whether undertaken mounted on a horse or, reluctantly, mounted in a tank, was the proud prerogative of the cavalry regiments. It was in fact suggested in due course that the tank brigade in the Mobile Division should be replaced by cavalry regiments when enough cavalry had been mechanized.

The dislike between the RTC and the cavalry was deep-seated and mutual.

CAVALRY MECHANIZATION

It is, actually, incorrect to say that apart from the 11th Hussars and the 12th Lancers cavalry mechanization began in 1935. This idea has taken hold because "mechanization" has become synonymous with "being equipped with AFVs". But mechanization originally meant the provision of motorized vehicles for supply transport and for fire-power transport from which the crew dismounted to fight. Orders for partial mechanization of this sort were issued to the cavalry in November 1927. As an example: in 1928 the horsed transport of the 3rd Carabiniers at Tidworth was replaced by 11 six-wheeled lorries, three motor-

Light Tank Company, R.T.C., in India being inspected by the Viceroy, the Marquess of Linlithgow. This was a farewell parade. Having instructed cavalry regiments in mechanization to take over from it the R.T.C. left India for Egypt in 1939. Company is equipped with Mark VIBs Indian pattern i.e. without cupola. (The Tank)

Ford Pick-up cars armed with a ·303 Vickers Berthier machine-gun were the equipment of the 8th King's Royal Irish Hussars when they were converted to a motor regiment in 1935 in Egypt. With the 7th Hussars (converted to light tanks) and the 11th Hussars they formed the Mersa Matruh Mobile Force. (Imperial War Museum)

Cars of the 8th Hussars in the Sinai Desert on their way to Palestine, June 1936. (Imperial War Museum)

A contrast with thirty years earlier—the equipment of the Queen's Royal Irish Hussars in Malaya in 1964: the Saladin armoured car. The Queen's Royal Irish Hussars was formed in October 1958 by the amalgamation of the 4th Queen's Own Hussars and the 8th King's Royal Irish Hussars. (Army PR)

cycles, and three motor-cycle combinations. At the same time, one of the three sabre squadrons was converted to a machine-gun squadron consisting of four troops of two guns each. This MG squadron was "to be mechanized in due course," i.e. when vehicles became available. Moving from Tidworth to Canterbury at the end of 1929 "The Carbs" took part in experiments "with a view to comparing the merits of the Morris six-wheeler light track vehicle with those of pack-horses as the best method of carrying the Vickers guns of a cavalry regiment." Other exercises were carried out in "the use of Austin-Seven motor cars as scouts." The regimental history of The Queen's Bays is another that records the issue of Austin Sevens for a scout troop and the provision of a mechanized machine-gun squadron in place of a sabre squadron. Thus, although it was "the Cherry-Pickers" and the 12th Lancers on whom the unwelcome blows of complete mechanization first fell the other cavalry regiments at home had a taste of it at the same time. "It was obvious," says the Carbs' regimental historian, Lieut.-Col. L. B. Oatts, "that complete mechanization was only a matter of time."*

But it was not obvious to all. Especially was it not obvious to all in the War Office. After the 1930 autumn manoeuvres the War Office decided to reverse the trend towards cavalry mechanization. There were now, once again, to be three sabre squadrons, the number of machine-guns was reduced to four, and the machine-gunners were to be mounted on

*I Serve, p. 246.

Frontier patrol in the Western Desert, 1940. A carrier at the "wire" which marked the frontier between Egypt and Cyrenaica.
(Imperial War Museum)

The 8th Hussars formed up in Abbassia Barracks, Egypt, at the outbreak of the Second World War in September 1939. The regiment was converted to a Cavalry Light Tank Regiment at the beginning of 1939. Its equipment was initially 11 Mark IIIs and 7 Mark VIBs, "cast-offs" of the 7th Hussars and the 6th Royal Tanks.
(Imperial War Museum)

Arrest of a terrorist suspect by a patrol of 8th Hussars in Palestine. The regiment returned to Egypt at the end of 1936.
(Imperial War Museum)

horses again with their guns on pack. The signallers and scouts were to be put in Austins. In passing it should be noted that much of this organization could not be put into practice, for the army was so short of men—as well as money and material—that the Carbs, for example, could not parade three squadrons; for annual training they had to form one composite squadron.

However, the evil day could not be put off indefinitely. In the autumn of 1934 the Inspector-General of Cavalry, Major-General Blakiston-Houston, announced to the assembled regimental commanders that "he could no longer see any future for horsed cavalry as such and that he proposed to ask that the bulk of the cavalry regiments be converted to armour. For this he requested their support."* In November the Colonel of the 3rd Hussars informed the commanding officer and the second-in-command that the Inspector-General, having been asked by the CIGS "to select a cavalry regiment to carry out an experiment in mechanization to replace horsed cavalry," had chosen the 3rd Hussars, which was just about to move from York to Tidworth. To sugar the pill a little they were told that by carrying out this experiment they would in no way prejudice their chances of remaining a horsed regiment if it was later decided that further cavalry regiments were to be mechanized.

The reaction of the 3rd Hussars, and indeed of all those against cavalry conversion, is well expressed in their regimental history where the choice of words perfectly portrays their feelings and sums up the cavalry dilemma. "Coupled with this unwelcome honour" of blazing a trail for future mechanization "was the threat that if the cavalry failed to find 'an adequate mechanized substitute for the horse,' still more regiments would have to be disbanded or be absorbed by the Royal Tank Corps, which had usurped the traditional rôle of the cavalry on the western front during the Great War." If the view of the enlightened minority of cavalry officers that there was no future for the horse in warfare "had prevailed, all the cavalry regiments would have been mechanized soon after the Great War, and they could have

*Major General W. R. Beddington, A History of the Queen's Bays, Warren & Son, 1954, p. 4.

Close up of a Light Tank Mark VI showing its two-piece radiator louvre, return roller on top of leading bogie, and round cupola which distinguish it from the Mark VIA (return roller attached to hull side, and octagonal cupola) and the Mark VIB (one-piece radiator louvre). (Imperial War Museum)

absorbed the youthful Tank Corps. As it was, when the old die-hards reluctantly accepted the principle of conversion, the Tank Corps had become a powerful and established arm of the service, and the cavalry had lost an opportunity which was never to recur. It would be idle to assume that either the officers or the troopers, who loved their horses in a way that Englishmen can never love machines, took kindly to their new task. But the regiment had led the way before, and they would do it again. At Tidworth, in December, 'after the most serious consideration and the fullest discussion,' it was decided that 'the only course was to give the experiment a real and whole-hearted trial'."*

The experiment was an imitation of the French army's *dragon portés*, horsed cavalry which had been converted into motorized troops. Only "A" Squadron of the 3rd Hussars was motorized to begin with. During 1935 it was reconstructed with a special establishment and trained throughout the year with a variety of wheeled and tracked vehicles. Then, early in 1936, the entire regiment was mechanized. The horses were replaced by "thinly-armoured scout cars and ungainly trucks—'to represent light tanks'."* Nor was it only the 3rd Hussars who lost most of their horses. The Army Council decided that eight cavalry regiments would be on a "mechanized basis" —in addition, that is, to the 11th Hussars and the 12th Lancers. Five of the newly converted regiments were to be "motorized cavalry", carried in a new type of light truck from which they could dismount instantly and fight on foot; the other three were to be light tank regiments.

These newly converted regiments were to form two brigades at home and one in Egypt. Each mechanized cavalry brigade at home was to have two regiments of motorized cavalry and one light tank regiment. The brigade in Egypt was to have one motor regiment and one light tank regiment, as well as the armoured car regiment, the 11th Hussars, already there. The two home brigades, together with the 1st Tank Brigade RTC, were to form the 1st Mobile Division. This organization, it will be noticed, was different from the one proposed in 1934 in that it was to have two mechanized cavalry brigades.

*Hector Bolitho *The Galloping Third*, John Murray, 1963, pp.242-3.

The conversion of the regiments in Egypt was actually begun in the late autumn of 1935. Throughout the summer the Abyssinian crisis had been developing and on October 3 Mussolini launched his attack. A "Mobile Force" was got ready in Egypt to defend the Western Desert against Italian attack in the event of the war spreading. The motor regiment was the 8th Hussars equipped with Ford V8 troop-carrying "pick-ups". The regiment to be converted to light tanks was the 7th Hussars. This Mersa Matruh Mobile Force was soon being called the "Immobile Farce" by the troops. Rain and violent sandstorms bogged down the vehicles and choked the engines.

As well as the 3rd Hussars the first regiments converted in England were the Queen's Bays, the 4th Hussars, and the 9th Lancers. It should not be imagined that conversion was an immediate process. Apart from the time needed to train the officers and men in driving and maintenance, wireless, and gunnery, there was much too to be done on the administrative side and in turning farriers and storemen into fitters, mechanics, and technical storemen. And most delaying of all was the appalling lack of equipment. The regiments lost their horses but got little in their place. Mechanization was not a matter of line upon line of armoured vehicles drawn up in tank parks waiting for a sympathetic War Office to persuade reluctant cavalrymen to accept them. In the case of the 3rd Hussars the first tanks did not arrive until 1937— and then only enough for one troop! By September 1938, at the time of the Munich crisis, only one squadron and regimental headquarters had tanks;

Light tanks of The Queen's Bays marching past their Colonel-in-Chief, H.M. Queen Elizabeth, in 1938. The Bays were one of the first cavalry regiments to be mechanized. They were part of 2nd Armoured Brigade in the 1st Armoured Division.
(Imperial War Museum)

In December 1938 the first delivery was made of the new cruiser, the A13, easily identifiable by its four irregularly spaced large suspension wheels. This was the first British tank with a Christie chassis. It was designated Cruiser Marks III and IV, the Mark IV, as seen here, (A13 Mark II) with extra armour on the turret. The Mark III is illustrated on page 75. (Imperial War Museum)

For each regiment the present badge, or the last badge before amalgamation or disbandment, is shown. Except where otherwise stated all are cap badges. See also note on page 167.

The Life Guards
(formed the composite 1st and 2nd Household Cavalry Regiments equipped with armoured cars)

Royal Horse Guards (The Blues)

1st King's Dragoon Guards

The Queen's Bays
(2nd Dragoon Guards)

3rd Carabiniers
(Prince of Wales's Dragoon Guards)

4th/7th Royal Dragoon Guards

5th Royal Inniskilling Dragoon Guards
Collar badge   *Cap badge*

The Royal Dragoons
(1st Dragoons)

The Royal Scots Greys
(2nd Dragoons)

3rd The King's Own Hussars

4th Queen's Own Hussars

7th Queen's Own Hussars

8th King's Royal Irish Hussars

9th Queen's Royal Lancers

10th Royal Hussars
(Prince of Wales's Own)

11th Hussars
(Prince Albert's Own)

12th Royal Lancers
(Prince of Wales's)

13th/18th Royal Hussars
(Queen Mary's Own)

14th/20th King's Hussars

15th/19th The King's Royal Hussars

16th/5th The Queen's Royal Lancers

17th/21st Lancers

Royal Tank Regiment

World War II

The Derbyshire Yeomanry

Royal Gloucestershire Hussars

Lothians and Border Horse

The Fife and Forfar Yeomanry

Westminster Dragoons

3rd/4th County of London
Yeomanry
(Sharpshooters)

1st Northamptonshire
Yeomanry

East Riding of Yorkshire
Yeomanry

North Irish Horse

Inns of Court Regiment

22nd Dragoons

23rd Hussars

24th Lancers

25th Dragoons

26th Hussars

27th Lancers

Royal Armoured Corps

Royal Wiltshire Yeomanry

Warwickshire Yeomanry

The Nottinghamshire Sherwood
Rangers Yeomanry

The Staffordshire Yeomanry
(Queen's Own Royal Regiment)

Close up of the unique identifying feature of the Matilda, Infantry Tank Mark II—the skirt with five mud chutes.
(Imperial War Museum)

A10E1—prototype of the Cruiser Mark II unmodified. Modifications included place for MG in hull front and rearrangement of engine louvres (see picture on p.74). This rearrangement was finalised as shown in pictures on page 75.
(Imperial War Museum)

Infantry Tank Mark I—the original Matilda. 4th R.T.R., the first army tank battalion was equipped with 50 of these tanks when it went to France with the B.E.F. in September 1939.
(Imperial War Museum)

Three-quarter rear view close up of an A9 (Cruiser Mark I) showing the features which distinguish it from the A10 (Cruiser Mark II): forward sub-turrets (one visible at left of picture) and arrangement of engine air louvres. (Imperial War Museum)

the other two squadrons had 15-cwts. The 4th Hussars, who were the first mechanized cavalry regiment to be fully equipped with fighting vehicles and trained personnel after the 11th Hussars and the 12th Lancers, received their first issue of light tanks (Mark VIBs) in November 1937.

Major-General Charles Norman, who later commanded the 8th Armoured Division and who in 1936 took over command of the 9th Lancers at the time of their mechanization, has pungently described the experience. "We were first issued with worn-out Carden Lloyd [sic] carriers, small, open, weaponless armoured vehicles whose over-heating Ford engines scalded the occupants with super-heated steam from their cooling systems. After every exercise the plain round Tidworth was dotted for miles with our mechanized casualties, which were recovered during the next 36 hours by the devoted labours of the Regimental and Ordnance Corps fitters. A special mobile meals service was arranged by the Quartermaster's department to feed the stranded crews.

"For the training season of 1937 the Carden Lloyds were replaced by ancient light tanks mainly of the earliest marks, though a small number of Mark V were issued. These actually carried machine-guns and wireless sets, and we began to feel that we were getting somewhere. True, the tanks had been returned as unserviceable from Egypt; their turrets still had desert sand upon the floors; the engines, transmission and tracks were in a sad state. The same routine of recovery and feeding of crews after an

exercise had therefore to be maintained, but at least they were real tanks.

"The early wireless sets, Nos. 1 and 7, gave plenty of scope for the display of humour and the practice of self-control—not always achieved. It was said on one occasion that the tail of the column half a mile away could hear the Commanding Officer over the air but not over the ether! The War Office felt obliged to send out a letter . . . to the effect that civilians were complaining about the language which their receivers were picking up and asking that messages should contain military nouns only, unqualified by superfluous military adjectives."[*]

Before all the eight cavalry regiments could be converted, in theory even if not in practice, there was a further change in the proposed organization of a mechanized cavalry brigade. It was now decided that each would have two light tank regiments and one mechanized infantry battalion. "Motorized cavalry" regiments would not be needed. This meant that mechanization was confined to the six regiments (four at home and two in Egypt) which had already started their training.

In 1937 there was yet another change: the mechanized cavalry brigade was to consist of three light tank regiments. Furthermore, the cavalry allotted to infantry divisions for close reconnaissance (one regiment to each division) were to be mechanized. On November 3, 1937, it was announced that five regiments would

[*]Ed. Joan Bright, *op. cit.* p. xxi.

be mechanized: the 1st King's Dragoon Guards (which arrived back in Aldershot from India in December and began its conversion to a light tank regiment the following month), the 4th/7th Royal Dragoon Guards, the 5th Royal Inniskilling Dragoon Guards (known as "The Skins"), the 10th Royal Hussars, and the 15th/19th The King's Royal Hussars.

The KDGs joined the 3rd and 4th Hussars in the old 1st Cavalry Brigade, now renamed the 1st Light Armoured Brigade. The 10th Hussars became part of the 2nd Cavalry Brigade, which was renamed the 2nd Light Armoured Brigade. From then on the Bays, the 9th Lancers, and the 10th Hussars remained together in the 2nd Armoured Brigade until after the war had ended in 1945 when the 10th Hussars left and the 4th and 6th RTR joined the brigade which was then commanded by Brigadier N. W. Duncan.

The 4th/7th Dragoon Guards, the Skins, and the 15th/19th Hussars became Mechanized Divisional Cavalry Regiments.

Mechanization was also ordered for the British cavalry regiments then serving in India. The 3rd Carabiniers, the 14th/20th King's Hussars (as it had now become), the 16th/5th Lancers and the 17th/21st Lancers all began their conversion to light tank regiments. The Carbs, stationed at Sialkot, said goodbye to their horses in January 1938 as did the 17th/21st Lancers who had their last mounted parade on January 4. The 14th/20th Hussars started their light tank training in October at Secunderabad. In India as in England the mechanization of the cavalry regiments was only made possible by the cadres of officers and NCOs from the Royal Tank Corps who were attached as instructors. Whatever the feelings between them it was the RTC which was instrumental in actually making the mechanization of the cavalry a practical fact.

The organization of the 17th/21st Lancers when it was mechanized as a light tank regiment in 1938 was a headquarters and three squadrons each of a head-

quarters and four tank troops—54 tanks, of which five were spare. The tanks the regiment had were Mk. IIs and Mk. VIs without wireless sets and without ·5 machine-guns. In 1939 the organization of a British light tank regiment in India was changed to a headquarters squadron and three squadrons of three troops each, with four light tanks in each troop. The establishment was 21 officers and 460 other ranks, and its full vehicle equipment was supposed to be 15 scout cars, 12 eight-cwt. trucks, 19 fifteen-cwts., 11 personnel carriers, 41 light tanks, 22 thirty-cwts., 2 Water Tank trailers, 1 motor-cycle, 1 van, and 1 breakdown tractor.

The other British cavalry regiment in India in 1938, the 13th/18th Royal Hussars (Q.M.O.), was not mechanized until it returned to the United Kingdom on October 31. It began training as the Mechanized Divisional Cavalry Regiment of the 1st Division on January 10, 1939.

Thus during 1938 mechanization was wholesale and only four regular regiments of horsed cavalry remained at the beginning of 1939: the Life Guards, the Royal Horse Guards, the 1st The Royal Dragoons, and the Royal Scots Greys. The last two regiments were in Palestine. There were also eight horsed yeomanry regiments: the Royal Wiltshire Yeomanry, the Warwickshire Yeomanry, the Nottinghamshire Sherwood Rangers Yeomanry, the Staffordshire Yeomanry, the Cheshire Yeomanry, the Yorkshire Dragoons, the Yorkshire Hussars, and the North Somerset Yeomanry. Eventually, before the end of 1941, all these twelve regiments lost their horses and were converted to other arms, the majority to armour.

RTC EXPANSION

When the 4th Bn. of the RTC was designated an "army tank battalion" in 1934 it had been announced that the second of these would be raised in 1937–38. In the interim the units of the 1st Tank Brigade, as well as taking part in brigade exercises, had been shuffled around individually in the assumed rôle of

Scout Carriers of the B.E.F. in France, September 1939. (Imperial War Museum)

Bren Carriers of the B.E.F. in France, November 1939. (Imperial War Museum)

Mark VIB light tanks and Scout Carriers of the 4th/7th Royal Dragoon Guards on an exercise at Bucquoy, near Arras, late 1939. Note Boys anti-tank rifles in front compartment of carriers and Bren LMGs behind. (Imperial War Museum)

Light Tank Mark VIB in France, October 1939. (Imperial War Museum)

Major C. Cokayne-Frith, "A" Squadron, 15th/19th The King's Royal Hussars, crossing the Franco-Belgian frontier near Wattrelos, south of Menin, 10 May, 1940, the day the German attack began. Apart from the 12th Royal Lancers in their armoured cars the 15th/19th in two columns (one led by Cokayne-Frith) was at the head of the B.E.F. (Imperial War Museum)

Scout Carriers of "C" Squadron, 15th/19th The King's Royal Hussars on the way back through Louvain, 14 May, 1940. (Imperial War Museum)

Matilda, Infantry Tank Mark I of 4th RTR in France, January 1940. A ·303 in Vickers machine-gun in the turret was the tank's sole armament. (Imperial War Museum)

"I" tank battalions with the infantry divisions. Although re-armament was now under way the decision had been taken to mechanize the cavalry rather than reduce it and expand the RTC as the means of providing the new armoured units that were clearly essential. So the raising of new RTC battalions was not immediately advanced by the growing urgency of the situation. It was not until May 21, 1937, that the RTC began to expand. On that date the old 7th, formerly "G" Battalion, which had been disbanded on Empire Day, 1919, along with most of the other battalions of the Corps, was officially resurrected at Catterick Camp as an army tank battalion. A year later, on May 16, 1938, the 8th Battalion was re-born at Perham Down, also as an army tank battalion.

In November 1938, after the Munich crisis, the RTC was further expanded by the creation of seven Territorial battalions. These were the 40th, 41st, 42nd, 43rd, 44th, 45th and 46th. They were converted from infantry. For example, the 40th (King's) Bn. was converted from the 7th Bn. The King's Regt. (Liverpool), the 41st (Oldham) Bn. from the 10th Bn. The Manchester Regiment, the 42nd from the 23rd Bn. The London Regiment, the 44th from the 6th Bn. The Gloucestershire Regiment, the 46th from The Liverpool Welsh.

At the same time the eight yeomanry regiments which had been converted to armoured car companies in 1920 (the 19th-26th Armoured Car Companies, RTC) were ordered to expand into battalions. Only the Derbyshire Yeomanry stayed as an armoured car unit in the long run. The Lothians and Border Horse, the Fife and Forfar Yeomanry, and the East Riding Yeomanry became Mechanized Divisional Cavalry Regiments. The Royal Gloucestershire Hussars, the 3rd County of London Yeomanry, and the Northamptonshire Yeomanry became mechanized cavalry regiments. The Westminster Dragoons became the tank element in a brigade of four officer-producing units.

On April 12, 1939 the War Office issued instructions for the doubling of the Territorial Army. Five more Territorial tank battalions were raised: the 47th, 48th, 49th, 50th and 51st. These came from existing battalions, e.g. the 47th from the 41st, the 48th from the 42nd, the 50th from the 44th. The yeomanry regiments also set about raising second-line units. The first to achieve this—within a fortnight—was the Fife and Forfar Yeomanry.

During the war the Royal Tank Regiment, as it had by then become, raised four more battalions: the 9th, 10th and 12th in 1940, and the 11th in 1941. Not all the 24 battalions, or regiments as they were re-designated, survived the campaigns. Some had to be broken up to provide reinforcements.

THE ROYAL ARMOURED CORPS

Army Order No. 58 of 1939 issued on April 4 was momentous for the cavalry and the Royal Tank Corps. It read:

"His Majesty the King had been graciously pleased to approve the formation of a new corps, to be designated The Royal Armoured Corps, to have precedence in the Army immediately before the Royal Regiment of Artillery."

The new Corps was to comprise the 18 cavalry regiments that had been mechanized, the eight mechanized yeomanry regiments that since November 1938 were being expanded from RTC armoured car companies to battalions, an old cavalry militia regiment that had recently been revived, and the Regular and Territorial battalions of the Royal Tank Corps. All the units of the former Royal Tank Corps, now re-named the Royal Tank Regiment, were to retain a corporate existence in the new Royal Armoured Corps by becoming battalions (later re-named "regiments") of the Royal Tank Regiment: for example, 3rd RTR, or 3rd Royal Tanks.

The 18 mechanized cavalry regiments were all those in "the 1922 list" on pages 141-2, except The Life Guards, Royal Horse Guards, 1st The Royal Dragoons, and The Royal Scots Greys. The old cavalry militia regiment was the North Irish Horse which had been disbanded after the First World War and was re-raised in 1938 as an Armoured Car Regiment (Supplementary Reserve). When the second-line regiments of the eight mechanized yeomanry regiments were raised these too were part of the Royal Armoured Corps. So too was the Inns of Court Regiment which as well as becoming an RAC officer-producing unit like the Westminster Dragoons, also, like the W.D's, formed a fighting regiment. The Inns of Court was an armoured car regiment.

At the end of 1940 and beginning of 1941 the RAC was expanded by the raising of six new cavalry regiments from cadres supplied by regular cavalry regiments. This procedure was adopted instead of the alternative of "unscrambling" some of the amalgamated regiments at the cavalry's own choice. The six regiments were:

22nd Dragoons, formed in December 1940 from the 4th/7th Royal Dragoons Guards and the 5th Royal Inniskilling Dragoon Guards;

23rd Hussars, formed in December 1940 from the 10th Royal Hussars and the 15th/19th The King's Royal Hussars;

24th Lancers, formed in December 1940 from the 9th Queen's Royal Lancers and the 17th/21st Lancers. (These three were all formed in England as armoured regiments, the designation adopted since earlier in the year for units in armoured brigades.)

25th Dragoons, formed in February 1941 at Sialkot, India, from the 3rd Carabiniers;

26th Hussars, formed in February 1941 at Meerut, India, from the 14th/20th King's Hussars;

27th Lancers, formed in December 1940 in England as an armoured car regiment from the 12th Lancers; originally it was to be formed in Northern Ireland and called the 2nd North Irish Horse.

In November 1940 one of the remaining horsed cavalry regiments, the Royal Dragoons, was converted to armour and became part of the RAC as an armoured car regiment. At the same time the Composite Regiment of the Household Cavalry (the Life Guards and the Blues), which had gone to Palestine in February 1940 with the horsed 1st Cavalry Division, became the 1st Household Cavalry Motor Battalion; later it was equipped with armoured cars and became the 1st

A13s Mark II (Cruisers Mark IV) of the Bays, 1st Armoured Division. (Imperial War Museum)

Household Cavalry Regiment. In September 1941 the 2nd Household Cavalry Motor Battalion, previously the Training Regiment, became an armoured car regiment in England and was designated the 2nd Household Cavalry Regiment.

The rest of the 1st Cavalry Division were the eight horsed yeomanry regiments listed on page 157. The division served in Palestine where the Royals and the Greys with their horses were already stationed. After only a few months it was announced that all or part of the division would lose its horses and be converted to other arms, but it was another year before the rôles of the various regiments were finalized. The Sherwood Rangers, for example, first became coastal gunners, then motorized infantry, then coastal gunners again (with two batteries in Crete, three in Tobruk, and one in Benghazi), until they were allotted their permanent rôle as an armoured regiment and became part of 8th Armoured Brigade in September 1941. The other armoured regiments in the brigade were the Staffordshire Yeomanry, who had also been part of the 1st Cavalry Division, and the Royal Scots Greys, who were the last cavalry regiment to be mechanized.

The other horsed yeomanry regiments which were converted to armour and became part of the RAC as well as the Sherwood Rangers and the Staffordshire Yeomanry were the Royal Wiltshire Yeomanry and the Warwickshire Yeomanry.*

In November 1941 and again in July 1942 the Royal Armoured Corps was expanded by the conversion of infantry battalions to armour. These were designated

*Six years later another of the ex-1st Cavalry Division yeomanry regiments was transferred to the RAC. The North Somerset Yeomanry which served from 1943 in the Royal Corps of Signals as 14 Air Formation Signals was converted in 1947 to a Divisional Armoured Reconnaissance Regiment in the RAC. In 1956 it was amalgamated with the 44th RTR and in 1965 the 44th was re-designated the Bristol Yeomanry, Bristol being the headquarters city of the 6th Bn. the Gloucestershire Regiment, from which the 44th had been originally converted in 1938.

as numbered regiments of the RAC. For example, the 5th Bn. The King's Own became 107 Regiment RAC, the 9th Bn. of the Sherwood Foresters became 112 Regiment RAC, the 7th Bn. of the Suffolks became 142 Regiment RAC, the 8th Bn. of the Essex Regiment became 153 Regiment RAC, and the 13th Bn. of the Sherwood Foresters became 163 Regiment RAC. Altogether, some 30 battalions were converted to become RAC regiments, though not all of them served for the rest of the war. Some were disbanded owing to casualties and the survivors reinforced other regiments; others reverted to infantry after a change of policy. The Royal Armoured Corps was at its maximum in the latter part of 1942 when it had 104 fighting regiments, 11 training regiments at Catterick, Bovington, Tidworth, Perham Down, Farnborough, Warminster, and Barnard Castle; an OCTU at Sandhurst; and Armoured Fighting Vehicle Schools at Bovington and Lulworth which had been vastly expanded from their pre-war size.

When the Royal Armoured Corps was formed a special badge for it was produced, consisting of the letters RAC surrounded by a wreath and surmounted by a crown. It was an unattractive badge, little worn. Even had it been more attractive it would still have been spurned. All units of the new Corps were allowed to keep their old designations, badges and distinctions. The RTR continued to wear the RTC badge, the cavalry regiments kept theirs. There was in fact nothing to show that they belonged to the same Corps—which was exactly what both wanted!

Camouflaged cruisers of the 9th Lancers in France, June 1940. Two A13s and an A9. The 9th Lancers were in 2nd Armoured Brigade, 1st Armoured Division. (Imperial War Museum)

A10 (Cruiser Mark II) of Regimental H.Q., the 9th Queen's Royal Lancers, in France during the fighting, May 1940. In the turret is the Commanding Officer (Lieut-Colonel C. H. M. Peto), standing on the rear the Adjutant (Captain K. J. Price). (Imperial War Museum)

In his short history of *The Royal Armoured Corps* written in 1942 Captain J. R. W. Murland of "The Skins" did not try to skate over the antagonism. "There are a few, a very few, pages in the history of the Royal Armoured Corps which do not make good reading, and which the new tradition must wipe out. The trouble dates from the formation of the Royal Armoured Corps. . . . The very idea of such a union of armoured units was loathed by everyone concerned, and this gave rise to considerable ill-feeling in the early days. The cavalry, robbed of their horses, had little love of things mechanical, which were *terra incognita* to them. The Royal Tank Corps, who had borne the burden in the lean years, were rewarded (as they saw it) by being reduced from a Corps to a Regiment, and, in addition, they had little in common with the cavalrymen. Both sought to retain their regimental identities with little or no thought for the Royal Armoured Corps as such, with the inevitable result that in the first two years the establishment of any Royal Armoured Corps spirit and tradition was seriously retarded."*

To aid in the retention of identity there was conceived to be a difference in function, stemming from the élan of the cavalry and the infantry-supporting origin of the Tank Corps. To the cavalry belonged— or at least wishful thinking would have had it so— the armoured cars, light tanks and cruisers of the

*Methuen 1943, p. 93.

A13 Mark II, Cruiser Mark IV, hors de combat in France, May 1940. Details of the A13 are described in Volume Three.
(Imperial War Museum)

Light Tank Mark VIC, 1940. Distinguishing features are absence of cupola and long barrel of 15-mm Besa. Mark VICs formed a large proportion of the tanks in the 1st Armoured Division in France. These particular vehicles belong to 50th R.T.R., 23rd Armoured Brigade, 8th Armoured Division. The brigade was re-equipped with Valentines before it first went into action at the First Battle of Alamein in July 1942.
(Imperial War Museum)

It was not only in Britain that there was a shortage of equipment at the beginning of the Second World War. Canada bought these old M1917 6-tonners at scrap value from the U.S.A. to provide vehicles for training. A train-load is seen arriving at Camp Borden, Canada, in August 1940. (Canadian Official)

reconnoitring and exploiting rôles, while the RTR had the slow-moving "I" tanks for the deliberate attack with infantry. In terms of formations this produced the idea, certainly among impressionable young officers and officer cadets, that there was something grander about an armoured division and that it was the special province of the cavalry. The reason for this illusion is not difficult to discern in the antagonisms of the inter-war years. For illusion, of course, it was. Furthermore, the experience of war brought the rôles of the cruiser and "I" tank ever closer together until eventually the distinction was seen to be artificial, and in 1944 Field-Marshal Montgomery asked for a capital or "universal" tank to replace the infantry and cruiser tanks.

During the war another RAC badge was produced. This has a mailed fist as the central design surrounded by a double "pincer movement". Even this, much more attractive as it was than the earlier badge, was not much worn until the infantry battalions were converted into numbered RAC regiments. Regimental loyalties remained paramount and those whose task it was to try to mould a Corps spirit found it all but impossible to overcome the primary allegiance to the individual regiment.

THE 1st MOBILE DIVISION, 1937

British rearmament began in a limited way in 1935. In 1937 a White Paper on Defence was published with a five-year plan for rearmament on a much larger scale. But the armour experts were not satisfied. Only two more army tank battalions were to be created— a quite inadequate gesture against the Germans who had just formed their fourth armoured division. Liddell Hart was asked by the Minister of Defence to prepare a paper suggesting how the army might be reorganized. It was completed by mid-June and was the starting point for the programme of army reform

When the 1st Canadian Army Tank Brigade arrived in the U.K. in February 1941 it was equipped with Matildas (Infantry Tanks Mark II)
(Canadian Official)

initiated by the new Secretary of State for War, Leslie Hore-Belisha. As far as armour was concerned Liddell Hart suggested that two armoured mobile divisions could be created at home and a third in Egypt. The army in India should also be able to form one armoured mobile division. Two armoured mobile divisions could also be organized from Territorial units.

In November Liddell Hart was asked to write another paper for the Cabinet. By this time he had been appointed personal adviser to the War Minister, an appointment from which he resigned in July 1938 "in order to be free to apply the spur of public criticism." His November paper on "The Rôle of the Army" was approved by the Cabinet as the basis for reorganization. Not surprisingly, armoured mobile troops were seen as the predominant need. Overseas there should be an armoured division on the frontiers of Italian East Africa, as well as one in the Western Desert of Egypt and one in India. At home the field force instead of having five infantry divisions and one armoured mobile division should have two infantry divisions and a minimum of three mobile divisions. There would therefore, in total, be three armoured mobile divisions overseas, three in the field force at home, and two organized from the Territorial Army, these latter initially on a training scale of equipment only.

In introducing the Army Estimates in March 1938 the Secretary of State for War announced that the army would be reorganized in divisions of two types: one, "a motorized division based on the light machine-gun"; the other, "a mechanized armoured division based on the tank." Although he did not say so, the number of these armoured divisions was still being argued about. At that time there was only one.

In 1937 it was at last decided to form the Mobile Division as from October 1. There was a prolonged argument between the Army chiefs and the new

Secretary of State for War as to who should command it. The War Minister was insistent that it should be an RTC officer, on the principle that as tanks were the striking power of the division the divisional commander should be someone with tank experience. The CIGS wanted a cavalryman—and those who supported him backed their argument with the proposal that the Tank Brigade should be left out of the Mobile Division and that its tank force should consist solely of two brigades of cavalry light tank regiments. In the event, as a compromise, an artilleryman was appointed, Major-General (later Field-Marshal Viscount) Alan Brooke. When Brooke was promoted the following summer the command of the division went to Major-General Roger Evans, ex-Royal Horse Guards and a former commanding officer of The Skins.

The 1st Mobile Division, with headquarters at Andover, consisted originally of the 1st (at Aldershot) and 2nd (at Tidworth) Light Armoured Brigades, the 1st Tank Brigade, together with divisional artillery, engineers, and signals. In theory it had 620 armoured fighting vehicles, but seven-eighths of these, even if they had all existed and some had not had to be simulated by trucks pretending to be tanks, were primarily reconnaissance machines. Only the Tank Brigade had heavier tanks and these were the obsolete Mediums. First deliveries of the new cruiser tanks, A13 and A9, were not made until December 1938 and January 1939 respectively. By that time the Mobile Division had been re-named the 1st Armoured Division, and its organization was about to be changed. The Secretary of State announced early in 1939 that two armoured divisions of handier pattern were to be created.

THE 1st ARMOURED DIVISION, 1938

The new organization for the 1st Armoured Division was a Light Armoured Brigade of three regiments

A10 Close Support with a 3·7in howitzer replacing the 2-pdr. in the turret. Only 30 of this type were built and were known either as Cruiser Mark IIA CS or A10 Mark IA CS—the A indicating two Besas, one co-axially in the turret, the other in the hull front next to the driver's position. A10 Mark I, of which only 13 were built, had a Vickers MG co-axially in the turret.
(Imperial War Museum)

A few Light Tanks Mark VIB were acquired from Britain by the Canadian Armoured Corps for training crews at Camp Borden.
(Canadian Official)

equipped with light tanks and cruisers, a Heavy Armoured Brigade of three regiments equipped with cruiser tanks only, and a Support Group consisting of a motorized rifle battalion, a motorized artillery regiment, and an engineer company. In point of fact, there were so few cruisers available that the distinction between a light and heavy armoured brigade was only on paper.

THE MOBILE DIVISION, EGYPT, 1938

Although little was done about forming an armoured division in India, the Munich crisis in September 1938 spurred the decision to improvise a Mobile Division in Egypt. Called originally the Matruh Mobile Force, it was more impressive than the "Immobile Farce" of 1935–6. It was even more impressive during the coming war when under the numbered title which it took in the spring of 1940 the "Mobile Division, Egypt" won immortal fame as the 7th Armoured Division.

Commanded and trained by Major-General Hobart, the Matruh Mobile Force was composed originally of a cavalry brigade, a tank group, and a pivot group. The cavalry brigade, re-christened the Light Armoured Brigade in 1939 and then the 4th Light Armoured Brigade in 1940, consisted of the 7th Hussars with two squadrons of light tanks (a mixture of Mk. IIIs, VIAs, and VIBs, without any ·5 ammunition for the VIAs and VIBs), the 8th Hussars with 15-cwt. Fords with Vickers-Berthier light machine-guns on improvised mountings, and the 11th Hussars with their Rolls-Royce and Morris armoured cars. Squadrons now had five troops each of one Morris carrying the troop leader with his wireless, and two Rolls-Royces. There were also Morrises at regimental and squadron headquarters.

The tank group, which became the Heavy Armoured Brigade and then the 7th Armoured Brigade, consisted of the 1st Bn. RTC complete to establishment with Mark VIBs, and the 6th Bn. RTC still having

Australian mechanized cavalry regiment lined up in the Western Desert, 1940. They are equipped with Universal Carriers and Light Tanks.
(Imperial War Museum)

only two companies which were equipped with old Mediums and light tanks. The pivot group, later called the Support Group, had the 3rd Regiment, Royal Horse Artillery, equipped with 3·7-in. mountain howitzers towed by "dragons". No. 5 Company, RASC, and the 2nd/3rd Field Ambulance completed the Force. Later the 1st Bn. King's Royal Rifle Corps arrived from Burma and after reorganization joined the pivot group as a motor battalion. By the outbreak of war the 3rd RHA had a mixture of 25-pdrs. and 37-mm. anti-tank guns, and "F" Battery, RHA, with 25-pdrs. had also been added to the pivot group. The first cruisers (A9s) were issued in October 1939.

In May 1940 after the brigades had been reorganized with one "heavy" and one "light" regiment in each, the cruiser state of the division was: 4th Armd. Bde. HQ—4, 7th Hussars—7 (out of 16 tanks), 6th RTR—23 (out of 36); 7th Armd. Bde. HQ—nil, 8th Hussars—nil, 1st RTR—23, of which eight were lacking 2-pdrs.

REORGANIZATION AND EXPANSION, 1939/40

Another result of Munich was that the reorganization and re-equipping of the Territorial Army was speeded up. But only one of the thirteen divisions proposed for its field force was to be armoured. When Hitler marched into Czechoslovakia in March 1939 the doubling of the Territorial field force was one of Britain's reactions. Added to the Regular Army's new model field force of four infantry and two armoured divisions that was being prepared, this meant a target of 28 infantry and four armoured divisions. The problem now was that there were neither the intructors nor the equipment available for bringing these divisions up to an active service scale. Indeed it meant that the existing field force, which included the 1st Armoured Division and the three army tank battalions, was deprived of some of the equipment needed to make it ready for war. The situation was exacerbated with the introduction of conscription in July—the trickle of new equipment had to be spread out even more widely, so that everybody had a little and nobody had enough.

The reorganization of 1st Armoured Division had reduced it to two armoured brigades, the 1st and 2nd, and a support group. The Tank Brigade, renamed the 3rd Armoured Brigade, left the division. Then in January 1940 when the 1st Armoured Division was still in England, the 1st Light Armoured Brigade, still consisting of the King's Dragoon Guards, the 3rd Hussars, and the 4th Hussars, came under command of the 2nd Armoured Division, and its place in the 1st Armoured Div. was taken by the 3rd Armoured Brigade, consisting of the 2nd, 3rd, and 5th RTR. It was also decided that both armoured brigades (the 2nd and 3rd) of the 1st Armoured Division would be equipped with cruisers to the extent that production allowed. There were changes too in the Support Group. A second motor battalion was added as well as an anti-tank/anti-aircraft regiment. But, as the 9th Lancers' regimental history records, "after the production of cruiser tanks it was decided that armour no longer needed artillery

support and so the 2nd Royal Horse Artillery left the Division."

The raising and training (so far as equipment allowed) of new armoured units and formations was also going on. In 1939 the 20th Mechanized Cavalry Brigade (later renamed the 20th Armoured Brigade), the 21st Army Tank Brigade, and the 22nd (Yeomanry) Armoured Brigade all began to be formed from Territorial Army units. But at this period these were formations in name only. Some of the units hardly existed and there was no equipment, not even training equipment, for them. Even trained units were without equipment. At the outbreak of the war on September 3, 1939, the 17th/21st Lancers, just back from India, were unarmed except for their rifles and revolvers and they were without transport. When they did manage to collect some training equipment in the next few weeks it consisted of four old Mediums armed with 3-pdrs., a few wireless sets, a handful of 15-cwts., one 2-pdr. without a mounting, and one Besa; later a Rypa (Roll, Yaw, Pitch apparatus) was added. Although they were designated a Heavy Armoured Regiment, and then in May 1940 an Armoured Regiment, there was no equipment to implement these organizations.

MOTOR MACHINE-GUN BRIGADES, 1940

At the end of May, when the German panzer divisions were over-running France, the 17th/21st Lancers were designated a Divisional Cavalry Regiment but with a special allotment of weapons and vehicles for a Motor Machine-Gun Regiment, which consisted of headquarters and three machine-gun squadrons carried in Austin "utilities". Together with the 16th/5th Lancers and 2nd Lothians and Border Horse, the 17th/21st formed the 1st Motor Machine-Gun Brigade, part of 12 Corps which had the task of defending south-east England. Two other motor machine-gun brigades were formed from the Divisional Cavalry Regiments that escaped through Dunkirk. These were equipped with a variety of hastily constructed armoured vehicles improvised on ordinary car chassis. The 14-h.p. Standard Beaverette was one type, the Humberette, with an open top armoured body on a Humber Snipe chassis, was another. Both were armed with a Bren gun and/or a Boys anti-tank rifle dismountable for ground action, and both were developed in later Marks. Their official name was light reconnaissance cars.

BRITISH ARMOUR IN FRANCE

While the 1st Armoured Div. was being reorganized and the 2nd was in embryonic form, both still in England, other British armoured units were in France. These were the Mechanized Divisional Cavalry regiments, an armoured car regiment, and one army tank battalion, all of which had gone to France in September 1939.

The army tank battalion was the 4th RTR. In 1939 it was grouped in the 1st Army Tank Brigade with the 7th and 8th RTR. But the 7th RTR and Brigade HQ did not go to France until the first week of May 1940, and the 8th RTR was left behind in England. The 4th RTR was equipped with 50 Mark I infantry

Light Tanks in Western Desert, 1940. A Mark VIB in the foreground, a Mark VI or VIA beside it. Mark VI lights formed the bulk of British tank strength in the Western Desert in 1940 and bore the brunt of many actions. (RAC Tank Museum)

A column of A13s moving up in the desert. These tanks still formed half the strength of 7th Armoured Brigade, 7th Armoured Division, in the offensive to relieve Tobruk in November 1941. They made a gallant departure from the battlefield at Sidi Rezegh. (Imperial War Museum)

View of a Scout Carrier showing the rear compartment on the right instead of on the left as with the Bren Carrier. These carriers of the Gloucestershire Regiment are on an anti-invasion exercise in the south of England, July 1940.
(Imperial War Museum)

Badges of Guards and Infantry Regiments which had at le

Grenadier Guards

Coldstream Guards

Scots Guards

Irish Guards

Welsh Guards

The Buffs
(Royal East Kent Regiment)
141st Regt. R.A.C.

The King's Own
Royal Regiment (Lancaster)
107th, 151st, Regts. R.A.C.

The King's Regiment
(Liverpool)
152nd Regt. R.A.C.

The Suffolk Regiment
142nd Regt. R.A.C.

The West Yorkshire Regiment
(The Prince of Wales's Own)
113th Regt. R.A.C.

The Green Howards
(Alexandra, Princess of Wales's
Own Yorkshire Regiment)
161st Regt. R.A.C

The Lancashire Fusiliers
108th, 109th, 143rd Regts. R.A.C.

The South Wales Borderers
158th Regt. R.A.C.

The Gloucestershire Regiment
159th Regt. R.A.C.

The East Lancashire Regiment
144th Regt. R.A.C. (later 4th R.T.R.)

The Duke of Wellington's
Regiment (West Riding)
*114th, 115th, 145th, 146th
Regts. R.A.C.*

The Border Regiment
110th Regt. R.A.C.

The Royal Sussex Regiment
160th Regt. R.A.C.

The Royal Hampshire Regiment
147th, 157th Regts. R.A.C.

The Essex Regiment
153rd Regt. R.A.C.

The Sherwood Foresters
(Nottinghamshire and
Derbyshire Regiment)
112th, 163rd Regts. R.A.C.

The Loyal Regiment
(North Lancashire)
148th Regt. R.A.C.

The Queen's Own
Royal West Kent Regiment
162nd Regt. R.A.C.

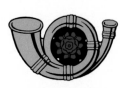

The King's Own
Yorkshire Light Infantry
149th Regt. R.A.C.

Battalion converted to Armour during World War II

The Manchester Regiment
111th Regt. R.A.C.

The North Staffordshire
Regiment
(The Prince of Wales's)
154th Regt. R.A.C.

The York and Lancaster
Regiment
150th Regt. R.A.C.

The Durham Light Infantry
155th Regt. R.A.C.

The Highland Light Infantry
156th Regt. R.A.C.

The Gordon Highlanders
116th Regt. R.A.C.

For each regiment the present badge, or the last badge before amalgamation, is shown. All are cap badges. The converted Guards battalions served in the Guards Armoured Division and the 6th Guards Tank Brigade. The converted infantry battalions became numbered Royal Armoured Corps regiments as indicated, some infantry regiments having more than one battalion converted and forming two, three, and even, in one case, four R.A.C. regiments. The Territorial battalions of the Royal Tank Regiment (40th–51st RTR) were also converted from infantry in 1938–39 e.g. 45th and 51st RTR from the Leeds Rifles (The West Yorkshire Regiment). The Royal Hampshire Regiment was granted the title 'Royal' in 1946; previously its badge had no crown and no 'Royal' in the scroll. The Green Howards badge was also re-designed after the war; previously the letter 'A' had "Alexandra" inscribed on the cross-bar and the scroll read 'The Yorkshire Regt' with 'Princess of Wales's Own' on another scroll below with a rose in its centre.

The following cavalry regiments whose badges are shown on page 154/5 have been amalgamated since World War II – Royal Horse Guards (The Blues) and 1st The Royal Dragoons, now The Blues and Royals; 1st King's Dragoon Guards and The Queen's Bays (2nd Dragoon Guards), now 1st The Queen's Dragoon Guards; 3rd Carabiniers (Prince of Wales's Dragoon Guards) and The Royal Scots Greys (2nd Dragoons), from 1971 Royal Scots Dragoon Guards (Carabiniers and Greys); 3rd The King's Own Hussars and 7th Queen's Own Hussars, now The Queen's Own Hussars; 4th Queen's Own Hussars and 8th King's Royal Irish Hussars, now The Queen's Royal Irish Hussars; 9th Queen's Royal Lancers and 12th Royal Lancers (Prince of Wales's), now 9th/12th Royal Lancers (Prince of Wales's); 10th Royal Hussars (Prince of Wales's Own) and 11th Hussars (Prince Albert's Own), now The Royal Hussars.

The 22nd Dragoons, 23rd Hussars, 24th Lancers, 25th Dragoons, 26th Hussars, and 27th Lancers were disbanded in 1948.

tanks, organized in three companies, each of five sections of three tanks, with one Mark I and one light tank at company HQ and two of each at BHQ. When the 7th RTR arrived in France it had 27 Mark I and 23 Mark II infantry tanks, and seven light tanks. It was these two units that gave the apparently invincible panzer divisions a nasty shock at Arras on May 21 and saved the BEF from being cut off from its escape-port at Dunkirk.

The Mechanized Divisional Cavalry regiments were the 4th/7th Dragoon Guards, the 5th D.Gs (the Skins), the 13th/18th Hussars, the 15th/19th Hussars, the 1st Lothians and Border Horse, the 1st Fife and Forfar Yeomanry, and the East Riding Yeomanry. The war establishment of fighting vehicles of each of these regiments was 28 light tanks and 44 armoured scout carriers. Together with the armoured car regiment, which was the 12th Lancers in their Morrises, the Mechanized Divisional Cavalry regiments were responsible for reconnaissance. In April 1940 they were grouped in two "armoured reconnaissance brigades" of three regiments each with the Lothians in GHQ reserve. After their return from Dunkirk they formed the 2nd and 3rd Motor Machine-Gun Brigades.

One other unit with an armoured element was also in France before the German attack. This started under the name of the "Hopkinson Mission" and was later known as Phantom. Its job was to discover information about forward troops and pass it to Advanced Air Striking Force HQ and to GHQ, BEF. Initially it consisted of a Headquarters Detachment; a "Phantom Squadron" of two armoured car troops, each of three Guy armoured cars, and a motor-cycle troop; and an Intelligence Section of six officers and six intelligence

Standard Beaverette Mark 3, 1940, was one of the improvised armoured vehicles on an ordinary car chassis, in this case a 14 h.p. The Beaverette Marks 1 and 2 were open-topped, the Mark 3 had a low turret with hinged lid. There was also a Mark 4 with a high open top turret. (RAC Tank Museum)

NCOs on motor-cycles. The armoured car and motor-cycle troops reported by wireless the information they obtained from reconnaissance and liaison, the Intelligence Section reported in person the information they obtained from liaison. From these small beginnings in France and Belgium in 1940, Phantom, which in 1941 was given the title of GHQ Liaison Regiment, developed into a unit of 150 officers and 1,500 other ranks which served in the Middle East, Tunisia, Italy, North-West Europe, and with the SAS. The present writer served with it from 1943 to 1945.

The 1st Armoured Division did not go to France until 1940. After a winter spent partly on anti-invasion duties in East Anglia and partly in training in the Poole-New Forest area it had been told that it would complete its training at the Tank Training Area at Pacy-sur-Eux in Normandy, moving there from England in May. It was still a travesty of an armoured division as far as equipment was concerned. When the Queen's Bays of 2nd Armoured Brigade went to Linney Head for battle practice in April there were still no guns for the Mark VIC light tanks. Each tank should have had a 7·92-mm. and a 15-mm. Besa, but "a sheet of three-ply wood covered the place where the gun-mountings would fit into the turret . . . When orders came on May 3 to be ready to go overseas within the next 12 days, no one had seen the Besa guns, except one or two NCO instructors, who had done a short course on the 7·92-mm. only."*

A number of A9, A10 and A13 cruisers now began to be issued to the regiments as they came off the production lines, in accordance with the decision that both armoured brigades of the division should be equipped with cruisers instead of one with cruisers and one with light tanks. This change-over was far from being complete by the time the division started to cross to France on May 17. Out of 284 tanks in the six armoured units 134 were light tanks. The Bays, for example, had four A9s, three A10s, and 22 A13s, a total of 29 cruisers as against 21 Mark VIC light tanks. Furthermore "very little was known about the driving and maintenance of the three different types of cruiser tank, as they had only just been issued.

"Dutchman" in British army service. This was one of the tanks built by Vickers for the Netherlands army and taken over on completion in 1939. Behind it is a Valentine, Infantry Tank Mark III. (Imperial War Museum)

*Major General W. R. Beddington, op. cit. p. 10.

View of a "Dutchman" light tank showing its distinctive hexagonal turret. The "Dutchman" was mechanically similar to the Vickers Light Tank Mark IV. (Imperial War Museum)

There were no spare parts or tools with them; these were to be made up on arrival overseas, as were the guns (Besa) for the light tanks, which arrived just before sailing to be put on board still nailed up in their packing cases."* Many of the cruisers lacked wireless sets, telescopes, and armour-piercing ammunition. As the 9th Lancers' history records, "the picture of 'C' Squadron Leader driving down the Southampton road in his private car handing out machine-guns, belt boxes and telescopes to his tanks [as they moved to the embarkation port] was a grim reminder of our appalling lack of readiness."**

By the time the 1st Armoured Division began to cross the Channel the opportunity for further training with the new tanks and weapons was gone. On May 10 —the day on which the division's billeting parties set off for France—the German blitzkrieg, conceived by Guderian from the teachings of Liddell Hart and the other British armour enthusiasts, erupted on the Western Front. The 1st Armoured Division would have to move straight into action and do the best it could.

Nor was it a complete division. Its field artillery support was gone, its two motor battalions had been removed to form part of a scratch brigade for a landing at Trondheim in Norway and when this was abandoned were not returned to 1st Armoured Division but on May 23 were sent to hold Calais. Its Support Group in fact consisted only of the mixed anti-aircraft/anti-tank regiment, the anti-tank batteries with the new 2-pdr., but the ack-ack batteries with only Lewis guns as the 40-mm. Bofors did not arrive until later. It was also short of one of its armoured units for the 3rd RTR had been detached for the defence of Calais. "It was with this travesty of an armoured division," wrote its commander, Major-General Evans, "a formation with less than half its proper armoured strength, without any field guns or a proper complement of anti-tank and anti-aircraft guns, without bridging equipment, without infantry, without air support, without the bulk of its ancillary services, and with part of its headquarters in a three-ply wooden 'armoured' command vehicle— that I was ordered to force a crossing over a defended,

*Major General W. R. Beddington, *op. cit.* p. 11.
**op. cit. p. 3.

unfordable river, and afterwards to advance some 60 miles, through four *real* armoured divisions, to the help of the British Expeditionary Force."

As the panzer divisions swept on there was incredulity in England. Surely, people said, the Germans were just advancing into a trap; our tanks would counter-attack and destroy them. Some of the German High Command felt the same. But had they seen the state of "A" Squadron of the 9th Lancers, for example, even before it went into battle and suffered casualties, the armchair strategists in England would have been less confident. There were only enough tanks to mount two of the four troops in the squadron. The second-in-command's close support A9 had no ammunition whatsoever for its 3·7-in. howitzer. There was, it is true, plenty of ammo for the Vickers but the gun had to be aimed by a telescopic sight and not only was there no such sight but there was not even a hole pierced in the front of the turret into which it could be fitted. So this theoretically powerful tank set out to stop the panzers with a rifle as its only effective weapon. The only weapons available in Second-Lieutenant Close's Mark VIC with its sheet of three-ply wood in the turret front was his revolver and rifle.

The remnants of the 1st Armoured Division were evacuated from Brest, St. Nazaire and Cherbourg on June 16, 17 and 18, by which time the French had asked for an armistice. Ill-equipped and ill-supported, the armoured units had fought almost without cease for nearly four weeks.

*Shortage of tanks was even more acute after the losses in France. Everything possible was put to operational use for the defence of Britain, including these Vickers Mediums Mark II** seen here with a Matilda in July 1940. The unit is the 48th Royal Tanks of 21st Army Tank Brigade.* (Imperial War Museum)

Christmas dinner, 1940, in the desert. 8th Hussars eat an improvised pudding of army biscuits, prunes, and marmalade against an A10 Mark IA (Cruiser Mark IIA).
(Imperial War Museum)

At the outbreak of the Second World War in September 1939 only two Matildas (Infantry Tank Mark II) were in service. Before production ceased in August 1943 nearly 3,000 had been built at the Vulcan Foundry, Newton-le-Willows, Lancashire. In this picture a squad at the 56th Training Regiment, R.A.C., is receiving instruction on a Matilda under the eye of Corporal Whalley, one of the Editor's staff when he was Assistant Chief Instructor there.   (Imperial War Museum)

"Tanks for Russia"—1: Canada built 1,420 Valentines (Infantry Tank Mark III) of which 1,390, including this consignment, were shipped to Russia under Lend-Lease arrangements.
(Canadian Official)

THE NEW ARMOURED DIVISIONS

After the baleful experience in France the organization of the British armoured division was changed in the autumn of 1940. An armoured car regiment was added, to carry out medium and close reconnaissance. There were still two armoured brigades but each now had a motor battalion as well as its three armoured regiments. The support group too was altered. As well as a Royal Horse Artillery regiment there was a full anti-tank regiment and a full light anti-aircraft regiment instead of one combined anti-tank and AA regiment. The two motor battalions having been removed to the armoured brigades, they were replaced by one lorried infantry battalion. Divisional troops, as well as the armoured car regiment, included two field squadrons of Royal Engineers and one field park squadron.

The total divisional strength was 13,669 (626 officers and 13,043 other ranks), plus 1,067 first reinforcements. Its fighting vehicles totalled 340 tanks, 58 armoured cars, 145 scout cars, 109 carriers, and nine armoured O.Ps. Other vehicles, excluding motor-cycles, totalled 3,002, and there were 918 motor-cycles. Grand total of vehicles—4,581.

The headquarters of each armoured brigade had ten tanks and nine scout cars. Each armoured regiment had 52 tanks and ten scout cars, and the motor battalion had 44 carriers. One of the field squadrons R.E. included six armoured vehicles scissor bridges, and the field park squadron had four armoured demolition vehicles. Divisional signals included nine armoured command vehicles.

When this organization was introduced there were three armoured divisions in existence: the 1st, being re-formed in England with the 2nd Armoured Brigade and the 22nd Armoured Brigade (which replaced the 3rd Armoured Brigade in September); the ill-fated 2nd, preparing to leave for the Middle East in November, with the 1st Light Armoured Brigade and the 3rd Armoured Brigade; and the 7th, fighting in the Western Desert against the Italians, with the 4th Light Armoured Brigade and the 7th Armoured Brigade.

Seven more armoured divisions were planned. The first of these to come into existence was the 6th Armoured Division which was formed in September 1940 with the 20th and 26th Armoured Brigades whose armoured regiments were the 16th/5th and 17th/21st Lancers and yeomanry regiments. Then came the 8th, formed in November, with the 23rd and 24th Armoured Brigades, all six of whose armoured regiments were Territorial units of the RTR. At the end of the year the 9th Armoured Division was formed with the 27th and 28th Armoured Brigades whose armoured regiments had all been Divisional Cavalry Regiments with the BEF and had then formed the 2nd and 3rd Motor Machine-Gun Brigades. In March 1941 the 11th Armoured Division was formed with the 29th and 30th Armoured Brigades from the newly-raised cavalry regiments and yeomanry regiments. The 10th Armoured Division was formed in the Middle East in August 1941 basically by the conversion of the 1st Cavalry Division, its two armoured brigades being the 8th and 9th. The other two armoured divisions were created by converting infantry, the Guards Armoured Division being thus formed in June 1941, and the 42nd Armoured Division, formerly the 42nd Territorial Infantry Division, being officially converted to armour in August. The two Guards Armoured Brigades were the 5th and 6th; the 42nd's were the 10th and 11th, which subsequently became tank brigades. Early in 1943 an eighth, and special, armoured division was formed, This was the 79th, which was the only all-armoured formation in the British army, and was equipped with a variety of specialized armoured vehicles. The commander of its 30th Armoured Brigade (for the 30th joined the 79th Armoured Division in November 1943) was Brigadier (now Major-General) N. W. Duncan.

Mark VI Triumphant! A Light Tank Mark VI of 3rd The King's Own Hussars with a captured Italian flag after the battle of Beda Fomm, February 1941. The 3rd Hussars at this time were in 4th Armoured Brigade, 7th Armoured Division.
(Imperial War Museum)

Valentines of the 8th Royal Tanks, 1st Army Tank Brigade, before the storming of Bardia, January 1942.
(Imperial War Museum)

"Tanks for Russia"—2: This photograph of Covenanters of "A" Squadron, 15th/19th The King's Royal Hussars originally appeared in October 1941 as a poster with the heading "Tanks for Russia"! At this period of the war the 15th/19th were in 28th Armoured Brigade, 9th Armoured Division. In August 1944 the regiment joined the 11th Armoured Division in Normandy as its armoured reconnaissance regiment in place of the 2nd Northamptonshire Yeomanry. Covenanter (Cruiser Mark V) was A13 Mark III—details of the tank are given in Volume Three.
(Imperial War Museum)

To begin with, many of these armoured divisions were hideously far short of the organization laid down. Some of the armoured regiments were that in name only. For example, at Christmas 1940 the 17th/21st Lancers in 26th Armoured Brigade were only one third equipped with a mixture of Valentines and Matildas. Not until March 1941 was the regiment fully equipped. By comparison, the 5th Royal Inniskilling Dragoons Guards at that date had only one squadron more or less fully armoured and the equipment of that squadron was: headquarters with one Crusader Mark I (Cruiser Mk. VI), one Light Tank Mk. VI, two Light Tanks Mk. VIB, one Light Tank Mk. IV; two troops each with three Covenanters (Cruiser Mk. V); one troop with four Humberettes; and one troop with one Light Tank Mk. VIB and two "Dutchmen". These "Dutchmen" were 40 light tanks which had been built by Vickers for the Netherlands army but were taken over on completion in 1939 by the British army. Mechanically they were similar to the Vickers Light Tank Mark IV but they had a simpler hull shape and a distinctive hexagonal turret.

The organization of an armoured division was changed again in the spring of 1942—this time more fundamentally. One armoured brigade was replaced by a motorized infantry brigade, the support group was removed, and the artillery was increased by an additional field regiment.

THE ARMY TANK BRIGADES

As well as the number of armoured divisions being more than trebled, there was a comparable increase in the number of army tank brigades. The 1st and 21st had been formed in 1939 and the 1st had seen service in France. To these were subsequently added the 25th, the 31st (later re-designated the 31st Armoured Brigade), the 32nd (which was the new designation of the 3rd Armoured Brigade from October 1941), the 33rd (later re-designated the 33rd Armoured Brigade, the 34th, the 35th, the 36th, the 10th and the 11th (which had previously been armoured brigades).

When the second armoured brigade was removed from the armoured division the junior brigade from the Guards Armoured Division became the 6th Guards Tank Brigade. Other displaced armoured brigades were either broken up, or served in an independent rôle, or in another armoured division, or became tank brigades.

The 13th/18th Royal Hussars (Queen Mary's Own) being inspected by their Colonel-in-Chief, H.M. Queen Mary, near Marlborough in April 1942. The 13th/18th served as a Mechanized Divisional Cavalry Regiment in France in 1939-40, then became part of 27th Armoured Brigade in the new 9th Armoured Division, went with the brigade to 79th Armoured Division and spearheaded the landings on Sword beach in Normandy on June 6th, 1944 with their DD tanks. In July 27th Armoured Brigade was broken up and the 13th/18th replaced the 24th Lancers in 8th Armoured Brigade. The vehicle on the right of the picture is a Loyd Carrier. (Imperial War Museum)

The tank which equipped the new Army Tank Brigades—the Churchill, Infantry Tank Mark IV, on which work began in July 1940. (Imperial War Museum)

174